SKILL
TRAINING
FOR SOCIAL
WORKERS

SKILL TRAINING FOR SOCIAL WORKERS

A Manual

Edited by

SUDHA DATAR, RUMA BAWIKAR, GEETA RAO
NAGMANI RAO AND UJWALA MASDEKAR

ESTD. 1983

SAGE www.sagepublications.com
Los Angeles • London • New Delhi • Singapore • Washington DC

Jointly published in 2010 by

SAGE Publications India Pvt Ltd
B-1/I-1 Mohan Cooperative Industrial Area
Mathura Road, New Delhi 110 044, India
www.sagepub.in

SAGE Publications Inc
2455 Teller Road
Thousand Oaks, California 91320, USA

SAGE Publications Ltd
1 Oliver's Yard
55 City Road
London EC1Y 1SP, United Kingdom

SAGE Publications Asia-Pacific Pte Ltd
33 Pekin Street
#02-01 Far East Square
Singapore 048763

Tata Institute of Social Sciences
P.O. Box 8313
V.N. Purav Marg
Deonar
Mumbai 400 088

Published by Vivek Mehra for SAGE Publications India Pvt Ltd, typeset in 10.5/12.5 pt Sabon by Star Compugraphics Private Limited, Delhi and printed at Chennai Micro Print (P) Ltd., Chennai.

Library of Congress Cataloging-in-Publication Data

Skill training for social workers: a manual/edited by Sudha Datar ... [et al.].
    p. cm.
  "Jointly published with Tata Institute of Social Sciences."
  Includes bibliographical references and index.
1. Social work education. 2. Social service. 3. Social service—Practice. I. Datar, Sudha. II Tata Institute of Social Sciences.

HV11.K54   361.3068'3—dc22   2009   2009039544

ISBN: 978-81-321-0238-0 (PB)

The SAGE Team: Rekha Natarajan, Jyotsna Mehta, Anju Saxena and Trinankur Banerjee

When I hear, I forget
When I hear and see, I remember
When I hear, see and reflect upon, I understand
When I hear, see, reflect upon and do, I know
When I hear, see, reflect upon and do again and again, I become skilled

To our students whose participation and feedback
reinforced our faith in skill training.

To all the directors of our institute who had faith and
confidence in our ability as skill trainers and encouraged to document our efforts.

CONTENTS

LIST OF TABLES AND BOXES

Tables

Boxes

LIST OF FIGURES

LIST OF EXERCISES

LIST OF IMAGES

LIST OF ANNEXURES

FOREWORD

Skill Training for Social Workers: A Manual developed by the Karve Institute of Social Service (KINSS) is an outcome of the detailed documentation of the sessions conducted by the faculty and outside experts during skill lab sessions. The skill laboratory conducted at the institute since the past many years is a unique self-designed module of learning and has become a brand of Karve Institute.

The informal dissemination of this manual is beyond the confines of the institute brought out of its utilities. It is indeed the recognition of this potential that led to the collaboration between the KINSS and the Tata Institute of Social Sciences (TISS) for publishing this manual by a reputed international publishing house like SAGE.

A skill manual for the trainee social worker is a comprehensive document which includes theoretical inputs, games and exercises on the theme of understanding perception, self-awareness, sensitivity, communication and working with individuals and groups. The Skill Laboratory Modules, which form an integral part of the training, especially during the first year, and the learning, which takes place through these laboratory sessions, is further concretised during the second year. The skill manual includes a variety of topics, role plays, songs, case studies, street plays and exercises on self-awareness, self-development, SWOT analyses, communication, goal setting, time management and stress management. Different types of communication skills are developed in the students which range from inter-personal communication skills to use of media through fieldwork training. The skill training is an academic exercise carried out in a scientific and professional manner. This facilitates a student to inculcate professional and global competencies essential for a social worker.

The skill development modules are designed in such a way that every student gets an opportunity to practically take part in the exercise. They are involved in each step and thus get a hands on experience of 'doing' and understanding the intricacies of the social work approach. This builds the confidence and strengthens knowledge, skills, aptitude and the attitudinal base of students. This manual will be a value addition to the faculty, professionals and students in strengthening, bringing uniformity and high quality standards in skill laboratory sessions, particularly in social work practice. It will go a long way in meeting the paucity of indigenous textbooks and teaching materials for use by social work educators, scholars and students.

The editorial team of this manual includes Sudha Datar, Ruma Bawikar, Geeta Rao, Nagmani Rao, Ujwala Masdekar and the contributors Anjali Maydeo, Anuradha Patil, faculty members of the Karve Institute, and Anand Pawar, Sameer Datye, Manjusha Doshi and Vidya Ghugari, who were the guest faculty, deserve special appreciation and thanks, for their invaluable contribution to this manual.

Last but not least, I must acknowledge the financial assistance bestowed by The Tata Education Trust and appreciate the continuous support of Rekha Mammen and her team members from TISS, and the SAGE Publications, for their painstaking efforts of editing and publishing this manual.

I am therefore, very much pleased to write this Foreword for such an important manual which would fill vital gap for indigenous material in social work training.

Dr Deepak Walokar
Director, Karve Institute of
Social Service, Pune

PREFACE

It all began with an invitation to the Tata Institute of Social Sciences (TISS), Mumbai, to host a conference of the Inter-University Consortium for International Social Development (IUCISD) in India in 2003. The enthusiastic committee that was formed decided to build up to the conference with several activities as part of a project titled 'Enhancing the Social Development Perspective in Social Work Education'—one of which was to revisit the social work curriculum.

As with other professions, social work has been constantly evolving and attempting to redefine its mandate as per the changing needs of society. The first curriculum developed by the TISS was based on 15 years of field experience of its founder, Clifford Manshardt, part of which was in India and on the curriculum for social work developed in America and Britain (Desai, 2002). Since then the curriculum has undergone several changes and now represents a combination of planned change at the level of the entire degree programme, and more ad hoc changes brought in through specialisation and individual courses at different points in time.

Today, the processes of globalisation and the ensuing problems have ensured that social work practice not only has to 'indigenise' but also needs to 'internationalise' strategies for practice. In India, one faces a duality of the phenomenon of technological changes and their impact on the one hand and on the other, a traditional feudal society and mindset. One sees newer forms of slavery through the processes of liberalisation, privatisation, and globalisation and its institutions. The role of civil society in strengthening democracy is increasingly being highlighted and recognised.

From a developmental perspective, it was felt that the dynamics of civil society, state and market forces need to be understood and integrated with development processes and ideologies in the context of social work practice. Therefore ideologies, approaches, methods, systems, clientele and emerging areas were identified for examination in each context of social work education and practice.

Based on a series of consultative workshops and meetings held with social work educators and practitioners including faculty from various schools of social work, we arrived at the following issues that need to be addressed:

1. Meeting the paucity of indigenous textbooks and teaching materials.
2. Need for developing strategies and approaches to suit the new socio-economic reality.
3. Re-organising the curriculum, fieldwork system and methods of teaching and research to integrate social and technical skills with the needs of the field.
4. The responses and experience of professionals/practitioners need to be taken on board.
5. Emphasis should be on development of applied theory.

The dearth of published social work literature relating to the Indian context has been expressed by social work educators and practitioners for more than three decades. There is a large body of unpublished, indigenous literature, student assignments, case studies, reports and the like, which are used as teaching training material for students, but not published formally. One of the reasons is that infrastructure for writing and publishing is not easily available to support knowledge development, even to faculty in the Institutions of Social Work Education(ISWE). Another factor is that social work practitioners are often more comfortable and skilled in the practice area and find it difficult to make time for this kind of writing. The Tata Education Trust kindly agreed to support this project that proposed to bring out four books, which would integrate 'objective' learning and 'subjective' experience:

1. *From the Abstract to the Concrete: Contextualising Practice-related Theories of Social Work*
2. *Skill Training for Social Workers: A Manual*
3. *Innovations through Praxis: The TISS Experience*
4. *Making a Difference with Social Work Education: Narratives from the Field*

These books aim to consolidate field and teaching experience in various sectors and contexts in order to review and build curricular material and plans in the social work curriculum relevant to the current context in India. Two broad areas were prioritised in the area of social work teaching and education:

1. Adaptation of social work theories for the Indian context.
2. Skill development of social work students.

Two broad types of contexts were identified in the arena of social work practice:

1. Field action projects initiated by social work institutions.
2. Social work practice as it has evolved outside the university context.

Three of these four themes were taken up by the faculty in the School of Social Work at TISS, Mumbai. The Karve Institute of Social Service (KINSS), Pune, was invited to work on the publication relating to skill development of social work students. The last two themes are still publications in the making, while the first of the above-listed themes, adaptation of social work theories for the Indian context, has been published in the form of an edited volume of the *Indian Journal of Social Work*.[1]

This publication is an outcome of the collaboration with KINSS. Faculty at the Karve Institute have for many years conducted skill laboratories with their students and had developed a standardised set of exercises that were given to the students every year. We learnt that there was also considerable demand from their alumni and others for copies of these exercise sets. The TISS project team worked with the KINSS editorial team to develop the manual further for publication by providing some research, editing, audio-visual and secretarial assistance. The manual also went through a round of peer review through the TISS Publication Unit before being taken up for publication by SAGE Publications, New Delhi.

The outcomes of this project would hopefully help schools of social work revise and reformulate their curricula and would also develop indigenous field-based theory that would be useful for teaching and practice. These publications are intended to serve as training source books for social work educators, practitioners and students in the context of integrating social development in social work education.

The pillars of this project have been our project team members: Neena Barnes Konnoth, Laxmi D. Jadhav and Ajitha Manjeshwar. We acknowledge with immense gratitude the financial support and encouragement of the Tata Education Trust for this project without which it would not have happened.

Rekha Mammen
Project Director
Assistant Professor (Senior Scale)
School of Social Work,
Tata Institute of Social Sciences, Mumbai

---

[1] LJSW Vol.69, Issue No.2, April 2008.

ACKNOWLEDGEMENTS

As social work educators, who are also closely associated with the field of practice, many of us have felt the need to develop consciousness in trainees regarding skills and attitudes for professional practice. These thoughts stimulated us to develop our skills training programme. The outcomes and experiences gained through skill training motivated us to prepare this manual. It has emerged out of collective efforts of many persons, over several years. We are indebted to all of them.

At the outset, we would like to thank the Tata Institute of Social Sciences (TISS), in particular Rekha Mammen and Sudha Ganapati for their persistent encouragement to the editorial team to prepare this manual for publication. Thanks to Mr Sawant for his creative photographs that so aptly brought out the spirit of the lab sessions and to Ms Ajitha for being the multi-purpose liaison between us and the institute. Thanks also to Mr Krishnan for assistance with the maps and Mr Vijendra Singh for assistance in creating tables/figures and in typing Marathi words.

We are deeply indebted to the peer reviewers for their painstaking review of our earlier working manual. Their comprehensive suggestions have helped us to enhance the content and quality of this manual.

We acknowledge the Managing Committee of the Karve Institute of Social Service (KINSS) and our former Director, Dr Cherian Kurien for the encouragement and support extended to us to prepare the manual for publication.

Dr Sunanda Koushik, former Director, KINSS, needs special mention as the source of inspiration behind documenting the skill lab sessions to prepare the manual.

Professor (Retd) Kalindi Muzumdar of Nirmala Niketan College of Social Work trained some of the faculty of the institute for the use of participatory methods in skill training. We are grateful to her for all that we learnt and also for some of the simulation games and poems that we have included in this manual.

We place on record the contribution of our former colleagues: Sumati Godbole, Meghana Marathe and Rashmi Tamuly. They have all contributed to the development of the content of this manual through the workshops they had conducted. Their valuable suggestions helped us in undertaking the task of preparing the manual. Our colleagues Anuradha Patil, Vishal Karuna, Anjali Maydeo and Sharmila Sahadeo have been a great support throughout.

Ms Sunita Pandhe and Mr Avinash Shirke went over the entire earlier version of the manual (both of whom are alumni and currently educators) and gave us several useful suggestions. We thank them for thus helping us enhance its quality.

It is with fond remembrance and gratitude that we acknowledge each batch of students for their enthusiastic participation during the skill labs and the challenges they posed during the sessions. This stimulated us to improvise as we went along, adding value to our experiences. They have been the backbone of our experiments and we learnt as much from them as they did from us.

We are deeply grateful to the following resource persons who conducted various workshops over the years and have added to the richness of our resource material:

1.	Theatrical games	Madhav Vaze
		Vidya Tamboli
		Manjusha Doshi
2.	Street theatre	Vilas Chaphekar
		Samar Nakhate
		Ujwala Paranjape
		Nilima Bale
		Dr Anant Lagoo
		Laxmi Narayan
		Anand Pawar
		Vilas Londhe
		Groups which performed street plays:
		Dropper Group, Pune
		Group of street children of Pune (Department of Continuing, Adult Education and Extension, SNDT University, Pune project on street children)
		Andhashradha Nirmulan Samiti, Pune
		Field workers of Mobile Creche Pune
		Kagad Kachpatra Kashtakari Panchayat, Pune
		Akshar Andolan, Pune Municipal Corporation
		Sahmat, New Delhi
3.	Posters making and poster exhibition	Nilima Chitale
		Vasudha Sardar
4.	Use of songs and other interactive visual media	Poornima Chikarmane

5. Traditional media	Uttam Zagade
6. Use of films	Jaya Modak
	Sumedha Lele
	Madhuri Abhyankar and SOFOSH Team
7. Puppetery	Manjusha Doshi
	Vidya Tamboli
	J. Vaishampayan
8. Use of songs, storytelling and dramatisation in working with children	Renutai Gavaskar
	Dr Sunita Kulkarni
	Late Leela Bhagwat
	Shobha Bhagwat

We are also grateful to the following who are still associated with our skill lab workshops and have also contributed in writing for this manual:

1. Anuradha Patil—Communication workshop
2. Anjali Maydeo—Photo language
3. Anand Pawar—Street play
4. Manjusha Doshi—Puppets and theatrical games
5. Vidya Tamboli—Puppets
6. Sameer Datye—Use of Internet in social wok practice

As part of using various media forms, we have put together a good collection of songs with social messages, prepared by practitioners using the traditional forms, street play scripts and *kirtan*s with social messages. Since these were drawn from field workers and activists they are in Marathi. Now that the manual is complete, we thought it is appropriate to have these translated into English by a person who not only has a good command over both languages but also possesses an understanding of the media. We are immensely grateful to Ms Vidya Vaidya for fitting this bill perfectly.

The Tata Institute of Social Sciences approached us for printing of this manual in 2003. It is being printed in 2009. The present Director of KINSS, Dr Deepak Walokar, supported us whole heartedly in carrying forward the process to a logical end.

The library and administrative support at KINSS and TISS helped us in ways both big and small. We thank all the concerned for this.

Last but not the least, we thank Ms Laxmi M. Vora (TISS) and Shri Arun Wasankar (KINSS) for the systematic and neat preparation of the draft of the manual.

Editors

INTRODUCTION

Social work is a profession with specialised know-how of working with people. Its practice involves the combined use of knowledge, attitudes and skills that are defined by the value base of social work. According to Dr Abraham Flexner, 'One of the important criteria of professionals is, they possess a technique capable of communication through a highly specialized educational discipline.' In the profession of social work, the skills essential for professional performance can be communicated. These skills may then be in a continuous state of being tested and refined.

If one refers to any English dictionary, we find the definition of skill. Most dictionaries define skill as expertness, ability to perform effectively due to repeated practice. According to Johnson (1995) skill is 'the practice component that brings knowledge and values together and converts them into action as a response to concern and need'. This implies that skills involve a complex organisation of behaviour directed towards a particular goal or activity. Through the use of skills a social worker displays her/his capacity to use interventions towards a goal-directed purpose. Skill is, therefore, the expression of a specific behaviour under the precise conditions which designate its use.

While the use of skill may often seem instinctive, commonsensical acts, the truth is that skills are developed and refined through exposure and experience. This also involves conscious, disciplined use of one's own self and one's abilities. The disciplined experience of social work training which exposes trainees to a supervised fieldwork experience helps to develop their skills to a certain extent. But while working in real-life situations, the focus has to be on the 'person in need' and the development of self as a worker may go into the background.

Students may also gain a limited knowledge of skills in the classroom through the theory they learn. But when we say that skill is an expertise and practice ability, then both the aforementioned training situations may have the following limitations:

- Since the human element is involved in the fieldwork situation, trainees cannot use trial and error method or repeated practice for development of specific skills.
- In the classroom, conceptual learning may reduce trainee participation because the focus is more on knowledge and information as a base for developing understanding.

The theory of social work emphasises understanding of human behaviour in the context of society at large. It also gives perspectives and insights into the analysis of problem situations and remedies or strategies to achieve the goals of development. The theory of social work is based on the philosophy of social work, out of which have emerged the principles of practice. The skill laboratory is a platform on which these principles are translated into practice skills, that is, 'learning by doing'. Through the experiential learning in the lab, insights are acquired to develop the personal self and the professional self. The trainees gain insight as to how appropriate social work skills are essential for the fulfilment of social work goals. We choose to use the laboratory approach because trainees are taken through each stage of skill development in the use of the methods of social work. Besides, the lab gives ample scope for experimenting till the trainees develop conviction. Demonstration can also be used to illustrate use of skills.

The lab also helps to reduce the element of unpredictability in the field situations. It endeavours to help trainee social workers (TSWs) to learn through simulated situations and reflections carried out in a relatively safe environment. With inputs from the facilitators, TSWs learn to bring likely field situations to enact in the lab. The process of observation, identification of lacunae in the way in which situations are tackled through immediate feedback and opportunity provided for relearning help trainees to prepare themselves for the field situation. They also learn to introspect. Group learning and peer support are important characteristics of the lab, which facilitate the process of introspection. Peer support not only helps in accepting the limitations in oneself but also helps strengthen the existing qualities in oneself because of the recognition and appreciation received.

The lab sessions thus help to stimulate imagination, enable critical reflection on implications of word and action and through this process the TSWs develop sensitivity, empathy and an ability to identify their own strengths and limitations. It also helps them to overcome fears and anxieties since they are better equipped to consciously face the real situations in the field. The lab also helps the trainees to translate theories of social work into practice.

This manual is an outcome of several years of experience and collective critical reflection of skill training through lab sessions, which were systematically documented, refined, used and developed to suit the training goals.

The manual thus concentrates on the following:

1. Development of self-awareness, that is, enabling the trainees to understand, develop and modify, if necessary, their own values, attitudes, abilities and talents.
2. Development of sensitivity to human problems.
3. Enhancement of abilities required to establish effective helping relationships.

4. Enhancement of skills in communication to facilitate effective intervention.
5. Providing opportunities to practice theory of methods in a controlled and guided environment.

At the end of the training one cannot expect a perfectly skilled social worker, yet one can say that these experiences will equip the trainee social worker with the confidence in use of self in various social work situations.

The manual has three sections. The first section gives the base or foundation for preparing oneself for working with people. It seeks to develop in TSWs an understanding about oneself, openness in perception, overcoming biases and rigidities and becoming conscious about sensitive use of the self in helping relationships.

The module on perception enables the trainees to perceive themselves and also others in an objective manner. Exercises on sensitivity are designed so that the trainees develop an ability to understand and empathise with the persons in need. The workshops on perception, self-awareness and sensitivity are a prerequisite for any skill training for working with people. The exercises should be conducted as a unit as they are complementary to each other. Since these are also foundation modules, these should be conducted at the beginning of skill training.

The section on communication is divided into two units, each of which contains two subunits. The first part focuses on the description of communication processes, followed by two workshops. The first workshop helps the TSWs to understand the basic concepts and process of communication and their elements. The second workshop in this unit would help the TSWs to understand various obstacles in communication and how these can be overcome.

In the second unit, the first part covers 'use of audio-visual media' while the second part is on 'innovative media in communication'. Each medium requires conducting independent workshops. At the end of these workshops, TSWs would have gained insight into the scope and preparation of each medium and developed skills in using media for effective communication.

The final section on methods deals with three methods of practice, namely working with individuals and families, working with groups and working with communities. The training module on working with individuals is designed to enable the trainees develop basic skills required for working with individuals throughout the helping process. It thus begins with skills required from first contact with the person in need till termination. The role plays take the trainees through the collection of information, process of assessing, arriving at a diagnosis and then formulating treatment goals and plans. The sessions also emphasise the skilful use of theory and the comprehensive use of principles, tools and techniques.

The module on group work has two parts. The first part focuses on three major areas of the group work process starting from identification of target group in relation to agency function, goals and scope. The exercises further emphasise the skills in developing achievable objectives on the basis of needs, problems and interests of members. Thirdly, the module enables trainees to achieve these objectives through use of appropriate activities, exercises and games. There is also an attempt to take the trainees through the stages of group development, namely, orientation, working and termination. The second part of this module contains games and activities for working with groups to make the TSWs more effective in achieving the objectives of group work. This part also gives techniques and tools of group work recording.

The module on community work emphasises various skills required for initiating contact and developing programmes at the community level. In the initial units covering this method, TSWs get insights into the importance and components of developing community understanding and how to establish contact and develop relationships in the community. The later workshops help TSWs understand the importance of preparing for and conducting activities and programmes in the community. Through these the TSWs develop insights about essential qualities and attitudes for working in communities and use of social mapping, community analyses and programme planning.

It is important to understand that the workshops in themselves are starting points for skill development. The learnings from the workshops need to be consistently reinforced through fieldwork supervision to ensure that these are translated in practice.

The lab sessions presented in this manual are reflective of the experiences gained in our institute. We look forward to others adapting these in their training and sharing with us their experiences while conducting the workshops. This will continue a process of mutual learning whereby the skill laboratory sessions can further evolve and become even more effective. We hope this manual will contribute to enhance skill learning components of TSWs and also the field practitioners.

NOTE TO THE FACILITATOR

Since the manual is to be used for skill training and has a definite set of objectives and expected outcomes, the following guidelines would prove useful.

1. Who should be the facilitator? The person/facilitator using the manual should preferably be a social work educator who has undergone skill training at least at some point of time in his/her career. He/she should have the conviction that skill training is an important part of social work education and skills can be developed through training.
2. The facilitator should necessarily be a person who has a good command over language, is alert and attentive, and is open to receiving new ideas. Ability to work in a team and take people along are essential qualities in the facilitator. He/she should be able to evoke participation and enthusiasm among participants to make the laboratory sessions vibrant.
3. Before setting off to conduct the training workshops, the facilitator should read the entire manual thoroughly.
4. The facilitator should be thorough in the theory base of the module on which he/she is to conduct training.
5. He/she should become familiar with the entire module and keep the training material ready.
6. Each session should be conducted sequentially, starting with the objectives and ending by highlighting and summarising the outcomes.
7. Skill sessions are more effective when conducted by a team of facilitators. It is therefore important that the group conducting a session should together take responsibilities for facilitating its various parts, observing and complementing one another and projecting excellent synchronisation. Therefore, they should jointly plan each session.

8. The workshops on perception, self-awareness, sensitivity and communication should be conducted as a unit before beginning the skill training modules.

DO'S AND DON'TS FOR THE FACILITATOR

1. The facilitator should ensure that theory of the module concerned is covered in the class prior to the session. If the theory subject is not part of the curriculum in the first year, give a brief overview of the relevant aspects of the theory and their field application.
2. The facilitator should show comfort and confidence while conducting the workshops. This requires proper and thorough prior preparation and clarity about the outcomes to be achieved.
3. The facilitator should provide ample opportunities for experimentation and innovation.
4. The situations presented in the module are indicative. The facilitator may develop situations that are reflective of their trainees' fieldwork experience.
5. Within the structure of the module, the facilitator should allow for as much flexibility as possible.
6. The facilitator should start with simple exercises and then move towards more complex situations while conducting role plays/exercises.
7. The facilitator should create space for voluntary participation. He/she should keep the environment positive and non-threatening.
8. The facilitator should acknowledge and appreciate volunteers for coming forward to participate.
9. The facilitator should encourage participation from as many as possible, but he/she should not force trainees if they are not comfortable.
10. The facilitator should encourage participants to bring their fieldwork situations to the lab.
11. The facilitator should ensure that the lab does not become a platform to target individuals and make scapegoats of them.
12. The facilitator should discuss the behaviour (verbal and non-verbal) reflected in the exercises rather than focusing on the individual participant.
13. Discussion and feedback may bring out defensive behaviour because of feelings of threat. The facilitator should handle it sensitively.
14. Under no circumstances should the facilitator become judgemental.
15. Sometimes the exercise may not bring out the desired effects necessary for the discussion to take off. The facilitator should then direct the situation to achieve desirable results.
16. The facilitator should have a mechanism for regular feedback from participants as well as team members as soon as each module is completed for achieving continuous improvement in sessions.

The figure illustrates the multiple roles that the facilitator must be equipped to perform.

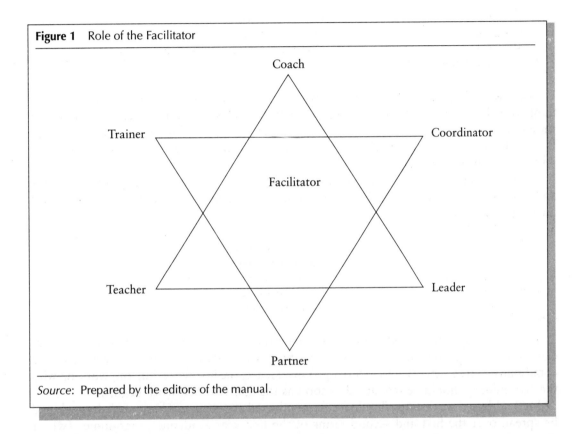

Figure 1 Role of the Facilitator

Coach

Trainer

Coordinator

Facilitator

Teacher

Leader

Partner

Source: Prepared by the editors of the manual.

PLANNING THE SOCIAL WORK SKILL LABORATORY SESSIONS

The timetable of the skill laboratory is very important. The first four workshops, that is, Perception, Self-awareness, Sensitivity and Communication need to be in the initial months of the training programme. For example, if the academic year begins in June and the field placements begin from July, then these workshops should be scheduled during June. They serve two purposes. Firstly, they prepare the trainee social workers (TSWs) for all the subsequent workshops and sessions that would be conducted through the year under the skills lab programme. Secondly, they would also help TSWs prepare for their field placements.

These workshops which are to be conducted in the first month of the academic pro-gramme could have the following schedule:

1. Perception   Half-day workshop
2. Self-awareness   One-and-a-half-day workshop
3. Sensitivity   One-and-a-half-day workshop
4. Communication   2-day workshop

These workshops could be conducted with a gap of one week, so that TSWs get time to think over their experiences. These have to be considered as one unit. Hence each workshop should start with a review of previous workshops and end with a link to the next workshop. During the first workshop on perception, the facilitator should present the objectives of this unit titled 'self-development'.

The workshops on 'use of audio-visual aids' need to be considered as independent modules and may be structured during the second term or some of these could also be organised during the second year.

1. Visual media   Half-day workshop
2. Audio-visual media   Half-day workshop
3. Innovative media   2-day workshop
4. Street play   1-day workshop
5. Puppets   1-day workshop

The workshops on methods will depend upon the fieldwork expectations and the theory classes. Usually during the first term of the first year, TSWs are expected to understand community, start casework and identify groups. Hence, the first workshop on 'working with the community' should be scheduled as soon as the first year fieldwork begins.

Method-based workshops should not be conducted at one time. These workshops should be spread over the first and second terms of the first year academic programme. Two or three half-day workshops on working with a community could be organised in the second week after the field training starts.

'Working with individuals' and 'working with groups' could start simultaneously. These could be organised once the concepts and basic principles of these methods are discussed in the theory classes.

WORKING WITH INDIVIDUALS

1. Intake interview   2 hours   First term
2. Social diagnosis   3 hours   Second term
3. Treatment   3 hours   Second term

WORKING WITH GROUPS

1. Planning for group work	3 hours	First term
2. Initial contact with groups	2 hours	First term
3. Conducting activities for modifying behaviour	Half-day workshop	Second term
4. Termination of groups	2 hours	Second term

WORKING WITH COMMUNITIES

1. Entering the community	2 hours	First term
2. Understanding the community (to be covered over three sessions)	6 hours	First term
3. Conducting meetings in the community	2 hours	Second term

The sequence of workshops is important, but the number of days depends upon the academic programme of that particular institute.

At the end of each module the facilitator should take written feedback or ask the TSWs to give a written feedback at the end of each term. A sample of evaluation form is given in Annexure A1. The facilitators should develop their own evaluation criteria. The feedback received should be analysed and the suggestions should be incorporated in the planning for next year as far as possible.

ANNEXURE A1 STUDENT FEEDBACK: SKILL TRAINING LABORATORY

1. List out titles of workshops conducted in the Skill Lab:
2. Are you clear about the objectives of the Skill Lab? (Please tick ONLY ONE):

   Clear ☐   Somewhat Clear ☐   Confused

3. Do you think the Objectives of skill training were achieved through the various workshops organised during the year?

   – Achieved to a very great extent ☐

   – Some of it achieved ☐

   – Not at all achieved ☐

   – Cannot say ☐

4. Which workshops did you like the best? (Give Reasons):
5. List the workshops you did not like (Give Reasons):
6. Do you think all workshops were

   Well planned   Yes ☐   No ☐

   Relevant   Yes ☐   No ☐

   Easy to understand Yes ☐   No ☐

7. Suggestion regarding conducted workshops
8. Suggestions regarding new workshops
9. Do you think these workshops are useful for your field work?

   Yes ☐   No ☐   Not Sure ☐

10. Give details of application of any workshop content in your field work.

    Name of the Workshop   How did you use the content of the workshop?

Note: This is just a sample feedback schedule. It can be adapted and modified according to the need of each institution.

Chapter 1

Understanding the Laboratory Approach in Skill Training

Sudha Datar and *Ruma Bawikar*

Certain skills are basic to social work practice and hence the trainee social workers (TSWs) need to be properly oriented to the concept of 'skill' right at the beginning. Since our formal education system does not encourage learners to participate in the process of learning, the trainees have to be exposed to the participatory methodology used throughout in the workshops that follow.

The following paragraphs explain the process by which skill labs can be introduced to the trainees. This, therefore, serves as the curtain raiser for the series of workshops to which the trainees will be exposed.

Objectives:

1. To help TSWs understand the basic principles of the laboratory approach.
2. To help TSWs understand the range of skills involved in social work practice.
3. To help TSWs understand the importance of their participation in the workshops for acquiring skills required in social work practice.

Time required: 3 hours.

Material required: Facilitator should prepare visual material—either OHP transparencies or charts—on the following topics:

1. Definitions of skill in social work practice.
2. List of basic skills required in social work practice.

Methodology used:

1. Brainstorming.
2. Role play.
3. Small group discussion.

Exercise 1.1 Concept of Skill

No. of participants: All.
Procedure:

1. Ask the participants to respond to the word 'skill' (brainstorming method).
2. List down the responses of the participants.
3. Select those responses which are relevant to social work practice.
4. Discuss in detail what a skill is and various definitions given in the context of social work practice.

Conclude: Skills are important in social work practice. One can develop these skills in various ways.

Exercise 1.2 Process of Learning in a Laboratory

Objectives:

1. To help TSWs in identifying skills required for relating to, and working with people.
2. To help TSWs to experience gains through feedback and introspection.
3. To help TSWs to understand the process of developing skills.

Method: Role play.
Time required: 1 hour.
No. of participants: This will depend upon the type of field situation. Some situations are given below:

1. The agency has a non-formal education class and a TSW has been asked to meet the Principal to collect a list of school dropouts.
2. On the first day of fieldwork, a TSW has to collect basic information about the agency from a *balwadi* [1] teacher.

---

[1] It is pre primary unit.

3. The superintendent of a residential care institution for children has asked a TSW to interact with them.

Ask participants to volunteer for the role play. Give time for preparation. Then ask the groups to enact the role play. After the enactment ask the observers to give their feedback on the process.

1. How did the worker approach the situation?
2. Do you think he/she was well prepared for the situation? How did you identify this?
3. How did he/she introduce himself or herself?
4. How did he/she seek information?
5. How did the receiver respond?

Then ask the actors to reflect on their enactment and review the process in the light of the feedback. Based on this reflection and feedback, highlight the areas that need to be changed. Finally ask the volunteers to try out specific suggestions given by others and observe and acknowledge the differences in performance.

Highlight the following:

1. Since these are simulated situations, they can be repeated.
2. Feedback can help in exploring alternatives which can be useful in changing our behaviour.
3. One can also gain from reviewing the situation objectively.

The facilitator should summarise this discussion by linking it to the lab approach wherein the participation of all contributes in benefiting each one. Willingness to share feelings and giving feedback enables in creating supportive environment.

Sometimes it may so happen that the fresh learner may feel inhibited to come forward to perform in role plays and the underlying skills may not emerge. If the institute or college has the required facilities, then the trainer can use film clips that demonstrate skills and ask the trainees to observe the skills and note them. Films depicting situations like a counselling session, a group meeting for a self-help group (SHG) and a health education session in progress could be used.

Exercise 1.3 Objectives for Skill Training

Objective: To help TSWs identify the objectives of skill training workshops.
Method: Small group discussion.
Time required: 40 minutes.
Procedure: Divide the class into small groups (8–10 members).

1. Ask each group to state their expectations from the lab sessions.
2. Ask each group to present their expectations.

The facilitator could summarise by highlighting the following objectives of lab sessions:

1. To help TSWs develop willingness to participate in the self-learning process.
2. To help TSWs to build their confidence so that they can develop their potential with practice.
3. To help TSWs understand the range of skills which are basic to social work practice and those that are specific to each method.

The facilitator could help the TSWs to make a list of basic skills used in the practice of social work:

1. Listening which leads to understanding.
2. Eliciting information in order to collect relevant data that would lead to assessment of a problem situation.
3. Building relationships for effective intervention.
4. Observing both verbal and non-verbal behaviour, which helps in the process of assessment.
5. Talking and listening skills that involve use of verbal language and body language. This leads towards developing a positive interpersonal relationship. This is also active listening which seeks to develop appropriate communication styles that promote understanding.

All skills could be classified into three categories—cognitive skills, procedural skills and interactional skills.

Cognitive skills are intellectual skills. A social worker requires cognitive skills in collecting relevant information for assessment and in order to arrive at a correct diagnosis. Skills in assessment and diagnosis are the highest cognitive skills required in a social worker. Other cognitive skills could be partialising, prioritising and setting intervention goals. Cognitive skills can be developed by developing critical and reflective thinking. Understanding of the self and others and understanding social issues, relationships and problems require cognitive skills.

Procedural skills are required in a worker because social work activities are based on certain logical, systematic and scientific steps which are to be procedurally followed, for example, collecting information is a step in all the methods of social work. Hence, skills in systematic gathering would come before any strategies for intervention. Some procedures are the same for all methods. History taking is the first step in case work but in group work, need assessment comes first. Some of the common procedural skills could be fact gathering, systematic intervention, skills in planning, evaluation and termination, recording skills, and so on.

Interactional skills are the most important in social work practice because interaction is the main medium/channel of all interventions. Interactional skills are reflected in the behaviour of the worker. Some of these are observation, listening, interviewing, establishing meaningful relationship, and so on. They come under the broad spectrum of skills covered in communication.

The facilitator needs to discuss the annual plan of skill lab sessions and the different methods that would be used in the sessions, especially:

1. Role play.
2. Group discussions.
3. Presentations.

4. Do it yourself exercises.
5. Games.
6. Demonstrations.
7. Audio-visual methods.

The facilitator can conclude this workshop with the following statement:
The more we do, the more we learn. Participation is the key to learning. Let us learn together to become effective social workers.

Section 1

SELF-DEVELOPMENT

MEANING OF SELF-DEVELOPMENT

Self-development is a sum total of many aspects, qualities and abilities that one possesses and how these are used to maximise one's effectiveness as a functioning individual.

As social workers, we look at self-development in the following context:

1. **Having a realistic self-concept:** This implies positive and healthy appreciation of oneself, understanding one's capacities and limitations, and overcoming negative and unrealistic ideas about oneself.
2. **Acquiring internal control over the self:** This means the ability to define 'self' independently. This understanding should not be coloured by what others feel about you.
3. **Understanding the cognitive, affective and behavioural aspects of the self:** This implies being sensitive to one's own feelings, sharpening emotional responses and developing a range of behavioural capacities which would be appropriate to different situations.
4. **Achieving congruence between different aspects of the self:** Behaviour is a reflection of our intellectual process and emotional reactions. This, therefore, involves achieving congruence among cognitive, affective and behavioural aspects.

NEED FOR SELF-DEVELOPMENT FOR SOCIAL WORKERS

1. Clear understanding of the self helps in understanding one's identity. It clears doubts and feelings of inadequacy. This results in clarity of role and improvement in professional performance.
2. Understanding oneself means knowing the factors or forces which build one's confidence, situations which bring out the best in oneself, how to relate to persons who are dissimilar to oneself.
3. Acceptance and respect of the self becomes the basis for accepting the other person's uniqueness, weaknesses, qualities and complexities. If we do not accept others as they are, we will not be able to value their experiences or encourage them to use their experiences for growth and self-development. The reciprocal relationship between acceptance and respect of the self and that of others can be explained with the following figure.

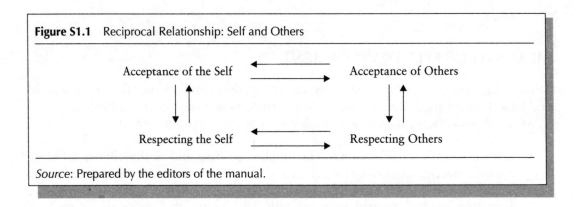

Figure S1.1   Reciprocal Relationship: Self and Others

Source: Prepared by the editors of the manual.

Respect indicates concern about the other person in 'totality'. Concern for others is fundamental in social work.

Understanding development of the self can be a context for understanding the other person's process of development. Social workers must be able to answer the question, 'How do I learn and grow?' This in turn helps social workers to appreciate the process of how others learn and grow.

In the process of self-awareness, one learns to be flexible and open. These qualities enable the social worker in building trusting relationships with others.

THE WORKSHOPS FOR SELF-DEVELOPMENT

In the section on self-development, three modules are to be conducted on the following topics:

1. Understanding perception.
2. Self-awareness.
3. Sensitivity.

Self-development is a goal of every individual. The professional needs to be consciously developed. One of the important components of personality is perception. Since we understand and interpret the world around us through the perceptual processes, our values and attitudes, our understanding of our own behaviour and that of others will depend upon how we perceive and interpret. Hence, understanding our own perceptions is the first step in self-development.

Similarly, self-awareness is a continuous and dynamic process. Trainee social workers (TSWs), need to continuously examine their own feelings, attitudes and behaviours, when they are interacting with others. The exercises on self-awareness take the trainees towards a step-by-step understanding of the process of self-awareness.

Sensitivity is also a prerequisite for helping others. Our attitudes and values affect our behaviour towards others and this in turn affects our relationship with others. Hence, purposeful use of the self is the most important tool in social work practice. The three workshops on perception, self-awareness and sensitivity should start in the trainees the process of consciously looking at oneself, which should be reflected through changes in behaviour and action and continued throughout their professional life. Hence it is important to conduct these workshops as a unit.

All the workshops that follow, whether communication or skill development in methods repeatedly focus on development of the 'professional self', since a skilled worker implies a self-aware professional who has consciously tried to inculcate values and attitudes of social work.

Through these workshops, TSWs would be confronted with the following questions:

- How do I perceive the world around me?
- Am I aware and open about my emotions and feelings?
- Am I willing to acknowledge that I am not perfect?
- Am I willing to face some pain in this process of understanding myself?
- Am I flexible enough to evolve alternative plans and strategies to change my feelings, thoughts and behaviour?

Confronting the above and becoming conscious about these in oneself would enable a TSW to appreciate the resistances and blocks one faces while bringing about change.

Hence one can say that these three workshops have a twofold benefit—one, understanding of the self and learning to adapt oneself as per the professional expectations and two, gaining insight into the client's thoughts and feelings while he/she is facing the problem and making efforts to overcome it by bringing about change in himself/herself.

Chapter 2

UNDERSTANDING PERCEPTION

Sudha Datar

Ability to observe the details, remember these and select the relevant amongst these, interpret and report them verbally or in writing are essential skills for a social worker. This largely depends upon our social perceptions.

To understand how perception plays an important role in our personality and also in our communication, we must first understand the basic concept of perception and factors affecting it.

MEANING OF PERCEPTION

To perceive is to observe, notice and understand with one or more of the sense organs and the mind, the reality around us. Human behaviour is determined to a great extent by the way in which the world is perceived. It refers to the world of experience—the world as seen, heard, felt, smelt or tasted by a person. It is a process of discrimination of the stimuli received from the outside world. The Figure 2.1 explains the process of perception:

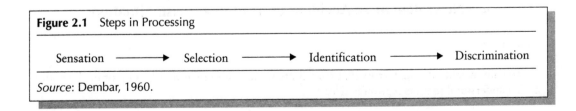

Figure 2.1 Steps in Processing

Sensation ⟶ Selection ⟶ Identification ⟶ Discrimination

Source: Dembar, 1960.

Perception is selective. The selection of specific from the whole depends upon the following.

Attention

This is an important factor which affects perception. It divides our field into focus and margin. For example, when we watch a cricket match, we focus on the ball and other things seen go in the margin.

Attention is not static. Attention shifts from one item to another. What is in focus at one time becomes marginal at another time. For example, if we get engrossed in reading a novel, we might forget our stomach ache.

Attention is influenced by external factors as well as by the internal factors in an individual. The external factors include:

1. Intensity of the event/problem.
2. Repetition of the event/problem.
3. Contrast in the stimuli.
4. Physical movement.
5. Novelty of experiences.

The internal factors include:

1. Interests.
2. Moods.
3. Motives.
4. Values.
5. Biases and prejudices.
6. Stereotyping.

To illustrate these, the following exercises would be helpful.

Exercise 2.1 Reactions to a Photograph Depicting an Accident or a News item of an Accident or any Other Crisis Situation

Objectives:

1. To gain insight into the factors that contribute to our interpretation of an event or the reality.
2. To understand that perception is selective.

No. of participants: All. To be divided into small groups of 10–12 members.
Material required: Photographs (or other material) depicting crisis situation (one for each group).
Time required: 45 minutes.
Procedure:

1. Divide the class into small groups.
2. Give one photograph to each group and ask them to see it.
3. Ask each member to write all the details seen in the photograph.
4. Ask the members to share their reactions in their group.
5. Conduct a discussion with all the participants.

Points for discussion:

1. Which factors, external as well as internal, helped in noticing the details in the picture?
2. Which parts of the picture were most frequently noticed? Why?
3. Did the reactions vary? Why?
4. Why people differ in their perceptions, even if the reality is the same?

   Through the discussion, highlight that there is no such thing as right or wrong perception. Perception is always subjective and, therefore, selective.

Exercise 2.2 Perceiving the Temperature of Water

Objective: To understand the influence of past experiences on perceptions.
No. of participants: 2.
Materials required: Three glasses of water: one containing ice-cold water, another tap water and the third containing hot water.
Time required: 15–20 minutes.
Procedure:

1. Ask one participant to dip his fingers in ice-cold water and ask the other to dip his fingers in hot water.
2. After 30 seconds ask them to remove their fingers and simultaneously dip them in the glass containing tap water.
3. Ask each one to describe the temperature of water in the third glass containing tap water.

Points for discussion:

1. Why was the temperature felt differently by both participants though the water had a constant temperature?
2. Can one relate this to real-life situations?

Highlight through discussion: Perception is always shaped by previous experience. It is therefore always relative.

Exercise 2.3 Expectancy and Perception

If we are expecting a visitor, then all that we hear is interpreted as a knock on the door or the sound of footsteps. If we are expecting someone to arrive, then we also hear the knock or the footsteps immediately.

Objectives:

1. To understand the influence of a sequence of a set of experiences on our interpretation.
2. To understand the influence of expectations on perception.

No. of participants: All.
Materials required: Enlarged separate sheets showing alphabets (Figure 2.2A) and numbers (Figure 2.2B).
Time required: 20–30 minutes.
Procedure:

1. First show the alphabet sheet and ask the participants to read.
2. Then show the number sheet and ask the participants to read it.
3. Finally show both sheets together and highlight the similarity between the alphabet 'B' and the number '13'.

Points for discussion: In spite of the similarity between the two, why were these figures perceived differently?
Highlight through discussion: Despite similarities in the stimuli, perceptions could be different because of differential expectations arising from the sequence learnt earlier.

Exercise 2.4 Developing Holistic Perception

Perception is not only a summation of all sensory experiences but also an organisation of facts. This is normal human tendency. The different ways in which facts are organised could be illustrated through all the following exercises.

Objective: To understand the ways in which a complete perception comes through organising facts.
Note to the facilitator: The facilitator could use figures given in the manual or other similar pictures from psychology textbooks.
Figure-ground Perception: In our daily life also we see the picture on the wall but not the wall which holds the picture. Sometimes, when two shapes are put together different figures may be perceived (Figure 2.3).

Figure 2.2A Sheet of Alphabets

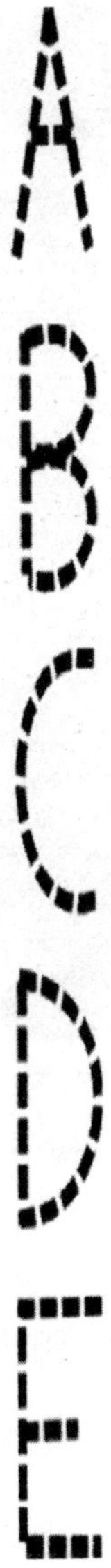

Figure 2.2B Sheet of Numbers

Source: Morgan et al., 1986.

Figure 2.3   Profile and/or Vase

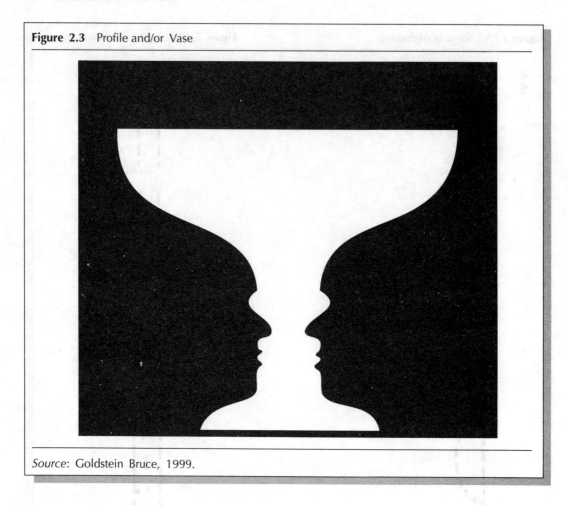

Source: Goldstein Bruce, 1999.

In reality also we need to see the problem against the background from which it emerges. This is holistic perception.

Grouping

Grouping of stimuli in a pattern is also an important way of organising facts. Proximity, similarities and continuation guide the process of organisation. Based on this, we group people together. For example, all people with fair complexion are beautiful or all people with grey eyes are deceptive.

Our cultural background also contributes to grouping. These create stereotypes.

Certain symbols have specific meaning for some people and these symbols stimulate certain feelings. For example, the symbol of swastika in India and the same in Germany will have different meanings.

A little modification in direction and placement changes our perception.

Show the participants two figures—one of two squares placed differently and another two lines equal in length enclosed within outward arrows and inward arrows (Figure 2.4). The same figures may be perceived either as a square or as a diamond. Similarly, the two equal lines may be interpreted as being unequal.

Figure 2.4   Orientation Influences Perception

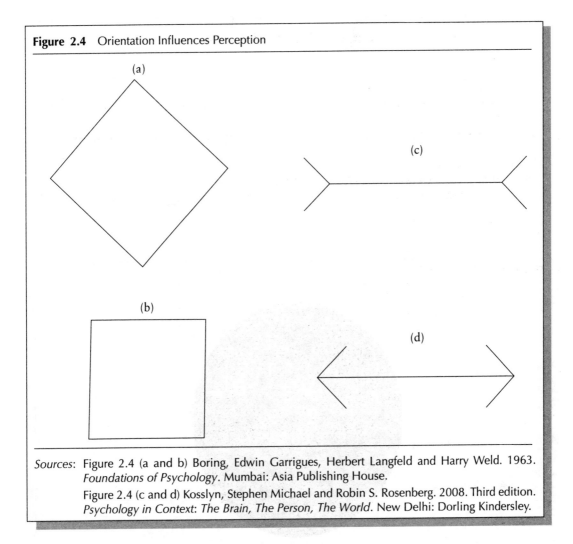

Sources: Figure 2.4 (a and b) Boring, Edwin Garrigues, Herbert Langfeld and Harry Weld. 1963. *Foundations of Psychology*. Mumbai: Asia Publishing House.

Figure 2.4 (c and d) Kosslyn, Stephen Michael and Robin S. Rosenberg. 2008. Third edition. *Psychology in Context: The Brain, The Person, The World*. New Delhi: Dorling Kindersley.

Distortions in Perception: Very often there is a tendency to generalise situations or draw conclusions based on partial perceptions. These are called fallacies. Fallacies in observation are of the following types:

1. Identification of part for the whole.
2. Either-or fallacy. For example, individuals are either good or bad. This is not true since people are a combination of both.
3. Partial view, focusing on some aspects, ignoring others.

Exercise 2.5 Black Circle

Objectives:

1. To understand that when we concentrate on a striking fact, we may ignore other aspects of reality.
2. To understand that perception of the reality should reflect the totality of a situation.

No. of participants: All.
Material required: One white drawing paper 12″ × 12″ in size.
Draw one-inch diameter circle on it and fill the circle completely with black colour (Figure 2.5).

Figure 2.5   Black Circle

Source: James, Bhaise, Marie, Brian of Training Animators in Conscientization and Education (1975) (TRACE Team), published by Janaseva Mandal, Nandurbar (Maharashtra).

Time required: 20–30 minutes.
Procedure:

1. Hold up the paper to display the black spot to all the participants.
2. Ask them just one question, 'What do you see?'
3. Note as many observations as possible on the black circle.

Points for discussion:

1. Where did the majority focus their attention?
2. Why did everybody concentrate there?

Highlight through discussion:

1. Selective perception distorts reality.
2. Holistic perception helps to understand the reality situation in its entirety.

Stereotype thinking:
This type of thinking contributes in adding more subjective information to the facts, which can lead to exaggeration of reality. Our perceived notions always influence our processing of external stimuli.

Exercise 2.6 From Fact to Fallacy

Objectives:

1. To understand the ways in which our attitudes, values and thinking distort facts.
2. To understand the process by which fallacy is believed to be fact.

Note to the facilitator: A picture could be drawn by a trainee social worker who is an artist and that could be used for this exercise.

No. of participants: All.
Material required: Draw a picture of man wearing a hat with a briefcase in his hand on a big chart paper (Figure 2.6).
Procedure:

1. Pin the picture on the blackboard.
2. Ask the participants to list out whatever they see in this picture.

Time required: 20–30 minutes.

Figure 2.6 Man with a Briefcase

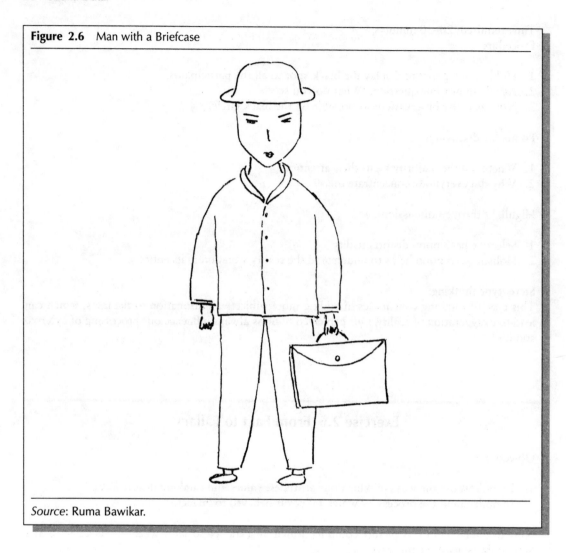

Source: Ruma Bawikar.

Points for discussion:

1. How are the inferences drawn?
2. What are the inferences based on?
3. Why do we believe in these inferences?
4. How do these inferences influence our responses?

Highlight through discussion:

1. Inferences drawn from subjective perception can lead to incomplete and incorrect responses.
2. They can create barriers in building positive relationships with others.

Table 2.1 shows the phenomenon of fact to fallacy clearly.

Table 2.1   Phenomenon of Fact to Fallacy

What happened	Mr. A says		Mr. B says	Comment
The event	I see a _ _ _	Fact	I see a _ _ _	No argument
		Human figure with a hat and a brief case (Figure 2.5)		
The label First inference	It is a man with a brief case	Fact	It is a man with a brief case	Because it could be a woman dressed like a man
Second inference	He is taking some work home with him	Fact	Spies some times use brief cases	Going off in a different direction
Third inference	He must be a very dedicated man to take work home with him	Fact	I would not be surprised if that man does not turn out to be a spy	Value judgement
Fourth inference	A man who is dedicated is bound to be successful in life and an asset to our community	Fact	This country is infected with spies and unless we do something about it we are in trouble	Adding opinion to statements
And so on		Fact		Misleading and leading to error

Source: Morgan et al., 1986.

This unit could be concluded after highlighting following points:

1. When we perceive our reality, our emotions and thinking processes affect the interpretation of it. Hence, there could be distortions in our perception.

2. Distortions in perception can adversely affect our relationship and communication with the client systems.
3. Efforts that we need to make to check our perceptions are as follows:

   (a) Examine the situation from all angles—holistic understanding is important.
   (b) Examine our interpretation by counter checking with others.

4. Developing objectivity and a non-judgemental attitude will help us in understanding our reality appropriately.

These exercises on 'Perception' will help the trainees to know the contribution of the perceptual process in understanding oneself and the world around us and also prepare them for the next unit, that is, Self-awareness.

Chapter 3

SELF-AWARENESS

Sudha Datar, Ruma Bawikar and *Geeta Rao*

MEANING OF SELF-CONCEPT

The most important part of a man's personality is the self-image. Self-image is awareness of how one consciously perceives oneself.

Self-concept is that part of the self about which one is aware. It includes the perception one has of one's own characteristics, feelings, attitudes, values and abilities. It is a picture the person has of himself. Although the core personality remains the same, the self-concept may change or develop over a period. This is because of environmental influences and life experiences. It is important to recognise that each person has a unique self-concept.

Exercise 3.1 Know Yourself

Objectives:

1. To enable trainee social workers (TSWs) to gain insight into their own personal characteristics.
2. To help them understand how inhibitions affect expression of self and self-revelation.

Materials required: Papers and pencils.
No. of participants: All.
Time required: 20 minutes.
Procedure:

1. Ask all participants to write five qualities they like in themselves and five qualities they do not like in themselves.

2. After two minutes ask participants who would like to read out what they have written.

Points for discussion:

1. Which qualities could you write immediately?
2. Could you write all 10 qualities?
3. If no, then why?
4. Why are qualities which we do not like in ourselves perceived as negative qualities?
5. Why are positives written quickly and why does it take longer to write down our negative qualities?
6. Why could some complete the list?
7. While reading out the list aloud, what did one feel especially about those characteristics which one does not like in oneself?
8. What is the basis for our likes and dislikes?

   We do know ourselves to a certain extent but we have not consciously allowed our understanding of the self to surface. Sometimes we fall short of words to express ourselves. We are also at times confused between positive and negative characteristics. With the help of a list of adjectives, we may be able to understand ourselves better.

Exercise 3.2 List of Adjectives

Objectives:

1. To enable trainees to understand themselves.
2. To help them get clarity regarding negative and positive qualities.

Material required: A lists of adjectives (Annexure A3.1).
No. of participants: All.
Time required: 30 minutes.
Procedure:

1. Distribute the list to all participants.
2. Ask participants to read the list and tick mark the qualities that describe them the best.
3. With the help of participants classify the qualities into positive, negative and neutral.
4. Ask participants to count positive and negative qualities in themselves from the list in which they have tick marked their own qualities.

Points for discussion:

1. How many more qualities have we identified in ourselves?
2. Which are negative and which are positive? What do we feel when some more negative qualities are identified?
3. What insights do we gain from this exercise?

Exercise 3.3 Mirror Reflection

Objective: To help TSWs understand the process of knowing themselves.
No. of participants: 2.
Materials required: Two mirrors (size 10″ × 6″).
Time required: 30 minutes.
Procedure:

1. Ask one participant to hold the mirror close to his face, touching the nose and look into the mirror and ask him to note what he sees of himself.
2. Then ask him to move the mirror in such a way so as to be able to see more of himself. Ask him to note whatever he has been able to see now.
3. Ask the second participant to hold the other mirror and ask the first to see himself with the help of both mirrors.
4. Ask the first participant to instruct the second participant what he/she wants to see while the other holds and both manoeuvre the mirrors accordingly. Ask the first to note what he/she sees.

Points for discussion:

1. What were the differences in these three situations?
2. What were the outcomes of each situation?

Points to be highlighted:

1. If we are very subjective, we may distort our understanding of the self.
2. Even if we try to understand the self, our efforts alone have limitations.
3. We require the help of others to understand the self.
4. To understand the self one requires to generate dialogue with others and should be willing to take help from others.

Source: David, W. Johnson. *Reaching Out-interpersonal Effectiveness & Self Actualization*
301.15 J50R, pg.22

Exercise 3.4 Openness of the Self

Note to the facilitator: If the group members are not familiar with each other, then this exercise is difficult to conduct.
Objectives:

1. To help trainees identify their own behaviour patterns.
2. To encourage the willingness to share.

3. To understand the perception of others about oneself.
4. To understand the differences between self-perception and perception by others.

Materials required: Photocopied lists of statements (Annexure A3.2) and pencils.
No. of participants: All.
Time required: 20 minutes.
Procedure:

1. Ask each participant to select one member they trust the most and form pairs.
2. Give the list of statements and a pencil to each participant.
3. Ask them to tick mark the statements which are applicable to them. This has to be done individually.
4. Ask the participants to share the list with their partner and tick mark his/her reactions in the 'agree/disagree' column without questioning the reasons. Both members of the pair have to share their list with each other.

Points for discussion:

1. How did the participants receive each others' disclosure?
2. Could the participants overcome their sense of discomfort in the process of being open?
3. What were the feelings while reading the list to the person they had chosen as the trusted one and when he/she chose to disagree?

This is presented in Figure 3.1 by partially making use of the Jo-Hari window:

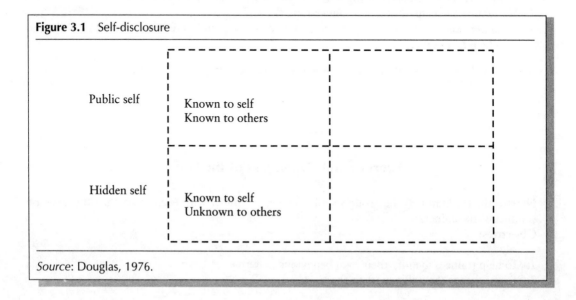

Figure 3.1 Self-disclosure

Public self	Known to self Known to others	
Hidden self	Known to self Unknown to others	

Source: Douglas, 1976.

We have tried to reveal ourselves to another person through these exercises.

One's self-concept can be realistic and idealistic. The ideal self-concept is defined as 'the organized conceptual patterns of characteristics and emotional states which the individual consciously holds as desirable for himself' (Rogers, 1961). We strive to achieve the ideal self-concept, but it is quite difficult.

For a realistic self-concept, we need to receive information from others also. One has to be open in giving information about oneself and at the same time one needs to have willingness to receive information from others regarding self.

Exercise 3.5 Mirror Reflection (Interpersonal Perception)

No. of participants: All.
Materials required: Papers and pencils.
Procedure:

1. Ask each participant to write five positive qualities and five negative qualities about themselves.
2. Ask each participant to select two participants whom they know and trust and form a group of three.
3. Ask all three from each group to write down five positives and negatives about the other two members on a separate paper with the name of the person written on the paper.
4. They should give the papers to the respective persons about whom they have written.
5. Ask them to check these lists with their own list and try to understand the similarities and differences.
6. Ask each member from the group of three to read out their lists to each other.

Points for discussion:

1. What was the first reaction of each participant when they received the lists?
2. What did each one feel while writing about the others' qualities?
3. What did each one feel when it was read aloud to each other?

After the discussion, complete the Jo-Hari window of the self (Figure 3.2).

The public self becomes larger because of the self-disclosure by the person and by receiving feedback from others. The broken line shows the expanding the public self.

In conclusion, we have learnt the following:

1. We behave on the basis of what we know about ourselves (this is our self-concept).
2. Others relate with us on the basis of what they know about us (their perceptions about us).

These two understandings may not be identical.

Figure 3.2 Jo-Hari Window

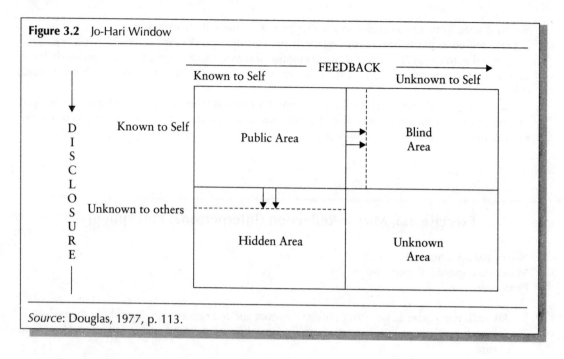

Source: Douglas, 1977, p. 113.

- When we come closer to some people, we are willing for self-disclosure thereby increasing the public self and reducing the hidden self.
- In this process, we also seek information regarding what others think of us or know of us, which we may not know.
- When others share their views regarding us it is called feedback.

How should feedback be given?

1. It is to be solicited and not dumped.
2. It should be specific and clear.
3. It should be descriptive and not evaluative.
4. It should be timely.
5. It should seek understanding.
6. It should describe one's feelings without putting motives to other's behaviour.

Feedback could be positive or negative. But if we introspect on the basis of this, we reduce areas of blind self and our public self becomes large. It has to be mutual sharing between two persons. If feedback is given in public and without consideration for the other person, strong emotional reactions can be stimulated.

Exercise 3.6 Reactions to Insult

Objective: To understand one's reactions to humiliating situations.
No. of participants: All.
Time required: 20 minutes.
Materials required: Photocopied lists of reactions to insult (Annexure A3.3) and pencils.
Procedure:

1. Distribute photocopies of the list (Annexure 3.3) to all.
2. Ask the participants to tick mark whichever are applicable to them.

Points for discussion:

1. To what extent do these reactions strengthen or weaken our relationships?
2. What type of feedback would be more acceptable?
3. Do we have any control on the person who gives feedback?
4. What factors influence the nature of our reaction?
5. How does one deal with feedback?

Highlight the following: Emotional reactions may be of anger, hostility, depression, retaliation, aggression, withdrawal, shock, revenge, giving back, and so on. One cannot compartmentalise reactions into 'right' or 'wrong' reactions.
    Ways of dealing with feedback.

- Listen carefully.
- Collect and explore facts in relation to feedback.
- Explain one's position if necessary.
- Try to understand (and analyse) emotions.
- You may choose to agree or disagree.
- If you agree, show willingness to change.
- If you disagree, base your opinion on facts rather than on ego or pride.
- Discuss limitations to change with a person you trust.

    We get feedback from significant others, from other individuals like people in authority, colleagues and other formal groups. This happens continuously due to our interactions. Therefore we can say that self-concept is not a static condition. We go on adding information. We continuously reflect or introspect on all our experiences. The core self is quite stable. A balanced understanding of the self is important for a positive self-image. A positive self-image helps us to feel comfortable with the self. This process of self-awareness influences in turn our thoughts, feelings and attitudes towards the self or others. Our values directly affect our relationships with others. These guide our behaviour.
    Hence, value reflection is an important component of the process of self-awareness. Value is defined as a belief upon which an individual acts by preference.

The characteristics of values are as follows:

1. Learnt.
2. Interrelated to one another.
3. Relatively stable and enduring.
4. Can change but force cannot be used for change.
5. Help to select facts and act as filters.
6. Have an evaluative function.
7. Indicate degree of acceptance of the self and others.

Exercise 3.7 Reactions to Events

Objective: To understand how different attitudes of different individuals affect responses to the same stimulus.
Time required: 30 minutes.
Participants: All.
Materials required: Cuttings of current news items, for example, on terrorism, communalism, railway accident and natural calamity, from newspapers.
Instructions:

1. Ask participants to read the news carefully and write down their reactions.
2. Then ask a few participants to read aloud the reactions to the group.

Points for discussion:

1. What do these reactions indicate?
2. Can we make a list of values, biases reflected through the reactions?

Highlight the following:

1. Values affect our thinking and actions.
2. Values are not consciously expressed.
3. Individuals may not be aware of influences of values on their interpretations or reactions to situations.

Exercise 3.8 Complete the Story

Objectives:

1. To gain insight and understanding into one's own values and individual differences in values.
2. To develop understanding regarding how our problem-solving process, decision making, and so on get affected due to our attitudes and values.

No. of participants: All.
Materials required: Paper and pen for each participant.
Time required: 30–45 minutes.
Procedure:

1. Narrate a story (Annexure A3.4) with no ending to a whole class.
2. Ask each participant to write the end of the story.
3. Ask a few participants to read out the endings.

Points for discussion:

1. Why are there so many different endings for the same story?
2. What wordings are used to end the story?
3. What is the tone of the ending?
4. To what extent our values affect our interpretation?
5. Is there a need to examine these values?

Conclude the workshop by highlighting the following:

1. Our self-concept could be positive or negative and this leads to the evaluation of the self.
   Our self-esteem is a personal judgement of one's own worth. This gap can be minimised
   by self-talk and open interactions with others. This is the process of self-awareness.
2. Attitudes and values can change if the process of self-awareness, acceptance of reality
   and willingness to change are consciously initiated.
3. Self-awareness opens the opportunity for development of an integrated personality. An
   integrated person is (Figure 3.3):

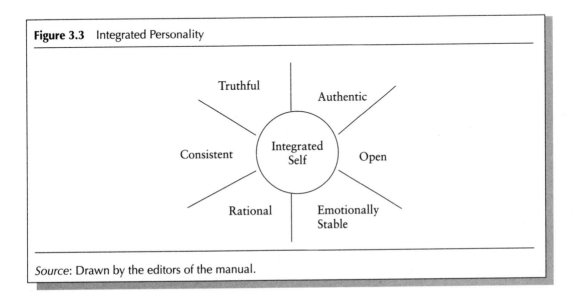

Figure 3.3 Integrated Personality

Source: Drawn by the editors of the manual.

4. Self-awareness is the first step in self-development. It helps the person to remove the 't' from the sentence 'I can't' and helps the person to believe in 'I can'. This is the key to self-development.
5. A person with a positive self-image usually:

   (a) visualises self as adequate, secure, open minded and satisfied;
   (b) visualises others as unique and accepts and allows them to grow and
   (c) is comfortable in building relationships, willing to share, understand, tolerate and welcomes differences of opinions.

These exercises in self-awareness initiate the process of self-development in the trainees. They need to consciously use this understanding of the self for setting self-development goals. Understanding of the self cannot be complete without being sensitive to other person's needs, emotions and behaviour and hence the unit on sensitivity.

ANNEXURE A3.1 LIST OF ADJECTIVES

1. graceful
2. cheerful
3. intelligent
4. aggressive
5. kind
6. harsh
7. brave
8. artistic
9. likable
10. happy
11. systematic
12. miser
13. irresponsible
14. attractive
15. nervous
16. irritable
17. enthusiastic
18. careless
19. critical
20. boastful
21. simple
22. confident
23. fair-minded
24. impatient
25. wicked
26. clean
27. formal
28. talkative
29. lazy
30. affectionate
31. reliable
32. alert
33. resourceful
34. modest
35. fussy

36. obstinate
37. delicate
38. friendly
39. vague
40. adventurous
41. unsteady
42. anxious
43. social
44. superior
45. curious
46. greedy
47. frank
48. impressive
49. quiet
50. optimistic
51. energetic
52. foolish
53. active
54. insincere
55. excitable
56. clever
57. shy
58. argumentative
59. jealous
60. disciplined
61. ambitious
62. quarrelsome
63. independent
64. tense
65. willing
66. efficient
67. thoughtful
68. serious
69. suspicious
70. sympathetic
71. inventive
72. honest
73. weak
74. contented
75. tolerant
76. idealistic
77. strict
78. obedient

79. shirker
80. humorous
81. mischievous
82. restless
83. bossy
84. selfish
85. rude
86. determined
87. punctual
88. broad-minded
89. bluffer
90. smart

Source: Daphne Lennox. 1982. *Residential Group Therapy for Children*. London and New York: Tavistock Publication.

ANNEXURE A3.2 INTERPERSONAL PERCEPTIONS

Tick mark whichever applies to you and or to your friend:

Are you someone who_____	Myself	My friend	Agree	Disagree
1. Keeps trying until you succeed.				
2. Listen carefully to news.				
3. Takes an active role in a group.				
4. Often interrupts others.				
5. Tends to decide in haste.				
6. Is work oriented.				
7. Waits for others to greet first.				
8. Prefers to work by yourself.				
9. Wants to do what is fun and does not worry about the future.				
10. Believes that most people can be trusted.				
11. Will let people take undue advantage of you.				
12. Is a difficult person to manage.				
13. Asks others for help.				
14. Is satisfied with yourself.				
15. Gets upset under pressure.				
16. Is much too independent.				
17. Makes friends easily.				
18. Has difficulty in saying no.				
19. Cannot keep a secret.				
20. Lacks control of emotions.				
21. Is serious.				
22. Is willing to consider and accept others' suggestions.				
23. Supports others.				
24. Takes personal responsibly for own performance.				
25. Finds it difficult to relax.				

ANNEXURE A3.3 REACTIONS TO AN INSULT

When someone (teacher or colleague) insults you in the presence of others, do you (tick whatever applies to you):

1. Get angry and retaliate.
2. Start laughing.
3. Insult him back.
4. Go into your shell and stop talking to people.
5. Read, sing, go for a walk, listen to radio, watch TV.
6. Pray in silence.
7. Keep quiet and discuss the matter with that person when everything is over.
8. Start a character assassination campaign against the person.
9. Avoid that person for sometime.
10. Start crying.
11. Go on sulking.
12. Any other action (specify).

Source: Prepared by the authors.

ANNEXURE A3.4 COMPLETE THE STORY

One couple lived in a remote village. The husband fell seriously ill. It was a stormy night and it was difficult to reach the PHC doctor who lived in the next village and to bring the medicine. The wife asked a truck driver for a lift. He was willing to help her on one condition that she should have sex with him. She agreed to this condition, got the medicine from the doctor on time. Her husband was completely cured. After a few months the husband comes to know about this incident. He feels …

Source: Prepared by the authors.

Chapter 4

SENSITIVITY DEVELOPMENT

Ruma Bawikar and *Nagmani Rao*

Social work being a helping profession relies on interpersonal relationships. The worker needs to develop meaningful and purposeful relationship with the clients. A relationship is an important tool which helps not only in collecting information but also in influencing change in the client.

If the worker develops the ability to respond appropriately to the client, it will help in developing a relationship. Appropriate responding is a reflection of the worker's sensitivity.

WHAT IS THE MEANING OF SENSITIVITY?

This word is derived from the word 'senses'. Sensitivity as per the dictionary meaning is 'All the five senses by which a living thing becomes aware of the external world.' It is an ability which is responsive to or helps to notice slight changes.

In social work, sensitivity implies the following aspects:

1. Receptivity of the worker.
2. Empathetic understanding of the situation.
3. Ability to differentiate the nuances.

We may define sensitivity as an ability to respond empathetically in accordance with the client's needs.

Sensitive responding helps the client to feel that he/she is understood, leading to a sense of comfort.

Sensitivity is expressed through

1. words—verbally;
2. non-verbal communication—facial expression, touch, actions, tone and
3. in the written form.

Both cognition and affect play an important role in our sensitivity.

HOW DOES SENSITIVITY HELP?

If a worker is sensitive, he/she will be able to help the person open up. Sensitivity in a worker enables him/her to develop a holistic understanding of individual, group or community situation (Figure 4.1).

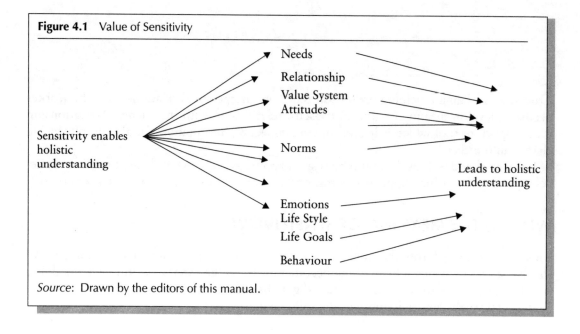

Figure 4.1   Value of Sensitivity

Sensitivity enables holistic understanding

Needs
Relationship
Value System
Attitudes

Norms

Leads to holistic understanding

Emotions
Life Style
Life Goals
Behaviour

Source: Drawn by the editors of this manual.

With understanding one is able to accept others and also can be an effective facilitator.

Sensitivity can be developed. It requires a conscious effort based on introspection and feedback. Trainee social workers (TSWs) could use the following methods to develop this ability:

1. reading case studies;
2. exposure visits;
3. observating professional social workers in the field and
4. discussing experiences with colleagues and professionals.

To help TSWs develop capacities to become sensitive, conducting workshops could be a very useful method.

The objectives of the workshop are as follows:

1. To understand the concept of sensitivity.
2. To understand the factors that help us to become sensitive. These are:

   (a) Clarity of the role of social worker.
   (b) Keen observation and acceptance of the uniqueness of individuals, groups or communities.
   (c) Understanding the feelings and thoughts of the person who is in a situation of deprivation or distress.
   (d) Understanding the difference between 'receiving help' and 'giving help' and the dynamics involved in these two roles.
   (e) Understanding the need for continuous examination of our values, biases or prejudices, which create blocks in our sensitivity.

3. To develop the 'will' in the TSWs to become a sensitive professional.

The workshop could be divided into two parts:

Part I: Understanding the concept of sensitivity.
Factors which contribute to our sensitivity. The facilitator should start this workshop with two 'do it yourself' exercises.

Part II: Understanding our perceptions about receiving help and giving help.

PART I

Exercise 4.1 Comfort in Relating with Others

Objective: Helping TSWs to understand the qualities that make a person approachable.
No. of participants: All.
Time required: 30 minutes.
Materials required: Nil.

Procedure:

1. Ask all participants to write down the names of the persons with whom they feel comfortable while communicating.
2. Also ask them to write down the names of the persons with whom they feel uncomfortable while communicating.
3. List out the reasons for both.
4. Give the participants 15 minutes for writing.

After the task has been completed, the facilitator can ask randomly some of the trainees to read out only the reasons. These reasons should be written on the blackboard in two columns.

Reasons Why I Feel Comfortable	Reasons Why I Feel Uncomfortable

Points for discussion:

1. Which are the common qualities that make us comfortable with a person?
2. Can we develop these qualities ourselves?
3. Can we identify those qualities in ourselves also?

Sum up the discussion by highlighting the most important qualities that help build appreciation and trust. This leads to a comfortable relationship.

Often there is a confusion regarding the word 'sensitivity'. Sometimes, a person who responds with disproportionate emotions to a stimulus directed towards him/her is mistakenly considered a sensitive person.

Whereas sensitivity is reflected in sharing empathetic understanding about a person's problem. This would be reflected through appropriate rather than exaggerated response.

The TSWs need to look at their own responses. For this purpose, the following exercise could be given.

Exercise 4.2 My Reaction

No. of participants: All.
Time required: 45 minutes.
Materials required: Copies of the exercise, one per participant.
Procedure: Ask the TSWs to individually respond to the following exercise.

Tick against the column which best explains your feelings:

Sr. No.	Statement	Always	Sometimes	Rarely	Never
1.	If I see my neighbour beating his wife, I want to stop him.				
2.	I feel very upset when I am scolded.				
3.	When I come to know my close friends from my college days are going to divorce, I feel very sad.				
4.	My friend has had an accident. I tell my family to manage things by themselves for some days so that I can stay with him/her and look after him/her.				
5.	When I read news items about rape and murder of women I feel I must do something to change the situation.				
6.	I think the farmers who have committed suicide due to drought and poverty are irresponsible.				
7.	When I see my friends quarrelling with each other I want to stop them.				
8.	When I see people in slums living in filthy surroundings I wonder how they can bear to live like this.				
9.	I feel insecure because of the growing violence in society due to religious and caste conflicts.				
10.	When I am not given an opportunity to participate in an event I feel neglected and resentful.				

1. After the exercise have an open discussion and on a chart paper/blackboard map the response trends.
2. Then conduct a discussion along the following lines:
    (a) What is the difference between sensitivity directed towards self and sensitivity directed towards others?
    (b) What is more helpful?
    (c) What are my areas of responding that I need to modify or change?
    (d) While working with people in need which type of sensitivity is more useful and why?

Conclude the session by highlighting that sensitivity has to move beyond the self while working with people.

In social work, our major concern is the marginalised groups. Deprivation and its impact on behaviour will only be understood if the social worker is sensitive. Such sensitivity can be developed by getting exposure through training.

Exercise 4.3 Willingness to Participate

Objective: To enable TSWs to gain insight into the feelings of an individual when he is not sure of the consequences of his behaviour.
Material required: Nil.
Time required: 30 minutes.
No. of participants: 10.
Procedure:

1. First ask five volunteers to come forward.
2. Then ask five more volunteers to come forward but warn them that they will have to take some risk.

Points for discussion:

1. How did each group of volunteers come forward?
2. Ask the volunteers to share their feelings in the process.
3. Why did some of the participants hesitate?
4. Why did some volunteers come forward in spite of the risk involved?

Highlight the following points:

1. Any action taken implies change. Change always is a risk, since we cannot anticipate the consequences. One needs to examine the attitudes towards risk taking.
2. As social workers, we need to understand that there are different kinds of people:

    (a) Those who are willing to take risks.
    (b) Those who are afraid to take risks.
    (c) Those who remain as apathetic bystanders.

We also need to understand the reasons behind such attitudes. The resistance could be due to fear of the unknown, apathy, feelings of helplessness, fatalistic attitude, disinterest, do not care attitude, like to be watchers, and so on.

Hence, as social workers, we need to handle people's resistance with empathy. We cannot pressurise people. We need to give them time for decision making and for trying out alternatives. Any change is threatening. This needs to be always remembered.

Exercise 4.4 Opportunity

Objectives:

1. To develop understanding in TSWs regarding deprivation.
2. To develop understanding related to resources, availability and unequal distribution.
3. To develop analysis regarding 'haves' and 'have-nots' in society, inequalities at all levels and how it affects relationships, feelings and attitudes.

Materials required:

1. One sheet of blank chart paper.
2. Six to seven pencils.
3. Two dozens of crayons/sketch pens.
4. Any other drawing or painting material if available.

Time required: 45 minutes.
No. of participants: Nine, divided into three groups of three members each.
Procedure:

1. Prepare three chits with the numbers '1', '2' and '3' written on them.
2. Ask each group to pick up one folded chit.
3. The group which gets the chit with number '1' on it starts the game.

Instructions to each group:

1. Draw or write on the paper.
2. Use any material that is available for drawing or writing.
3. Each group gets 2 minutes to work on the blank paper.

   After the first group picks up the material for drawing, the facilitator should add one more instruction, that is, the second group will not be able to use the material used by the first group. The same would apply for the third group also.

Points for discussion:

1. How did each group get the opportunity? Was it based on any criteria or luck?
2. How did each member behave within the group with respect to resources available and the space available to them? How were the intra-group interactions?
3. What were the feelings experienced by each group during the process?
4. How was the opportunity used by each group?
5. Did group members think of the need of opportunity for others?

   This discussion will help the TSWs to gain insight into their behaviour and also understand the behaviour of others. The micro- to macro-level inequalities need to be highlighted in the context of opportunity and deprivation in society. The TSWs can use this exercise in their own fieldwork situations especially in the following contexts:

1. Leadership training programme.
2. Grassroots level functionary training.
3. Awareness training programmes in communities and organisations.

Exercise 4.5 Blindfolded Person

Objectives:

1. To develop sensitivity towards people with disabilities.
2. To gain insight about our own feelings and behaviour while relating to a disabled person.
3. To experience the feelings a disabled person experiences in his/her interactions with others.

No. of participants: 2.
Material required: One big handkerchief.
Time required: 40 minutes.
Procedure:

1. Ask the participants to decide who would be blindfolded.
2. The blindfolded person has to reach a specific point in the room.
3. The way is blocked by different obstacles.
4. The sighted person has to help the blindfolded partner travel through these.
5. The remaining group of trainees should be instructed to carefully observe the process and responses and behaviour of the two participants.
6. At the end of the exercise ask the volunteers, starting with the blindfolded persons to express their feelings about themselves and about each other during the experience.
7. Then ask all the observers to give their feedback.

Highlight at the end, the need to be sensitive to disabilities and support the disabled. The TSWs should be helped to understand the approach in the enabling process and their perception of the disabled person. After the discussion, read out the two poems 'Dear Mom and Dad' and 'Tell me' (Annexures A4.1 and A4.2).

Exercise 4.6 Power Walk

Objectives:

1. To develop sensitivity about class, caste and gender inequalities.

2. To enable analyses of structural factors in discrimination and subordination.
3. To develop sensitivity about inequality, discrimination and injustice.

Materials required:

1. Wide space to enable walking
2. Chalk
3. Chart paper
4. Sketch pens and
5. Placard.

Time required: 1 hour.
No. of participants: 10 (five males and five females).
Procedure:

1. Ask the participants to come forward.
2. Draw a straight line at the centre of the space kept for the exercise.
3. Divide the group as follows:

   (a) An upper caste, rich farmer male/female.
   (b) A landless *adivasi* male/female.
   (c) A Dalit agricultural labourer male/female.
   (d) Urban, upper class male/female.
   (e) Urban informal sector working-class male/female.

4. Have each of them hold a placard stating their role and stand on the central line.
5. Read out each given statement one at a time and let the volunteers take a step forward or backward.
6. After the exercise, highlight differences in society due to class, caste and gender inequalities.

Instructions to the trainees:

1. At the beginning, ask all the males/females to stand at the same level on the horizontal line.
2. For every 'Yes' answer to the statement, each individual move one step forward.
3. For every 'No' answer to the statement, move one step backward.
4. The audience should observe the movements of the participants and correct them, if necessary.
5. At the end of the 10 statements, distances between the individuals are to be observed.

Statements: (These may be adapted and modified according to the local situation.)

1. I am the dominant person in my family.
2. I can buy and hold property on my name.
3. I can move about freely at any time of the day or night.
4. I am the key decision maker on matters related to my children's education, marriage, and so on.

5. I need not fear sexual violence.
6. I can acquire as much education as I desire.
7. I am capable of buying the luxury goods required for my living.
8. I can actively take part in political processes.
9. I can exercise the choice of selecting my marital partner.
10. I enjoy equal position in society.

Points for discussion:

1. Factors leading to discrimination and subordination.
2. The social construction of inequality based on class, caste and gender and vulnerability to exploitation and injustice.
3. Obstructions to free participation in development.

Highlight through discussions: Exploitation, injustice and violence emerge from inequalities in society. To remove inequalities, one has to be sensitive to the lack of choices of powerless, subordinated sections. Inequalities are not desirable in a democratic society. Therefore, social workers need to focus their work with more sensitive understanding about these powerless sections. Positions taken by them have to reflect an attitude in favour of marginalised and subordinate groups. For these values of equality, justice and non-exploitation must be internalised.

PART II

Exercise 4.7 Giving Help–Receiving Help

Objectives:

1. To help the TSWs to gain insight into the two roles of giving help and receiving help.
2. To enable the TSWs to understand the feelings a receiver of help would experience.
3. The facilitator should start with the exercise on 'giving help'.

Material required: Photocopies of the exercise 'Learning to help' (Annexure A 4.3).
Time required:

1. 30 minutes to fill in the forms.
2. 30 minutes for discussion based on compiled reactions.

Each of these sessions is to be conducted separately.

Procedure:

1. Get the forms filled by the participants.
2. Compile the response and present on a chart.
3. In the next session, display this chart and discuss the responses highlighting the biases and values of TSWs as helpers.

Giving:
Discussion on the first exercise on giving help could be conducted with the help of the following points:

Statements 1a and b

- How long is our list of all the things that are wrong?
- Is life full of negative things?
- In spite of negative things, there are many good things in life.
- In our profession we often focus on problems forgetting the positives. Why do we get conditioned?
- Do people require help only when things go wrong?
- Highlight the positive reasons for seeking help listed by the TSWs.

Statement 2: Priority listing
Discussion on the priority listing should include the following points:

- Why do we need to understand our feelings and thoughts in listing our priority?
- Will it affect our acceptance and respect for the client?
- Do we need to keep aside our personal values in professional situations?

Statement 3: What does asking help indicate? This statement could be discussed on the following points:

- How there are multiple ways in which one can perceive the person who seeks help.
- How our perceptions would affect our responses to the client.

Highlight positive aspects in asking for help.
The complete exercise should be summarised with the help of the following points:

- Social workers should not have only problem orientation.
- Our perceptions regarding the person in need have to be examined.
- Our professional relationship should not get affected by our personal life value preferences or our personal life decisions.
- Our perceptions about the person in need also affect our perception of the value of the helper (worker).

Receiving Help

The second exercise 'receiving help' needs to be discussed in detail on the following points:

- Why do we hesitate to take help?
- Why do we approach only those whom we know, especially only our friends?
- What feelings are generated while receiving help?
- Is the decision easy?

To sum up both exercises, the facilitator can use the following points:

- Giving help is easier than receiving help.
- If we are comfortable in receiving help, we will be able to accept and respond positively to people who seek help.
- The role of the giver need not be at the higher level. Both the giver and the receiver gain through the helping process and therefore are at an equal level.
- Taking help is not an easy decision.

  Conclude by stating that we need to understand the feelings of a person in need. We need to respect and appreciate his/her efforts and respond appropriately.
  Source: Priestle and McGuire, 1983.

Exercise 4.8 Black Spot (Refer to Figure 2.5 in Chapter 2)

When one is working with individuals who show symptoms of dysfunction, we might focus on the individual alone. One tends to label the person and his problem. In doing so, we tend to ignore the other factors which have triggered the problem or contributed in the dysfunctioning of the person. To gain insight into the holistic approach in social work practice this exercise can be used.

No. of participants: All.
Material required: A white paper with a black circle drawn on it at the centre. The circle is painted black.
Time required: 30 minutes.
Procedure:

1. Hold the paper in such a way that all participants can see it simultaneously.
2. Ask the participants to report what they see within 2 minutes.
3. Write down all the responses on a blackboard.

Points for discussion:

1. How one concentrates only on the black spot and other things seen are ignored.
2. One should learn to look at the individual and his behaviour in the context of his/her environment.

3. Understanding an individual in totality is important in helping situations.
4. We tend to label the person and become judgemental when we concentrate only on the person/client.

The facilitator needs to give many examples to illustrate this point. For example, when a child does not have bath everyday, we tend to label him as a dirty child—without being sensitive to his environment where water is scarce.

Conclusion: Sensitivity is not a one-time effort. A mind which is alive to its surrounding will always respond sensitively. Sensitivity is contagious. If the helper is sensitive to the person in need, the person in need in turn tends to be sensitive to his/her surroundings, relationships and to other people's needs. Read the poem 'Smile' (Annexure A4.4). Sensitivity enables the person to develop the conviction and commitment required in the social work profession. Read poems 'Commitment' and 'Beware' (Annexures A4.5 and A 4.6).

In summary, we can present all three components of self-development as shown in Figure 4.2.

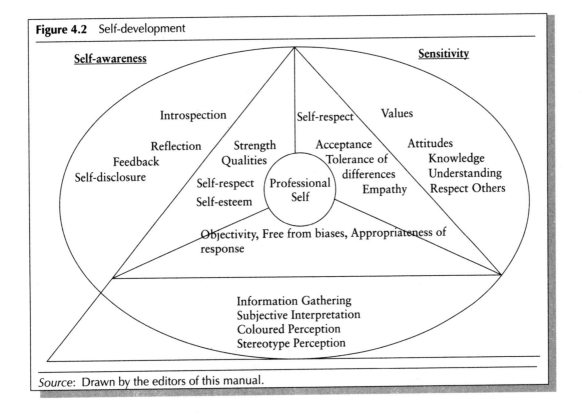

Figure 4.2 Self-development

Self-awareness

Sensitivity

Introspection Self-respect Values

Reflection Strength Acceptance Attitudes
Feedback Qualities Tolerance of Knowledge
Self-disclosure differences Understanding
Self-respect Professional Empathy Respect Others
Self-esteem Self

Objectivity, Free from biases, Appropriateness of response

Information Gathering
Subjective Interpretation
Coloured Perception
Stereotype Perception

Source: Drawn by the editors of this manual.

ANNEXURE A4.1 DEAR MOM AND DAD

Son :   The war is over now
        My task at last is through
        Mom and Dad, there is something
        I must ask of you

        I have a friend, oh, such a friend
        He has no family you see
        So Mom and Dad, I would like to
        Bring him home with me

Mom :   My son, of course, we don't mind
        If someone comes home with you
        I'm sure that he can come
        And stay a day or two

Son :   Mother, you don't understand
        What I'm trying to say
        I want him to stay with us
        As long as he may, but Mom I must tell you
        Please, don't be alarmed
        My friend, you see in battle
        Just happened to lose an arm

Mom :   My son, don't be ashamed
        To bring him home with you
        He can stay a week
        Or may be even two

Son :   Mom, before you give your answer
        There is something I must say
        My friend he fought a battle
        In which he lost a leg

Mom :   My son, it hurts me to say this
        But the answer must be NO
        Your father and I have no time
        For a boy who is crippled so

        Some time later, a letter came
        Saying their son has died
        When they read the cause of death
        The letter said suicide

        Later in a casket, draped
        With the Nation's flag
        They saw their son lying there
        Without an arm and a leg

                                Pushda M., X(a)
                                Birla Public School

ANNEXURE A4.2 'TELL ME'

Tell me what is the colour of the sky?
How high are the mountains?
And how do the ripples dance on the sea?
What makes a rose different from a lily?
What is the colour of the scorching sunshine?
Does the rain fall in drops or strings?
How white is the whiteness of snow?
And how dark is the darkness of night?
How small is the sparrow that chirps?
And how big is the tiger that roars?
And just a last query, my friend,
Tell me what is the colour of my hair?
And what is the shade of my eyes?
Tell me, for I am blind.

Lita Nadkarni

ANNEXURE A4.3 LEARNING TO HELP: A LEARNING MODEL

Giving:

1. Complete the sentence
   (a) People need help because...
       (Give 10 reasons) ....
       ....
       ....
       ....
       ....
       ....
       ....
       ....

   (b) What is wrong with the societal system today is that ....
       (Five sentences) ....
       ....
       ....
       ....
       ....
       ....

2. Give priorities according to your willingness to give help ....

    (a) • A very old pensioner with money problems   ( )
          • A child suffering from polio   ( )
          • Unmarried pregnant woman   ( )
          • Attempted suicide of a boy due to failure in SSC   ( )
          • A wife with an alcoholic husband   ( )
          • A woman practicing prostitution   ( )
          • A 30-year-old man caught in stealing   ( )

    (b) Give the reasons for the first and the last priorities.

3. When a person asks for help from others it indicates (tick mark)

    (a) Inadequacy
    (b) Better way of solving the problem
    (c) Helplessness
    (d) Awareness of one's problem
    (e) Dependency
    (f) Openness to accept problem situation
    (g) Any other (please specify)

Receiving:

Imagine that the last date of paying your examination fees is tomorrow and

1. You have not received your money order.
2. You have exhausted all your money.

    (a) What will be your reaction?
    (b) What help would you take under these circumstances?
    (c) What do you feel others will think of you?
    (d) If you avoid taking help, what are the reasons?

ANNEXURE A4.4 SMILE

A smile is such a funny thing
It wrinkles up your face
But when it is gone, you will never find
Its secret hiding place
But still more wonderful
It is to see what a smile can do
I smile at you, you smile at me
And so one smile makes two

Source: Emily Dickinson.

ANNEXURE A4.5 COMMITMENT

If I can stop one heart from breaking,
I shall not live in vain
If I can ease one life the aching,
Or cool one pain,
Or help one fainting robin
Unto his nest again
I shall not live in vain.

Source: Anonymous.

ANNEXURE A4.6 BEWARE

Surgeons must be very careful
When they take the knife!
Underneath their fine incisions
Stirs the culprit, Life!
Social workers must be very careful
When they accept the task!
Underneath their sincere intentions
Stirs the culprit: Human mind!

Source: All poems are compiled by retired Prof. Kalindi Muzumdar, Nirmala Niketan College of Social Work, Mumbai. As editors we have taken the freedom and added one more stanza in the poem 'Beware'. This was done by retired Prof. Sumati Godbole, Karve Institute of Social Service.

Section 2

COMMUNICATION

VALUE OF DEVELOPING COMMUNICATION SKILLS

Communication is the main tool in social work practice. A worker who has developed sensitivity towards a person in need will always consciously use appropriate words, tones and body language for developing a trusting relationship. The earlier workshop on self-awareness will also help trainee social workers to examine their potentials and limitations in communication. This, in effect, will help the trainees to develop the essential skills required for effective communication. We believe that a change is not possible without communication. Hence, in this manual, much emphasis is given for the development of communication skills.

Although most of our communication is verbal, non-verbal means of communication also strengthen, weaken or contribute substantially to our message. Even attitudes are more explicitly expressed by facial expressions and behaviour rather than only by words. Words without expression are meaningless stimuli.

Communication encompasses a meaningful expression, sharing of experience and interactions between a person and the environment. Hence, the communicator has to be a keen observer and a sensitive listener and a person with good command over language. Each language has its own potential and also built-in limitations. A good communicator hence needs to understand these aspects about language usage.

This section covers two aspects of communication: one, theoretical components of the communication process and two, on specific abilities required to develop communication skills on a one-to-one, one-to-group and one-to-many situations. Keeping in mind the multiple roles and functions social workers perform, we have included in this section a wide range of communications, the skills required and the ways of enhancing one's communication in different situations. The theoretical component of communication given in Chapter 5 is chosen with a definite purpose. It covers specific aspect of communication relevant to the practice of social work methods. It will facilitate skill training while conducting laboratory sessions on methods. The facilitator needs to refer to the chapters in this section not only for conducting communication workshops but also for developing specific communication skills relevant to each method.

Chapter 5

UNDERSTANDING COMMUNICATION: A THEORETICAL FRAMEWORK

Sudha Datar, Anuradha Patil,
Ruma Bawikar and Nagmani Rao

DEFINITION AND CONCEPTS

Many experts have given definitions of communication. If we go through some of them, we might get a broad perspective of the concept.

1. Communication is a process of passing information and understanding from one person to another.
2. Communication is the sum total of directly or indirectly and consciously or unconsciously transmitted feelings, attitudes and wishes.
3. Communication is the sum total of all things that one person does when he wants to create understanding in the mind of another. It involves a systematic and continuous process of telling, listening and understanding.
4. It is an art of transmitting information, ideas and attitudes from one person to another. It is a meaningful interaction between a person and his environment.

It is an art of giving information or a message, to communicate means to convey, reveal, impart or give or exchange information. In the process, one person is made aware of the ideas in the mind of the other person and thereby responds to the same.

PURPOSE OF COMMUNICATION

The purpose is not uniform. Purpose differs from situation to situation. Purpose influences the process of communication. Some of the purposes could be listed as follows:

- To get across an idea or an information.
- To pass on instructions or orders.
- To give advice, suggestions and guidelines.
- To persuade, motivate and encourage others.
- To raise morale of others.
- To educate, train and develop skills.
- To give warning.
- To resolve problems.
- Change attitudes, and so on.

PROCESS OF COMMUNICATION

Five important elements in the process of communication are as follows (Claude and Warren, 1949):

1. Source (sender).
2. Transmitter (channel).
3. Message.
4. Receiver.
5. Destination or goal.

Aristotle in his systematic study of the process of communication has specified three elements, namely, the speaker, the speech and the audience.

The receiver could be one person or a group of persons or even an institution. How the source and receiver would function depends upon their skills, attitudes, knowledge, values and the social system. These factors work as filters in communication.

The message is an idea to be presented. The content needs to be scanned, organised and isolated. The message must be clear to the source. It has to be encoded by the sender and decoded by the receiver.

The transmitter (channel) means the use of five sense organs for sending and receiving a message. This means that the message may be seen, heard, touched, smelt or tasted. More the channels involved in communication, more effective will be the communication.

The following sentence briefly describes the communication process:

Who (source), for what reasons, says *what* (message) through which *sense organ* (channel) to which *audience* (receiver) with *what effects* (reaching to goals of the source).

The steps in the process of communication are as follows:

1. Ideation by the sender.
2. Encoding of message, that is, verbal or visual.
3. Transmission through a channel.
4. Receiver receiving the message.
5. Decoding the message, that is, from words to idea.
6. Action by receiver: can be storage of information or active responding.
7. Feedback—receiver gives it to the sender (this is an important step, which is often ignored).

CHARACTERISTICS OF THE PROCESS OF COMMUNICATION

Communication is an Ongoing Activity

This is a process in which we are constantly engaged. We are continuously decoding signs from our environment, interpreting these signs and encoding the message. It is misleading to think of communication processes as starting somewhere and ending somewhere. It is a continuous process.

Communication is a Two-way Process

The receiver receives a message and sends a meaningful feedback to the sender. Unless the receiver's responses come back to the speaker and the speaker adjusts the message to fit the responses of the receiver, the cycle of communication is not complete.

   The receiver might strongly disagree with the sender because of the personality differences or due to differences in their value systems. If this is communicated through the cycle of communication process, it helps in increasing understanding. Feedback is an integral part of communication (Figures 5.1, 5.2, 5.3 and 5.4).

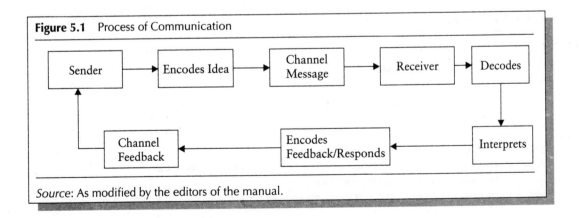

Figure 5.1   Process of Communication

Source: As modified by the editors of the manual.

This return process is called feedback. This helps in understanding the interpretation of the message.

The receiver might respond bodily (non-verbal responding), she/he may respond in writing, in symbolic gestures or verbally. Communicator needs to be attentive to the feedback and modify message in light of what is observed or heard from the receiver. We also get feedback from our own messages. We hear our own voice and correct our tone or mispronunciation. We read our written submission after we finish writing and correct it.

Both roles of the sender and the receiver get exchanged in the circle of communication. Hence the sender also becomes the receiver and gives feedback.

How to give feedback:

1. Feedback has to be specific rather than general.
2. It should be solicited and not imposed.
3. It has to be immediate but well timed.
4. It should not be given to satisfy our needs, but to help the sender.
5. It must be appropriate and proportionate.

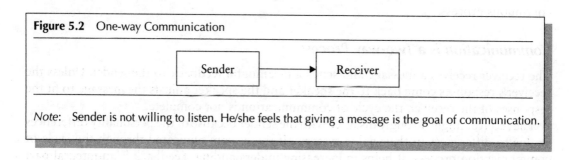

Figure 5.2   One-way Communication

Note: Sender is not willing to listen. He/she feels that giving a message is the goal of communication.

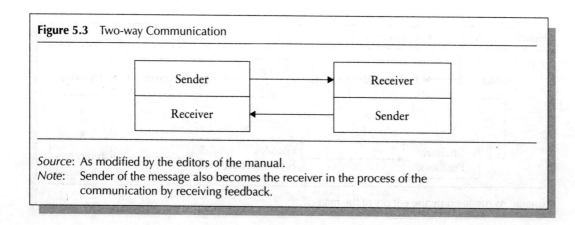

Figure 5.3   Two-way Communication

Source: As modified by the editors of the manual.
Note: Sender of the message also becomes the receiver in the process of the
          communication by receiving feedback.

Each Situation is Unique in Communication

The same message in different situations would have different impacts. What appeals to one receiver may not be appealing to another. Hence feedback will also be unique.

A Message Always has Two Elements

1. Facts—objective reality, cognitive aspects.
2. Emotions—subjective reality—verbally or non-verbally expressed.

CHANNELS OF COMMUNICATION

We use our sense organs to communicate. Five sense organs are usually used in combination. There can be two types of channels used in communication depending upon the purpose or objective of that communication.

Two-way Channels of Communication

1. Face-to-face

   Diad situations
   Psychodrama, Socio-drama
   Demonstration

2. Distance

   Letters
   Fax
   Email

CHARACTERISTICS OF TWO-WAY CHANNEL

1. Could be formal or informal.
2. It is more flexible.
3. Immediate modification is possible due to feedback.

One-way Channels of Communication

1. Written
   (a) Circulars
   (b) Notices
   (c) Newspaper
   (d) Books

    (e) Printed matter
    (f) Brochures
    (g) Leaflets
    (h) Hand bills

2. Visual

    (a) Charts
    (b) Posters
    (c) Photographs
    (d) Pictures
    (e) Maps
    (f) Slides
    (g) Models
    (h) Diagrams

3. Audio

    (a) Radio
    (b) Cassettes
    (c) Records
    (d) Bells
    (e) Buzzers

4. Audio-visual

    (a) Videos/TV
    (b) Films
    (c) Drama
    (d) Fine art performances
    (e) Puppet shows
    (f) Street plays
    (g) Demonstrations

Use of Multiple Channels

It is always better to use multiple channels for effective communication. Usually, we send the primary message in a single channel. For example, when we speak to a person the sound waves from our voice send the primary message. But there are other channels like expressions on the face, gestures and the relation of the given message to the previous message. Even the primary message conveys information at several levels. It gives the receiver words to decode. The sender emphasises certain words over others. The words are presented in a pattern of intonation and timing which contributes to the total meaning. The quality of the sender's voice (deep, high, shrill, rich, low, loud, soft) itself carries information about the sender and what he wants to convey.

In mass communication also, multiple channels exist. For example, in a newspaper, the meaning is conveyed not only by the words used in a news item but also by the size of the headline, the location on the page, the page number, whether photographs are used, and so on. All these tell us something more about the information than the words.

Many channels flow parallel from source towards the destination. These parallel relationships are complex, but have a general pattern. A communicator can emphasise a point by adding as many parallel messages as felt necessary. If she/he is communicating verbally, she/he can stress a word, pause just before it, use gestures, make use of eye contact or she/he can keep all the signals parallel except one. For example, she/he can stress a word in a way that makes it mean something else. One could say 'That is a fine job you did' in such a way that the secondary meaning of sarcasm or doubt is communicated.

TYPES OF COMMUNICATION

Communication can be classified in the context of different perspectives like the number of people involved, level of understanding and receptivity of people involved, status of people and methods used in communication. This context directly indicates the abilities required of the sender. Hence, understanding the characteristics of each type of communication is important to be an effective communicator.

Verbal Communication

Verbal communication is part of our daily lives. It is a learnt ability. Sometimes judgements are formed about people on the basis of their language ability and style of speech.

Verbal communication can be in one-to-one, one-to-group or one-to-mass situations. Mass media also makes use of verbal tools.

Words are used to express feelings, opinions, thoughts, attitudes, and so on. Use of words directly or indirectly expresses the sender's personality. Proper selection of words is very important in verbal communication. Words once spoken cannot be taken back.

Words break or build relationships. Words trigger negative emotions or help to soothe the person. Words are the base for all of our activities.

Verbal communication has two components:

1. Cognitive—factual.
2. Affective—emotional.

These components are interlinked and influence each other. The type of factual information affects our emotions. And these stimulated emotions, in turn, affect the cognitive content.

Verbal communication can be either oral or written. Written communication is used when the person is far away or when one wants to reach many at the same time. Written communication is better worded, exact, clear and may have a long-lasting effect. We use written communication extensively. Therefore developing one's abilities in this is important.

Guidelines for effective written communication:

1. Meaning should be clear.
2. Use short sentences.
3. Use the reader's vocabulary.
4. Use direct speech rather than indirect speech and use active speech.
5. Use positive statements rather than negative statements.
6. Use personal phrases rather than impersonal ones and use personal pronouns.
7. Use illustrations, examples and charts to simplify and clarify information.
8. Arrange ideas in a logical sequential order.
9. Economise on words.

Writing is a skill, which can be developed only with practice and conscious use of the feedback received. Written communication cannot be complete unless it is read. Reading requires concentration.

Non-verbal Communication

When we talk we are not only using language but also using our body through facial expressions, gestures, postures and movements. Our body movements cannot be separated from our verbal communication. The body is used to emphasise or substantiate our verbal communication. This is especially true in a face-to-face communication, for example, a wink of an eye, a shrug of shoulders, patting the other person's back, clapping. The sender requires understanding of the use of the body as an enabling or a hindering factor in the process of communication.

COMPONENTS OF BODY LANGUAGE

Physical appearance and traits: This makes the first impression on the receiver. Body structure—height, weight, hairstyles, everything gives certain messages. Hence, outward appearances should be in keeping with the situation and culture of the receiver.

Body movement: Slow and controlled movements indicate that one is sure of oneself. Jerky and less controlled movements indicate that one is unsure of oneself. Specific body movements have accepted meanings in our culture. These may change from culture to culture. Some gestures have universal meaning, which are usually understood by all uniformly. For example:

- Handshake—greeting
- Shrug of shoulder—I don't know
- Leaning forward—involvement
- Leaning backward—disinterest
- Shaking of head—disagreement
- Nodding of head—agreement

Facial expressions: While speaking, our facial expressions communicate our feelings. Without words also our facial expressions convey messages. It is said 'A human tongue can invent a lie, but a human face can never lie'. Eyebrows, eyes and lips are used in non-verbal communication. The facial expressions are also influenced by culture.

Vocal sound: Pitch indicates feminity–masculinity. Certain tones indicate certain messages. Softer tones and harsh tones give specific messages, which may not be expressed only through the words. Pitch and volume are also important in communication. A whisper indicates secrecy or intimacy. A loud voice indicates anger, hostility and aggression. Accordingly the receiver will receive the message.

Eye contact: With proper eye contact, distance between the sender and the receiver is reduced. Eye contact when used adequately encourages feedback, shows involvement, reduces distance and opens communication. When eye contact is avoided, it increases the distance or the gap between the sender and the receiver, reduces social contact, hinders expression of feelings and makes the receiver feel uncomfortable.

Personal space: This depends upon the quality of communication and on the number of people involved in communication. If this is not maintained, it might lead to defensive behaviour which blocks communication. This is indicated through moving and maintaining distance, holding the body rigid, leaning back and using inanimate objects to create distance.

Touch: Touching becomes part of the content of the message by the sender. It is especially very helpful while interacting with children or handicapped persons. Touch communicates different feelings—affection, support, appreciation or anger. A range of emotions can be expressed through touch. It is also an interactive signal, for example, shaking hands or patting on a receiver's back.

Conclusion

The totality of communication is divided as follows:

1. Verbal communication is only 7 per cent.
2. Non-verbal communication is 93 per cent, which is further broken down into body language—58 per cent—and tone of voice—35 per cent.

Matching of verbal and non-verbal expression is important in communication. Verbal and non-verbal expressions need to be consistent in conveying a message. The sender also has to learn to strike a balance between the two.

Formal Communication

This type of communication is part of any formal organisation. In an administrative hierarchy of an organisation, what position a person holds, where he is, what message he wants to give determines the channel, manner and method of his communication. It can be written or oral. It can also be upward or downward. Formal communication is concerned with specific objectives of giving instructions, orders, information, procedures and warnings that require to be followed. Feedback is also an important aspect of formal communication.

Informal Communication

This is part of our daily communication in informal groups. Along with formal communication in the formal set-up, informal communication also develops. This happens because formal communication does not provide room for personal relationships. It helps people in stabilising and being comfortable in their jobs. The groups and subgroups that develop have their own norms and values because of informal communication.

Sometimes informal communication leads to 'grapevine' communication. It arises out of casual social interaction and hence it is fickle, ever changing and distorted. Usually, grapevine communication is incomplete and hence can be misinterpreted. This communication is more active in periods of excitement and insecurity. This type of communication travels very fast.

Rumour is an undesirable feature of grapevine communication. It is communicated without evidence. Rumour is impure and injudicious communication. Being generally incorrect, it is undesirable. Hence one should be able to handle rumours. Following are some of the guidelines:

- Know what rumour is: It is a widely spread opinion without evidence of its truth. Two factors which contribute in rumour: It is a matter of importance and it is a matter concerning which there is ambiguity, uncertainty or doubt.
- Know when to expect rumour: Expect rumours during national emergencies, wars, disasters (natural and/or man-made), communal riots, food shortages, strikes, and so on, or in other words when there is a major crisis. These are all important issues that arouse fears, hatred and other strong feelings and the facts of the matter are hard to reach to all.
- Realise that rumour lives on prejudice: Human beings do not like to live with uncertainty or ambiguity. So where there is lack of evidence, we tend to substantiate on our own and this evidence comes not from the outside or from the facts, but from within, from our prejudice.The best remedy for rumours is to release a steady flow of accurate information to all concerned.
- Never repeat, never act on the basis of a rumour: Find out facts, track down the sources of distortions and help to make the communication accurate.

DIRECTION OR LEVELS OF COMMUNICATION

1. Downward.
2. Upward.
3. Horizontal.
4. Cross.

Downward Communication

This is usually from an authority to a subordinate, hence quite official. It is instrumental and not expressive. Five categories of communication that travel down have been described as follows (see also Figure 5.4):

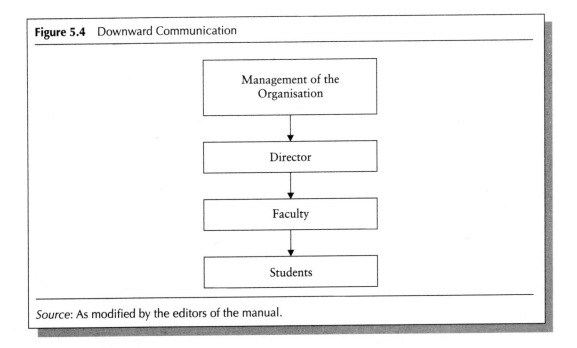

Figure 5.4   Downward Communication

Source: As modified by the editors of the manual.

1. Organisational policies.
2. Organisational practices.
3. Goal, rationale.
4. Job instructions.
5. Feedback on job performance.

In our daily life, we do see downward communication in families. This may vary from family to family, depending upon the type of family relationships.

Upward Communication

This communication is more expressive than instrumental. It communicates what the subordinate thinks and feels. The feelings could be about themselves, post, pay, performance or problems. Ideas and suggestions for what needs to be done, by whom and how, can also flow upward. Reporting of work done is an important function of upward communication (Figure 5.5).

Figure 5.5 Upward Communication

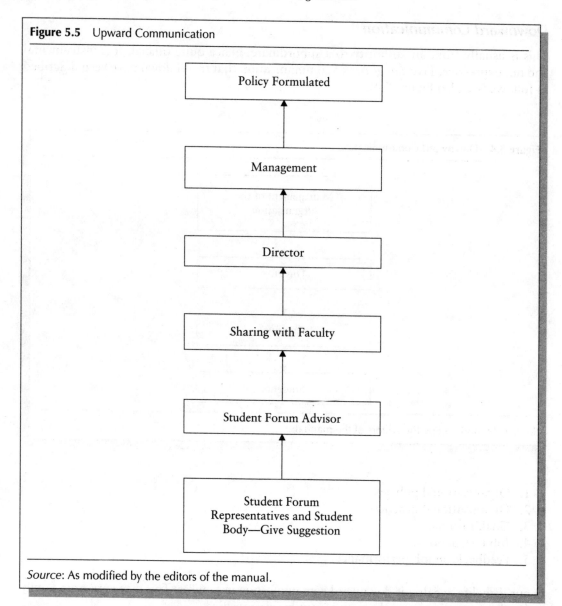

Source: As modified by the editors of the manual.

Horizontal Communication

These channels are to be kept open as these give socio-emotional support and coordinate activities. It is a powerful social stimulus. It is essential in our day-to-day life. Horizontal communication can be either formal or informal. It is between people who are on the same level or equals (Figure 5.6).

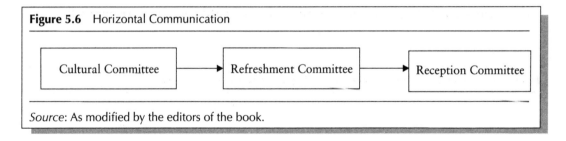

Figure 5.6 Horizontal Communication

| Cultural Committee | ⟶ | Refreshment Committee | ⟶ | Reception Committee |

Source: As modified by the editors of the book.

Cross Communication

This exists when people communicate with persons who are outside the approved channels of communication. For example, consulting other lecturers regarding difficulties related to fieldwork instead of consulting the appointed fieldwork supervisor (Figure 5.7).

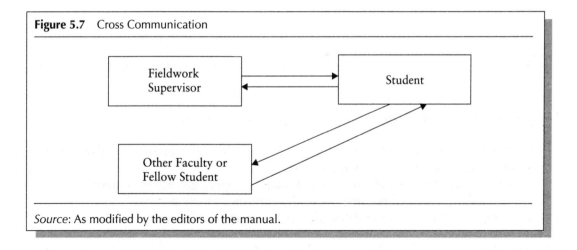

Figure 5.7 Cross Communication

Source: As modified by the editors of the manual.

CLASSIFICATION OF COMMUNICATION

Based on Number of Receivers

Communication gets affected depending upon the number of people with whom one communicates at a given time. Based upon the number of receivers we can classify communication as follows:

1. With self (intrapersonal).
2. One-to-one (interpersonal).
3. One-to-group.
4. One-to-mass.

These types can be presented in the form of a 'V'-shaped continuum (Figure 5.8).

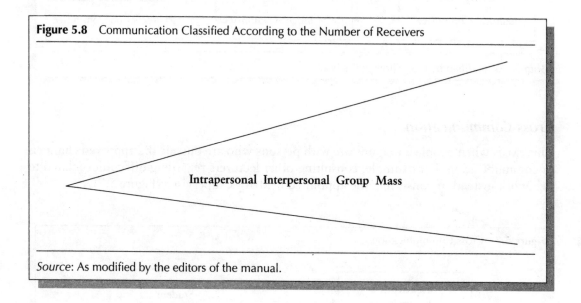

Figure 5.8   Communication Classified According to the Number of Receivers

Intrapersonal Interpersonal Group Mass

Source: As modified by the editors of the manual.

Four major changes gradually occur as we move from left to right:

1. Number of people involved increases dramatically from one person to millions, making the process of communication complex.
2. The message becomes less personal in focus and more general in content.
3. The persons involved become physically and emotionally distant.
4. Complex organisations and complex technological devices become essential.

In spite of these differences, the basic structure and components of communication remain the same.

INTRAPERSONAL COMMUNICATION

The chapter on self-awareness has emphasised the use of self-talk in understanding 'self'. If self-talk is based on introspection and feedback, it enables the process of the other three types of communication.

INTERPERSONAL COMMUNICATION (ONE-TO-ONE COMMUNICATION)

In our daily life, most of our communication is interpersonal. It involves two people: a sender and a receiver. It is an interaction between two persons (Figure 5.9).

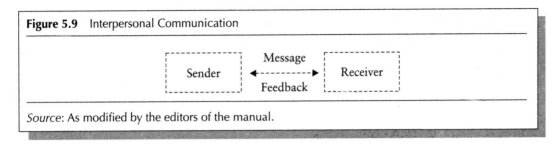

Figure 5.9   Interpersonal Communication

Source: As modified by the editors of the manual.

Here both roles are intermingled and hence both persons are sender and receiver at the same time. There has to be proper tuning between the receiver and the sender for effective communication cycle to be established.

These two circles indicate accumulated experiences of the two individuals who are communicating (Figure 5.10). The source can encode and the destination can decode only in terms of the experiences each one has had. If the circles have a large area in common, then communication is easy. If the circles do not meet, if there has been no common experience, then communication is difficult. This happens when a technical person talks to a lay person, an urban-based individual talks to a tribal in a language or with content that the latter cannot understand. Encoding of the message is important and how the message is given is also important.

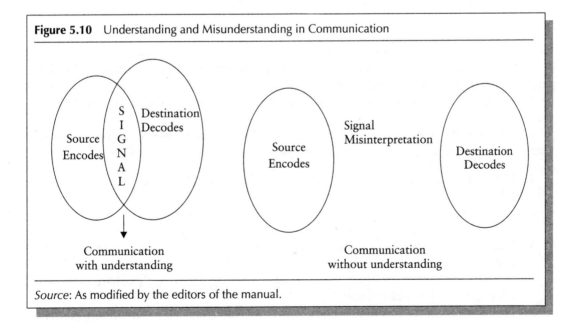

Figure 5.10   Understanding and Misunderstanding in Communication

Source: As modified by the editors of the manual.

Communication is influenced by the sender's personality. Similarly, the personality of a receiver in turn influences the receptivity and interpretation.

This filter consists of age, sex, education, upbringing, values, attitudes, culture, previous experiences, and so on (Figure 5.11).

Figure 5.11   Filters in Communication

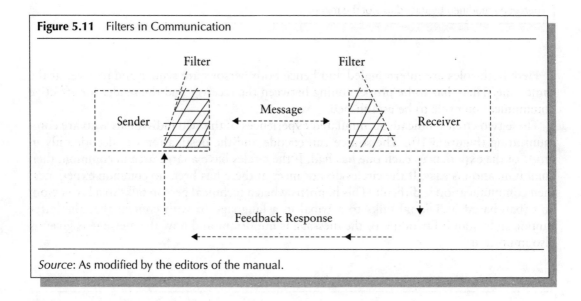

Source: As modified by the editors of the manual.

The sender has to be aware of the filters because they determine the interpretation and feedback. No communication is complete without a feedback. To understand the feedback and to act on the basis of the feedback, the sender has to develop skills of observation and listening. It is especially so in a helping relationship where the treatment is mainly administered through the medium of communication.

A communicator requires the ability to listen. How to listen requires to be consciously learnt. Responding indicates how and what the communicator is listening to.

1. Listen empathetically—give enough time, respect and allow the other person to express himself freely.
2. Listen patiently—show you want to listen by looking at the sender, not engaging in any other activity.
3. Understand the feelings—of the other person expressed along with the intellectual content of his talk.
4. Avoid interruptions or distractions—either coming from one's preoccupations or coming from the environment.
5. Listen to what is not said—body language and silences in communication are meaningful.

Common deterrents to effective listening are as follows:

- Assuming in advance that the content of the message is inherently uninteresting, unimportant, irrelevant or already known to you.
- Haste, impatience hinders listening.
- Believing that listening is passive.
- Behaviour that indicates our weakness.
- Distractions from within or from the environment.
- Preoccupation with our own thoughts.
- Selective forgetting.
- Omitting.
- Distorting.

For effective interpersonal communication, just listening intently is not enough. Communication is a dynamic process where the entire personality of a communicator is very important. For an effective and complete communication, the following guidelines are useful:

1. Stop talking to yourself.
2. Show your willingness to listen.
3. Encourage the receiver to talk (let him become the sender).
4. Give honest replies, that is, say what you mean (give proper feedback).
5. Modify or adapt your communication as per the demands of the situation.
6. Do not ask direct questions which can be embarrassing.
7. Maintain professional distance by avoiding loose talk (for example, commenting on the looks, dress).

Finally, remember that although both sender and receiver are responsible for making communication complete and meaningful in a helping relationship, the responsibility lies more on the worker who is continuously playing both the roles while dealing with the person in need.

One-to-group Communication

A small group, homogeneous in nature, is important in a one-to-group communication. Group members are usually not passive recipients of information; everyone is involved in the entire process of communication.

Due to group support, discussion gets stimulated. Through participation social consciousness can be developed. New insights are obtained and attitudes can be changed. Exchange of information and ideas flow freely. There is multiple interaction and feedback.

The communicator's behaviour in a group affects the group atmosphere. The communicator's behaviour and style is important in one-to-group situations, since it requires simultaneous acceptance or approval of all the group members.

If one uses a democratic approach, participation increases in a group. In the democratic style, the communicator is attentive, supportive, concerned and helpful, and encourages interpersonal relationships, gives freedom to talk, attempts to summarise, respects others, believes in equality and accepts others as partners in the process of communication. The atmosphere becomes informal, supportive and cooperative. People feel united and free. Enthusiasm is stimulated and groups become productive.

If a communicator is autocratic in his/her style, then participation is hindered. An autocratic communicator is dominating, critical and tries to control rigidly. She/he likes to preach and imposes decisions on others. She/he is not a good listener and loves to talk high handedly.

If this approach is used continuously, then the atmosphere in the group becomes hostile, participation is reduced. Members get divided. Sometimes apathy develops or unhealthy competition is stimulated.

The behaviour of a communicator affects the participation in the group as follows:

1. The number of members who contribute decreases or increases.
2. The frequency of each person's contribution varies.
3. The extent of group supportiveness is either good or inadequate.
4. The frequency of interruptions and obstacles created by members increases or decreases.
5. The willingness to listen to each other is seen or people become impatient and intolerant.

In group communication also, the communicator needs to be a good listener and observer. She/he has to play many roles and enable others to talk. When each member of the group derives satisfaction by listening and by contributing, then that is the success of a one-to-group communication. This is illustrated in Figure 5.12.

Mass Communication (One-to-Many/Group to Many)

When mass communication is required in a face-to-face situation, one needs to develop the art of public speaking. The skills required are much more complex than for one-to-one or one-to-group communication.

The criteria for becoming an effective public speaker are as follows:

1. Possess adequate knowledge and information about the subject matter.
2. Have clarity of purpose—whether it is just to impart information or create an opinion through emotional appeal or initiate action from the receiver's end.

It is formal communication, hence the speaker requires to prepare well in advance for the public speech.

Any speech requires understanding of the following elements:

1. Content—How much information requires to be included.
2. Emphasis—What stand is to be taken.

Figure 5.12 One-to-group Communication

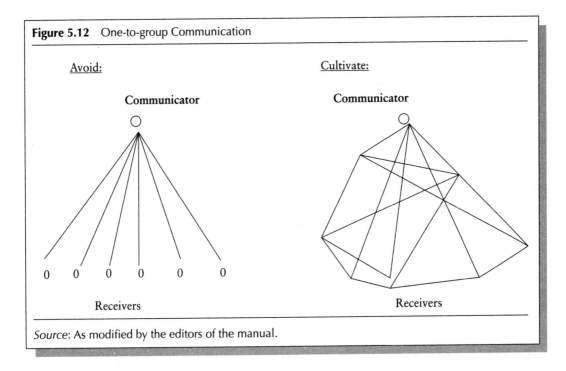

Source: As modified by the editors of the manual.

3. Elaboration—Which arguments are to be used, which illustrations are to be used; reference to views expressed by others related to the topic.
4. Body of the speech—

   (a) The beginning or introduction;
   (b) The core: the main subject
   (c) Substantion with convincing illustrations
   (d) Summarising, recapitulation
   (e) Concluding: re-emphasising the points

QUALITIES ESSENTIAL IN AN EFFECTIVE PUBLIC SPEAKER

Confidence, boldness, calm and collected nature, physical stamina, knowledge, precision, language ability, sense of humour, sense of time, positive self-image, flexibility, patience, resourcefulness, conviction in the subject of speech and willingness to prepare in advance. These qualities are not just to be accepted at an intellectual level but need to be reflected in the actual practice of public speaking.

This could be achieved through reading aloud, presenting in front of the mirror and later presenting in front of a small group of friends to get their critical feedback. Another way to improve presentation skills is by carefully hearing your own tape-recorded speech. This can help modifying your speed, tone, voice modulation, and so on.

Inadequate preparation leads to the following:

1. Audience not understanding the subject matter.
2. No illustrations ready at hand which are familiar to the audience.
3. Inadequate organisation of content leading to confusion.
4. Forgetting important points resulting in repetition.
5. Boredom in audience.

These may in turn lead to nervousness and fumbling and the speaker may lose control over the audience.

The skills required by the speaker are as follows:

1. Body language

   (a) Ability to evoke emotions through facial expressions.
   (b) Skill in using hand movements.
   (c) Use of body posture (so as to display confidence, enthusiasm, and so on)
   (d) Eye contact that includes everyone in the audience.

2. Verbal expression and tones

   (a) Speed of talking (not so fast as to sound jumbled or so slow as to become monotonous).
   (b) Pauses—to be used for dramatic effect rather than showing hesitation or cutting the flow of the speech.
   (c) Pitch: modulation according to the flow of the content.
   (d) Word usage and fluency in keeping with the level of the audience.
   (e) Supplementing the oral presentation with the help of different aids.

3. Observing audience response

   (a) Looking for signs of audience attention of boredom distraction.
   (b) Noting the response of the audience evoked by the speech.

4. Skills to improvise according to observed audience response

   (a) Pausing.
   (b) Altering speed and tone.
   (c) Making statement to draw attention (rumour, and so on).
   (d) Winding up without seeming abrupt.

The audience is an important factor in the process of mass communication. The speaker must be able to judge the level of the audience and approach them with a smiling and pleasant bearing. The behaviour of the masses is often unpredictable and any small provocation might lead to a break in communication. The speaker must have the capacity to touch the chord of the audience. If the audience is won, the speaker becomes successful.

Having gone through this theoretical component in communication, the facilitator must keep in mind that these are reinforced through the workshop sessions described in the following chapter.

Chapter 6

WORKSHOPS ON COMMUNICATION

Sudha Datar, Anuradha Patil and *Ruma Bawikar*

WORKSHOP 1

The trainee social workers (TSWs) need to develop an understanding of communication processes; hence the workshop is focused on two aspects:

1. Understanding the basic principles of communication.
2. Process and obstacles in communication.

At the end of the workshop, the TSWs would be able to identify abilities required for good communication and their responsibilities as social workers in using communication as a tool in achieving the objectives.

Exercise 6.1 Purpose of Communication in Social Work

No. of participants: All.
Material required: Chalk and blackboard.
Time required: 30 minutes.
Procedure:

1. Ask the trainees to state the purpose of communication in day-to-day life.
2. Then ask them to list out the reasons/purposes if they have to communicate with

(a) a husband who beats his wife and the wife has come to the center for help or
(b) a child who has been brought to the observation home because of stealing.

3. They have to highlight the purpose of the worker for communicating.
4. Write down both lists on a blackboard.

Points for discussion:

1. What are the similarities and differences in purpose?
2. What creates these differences?

The facilitator should summarise by highlighting the following purposes in professional communication.   •

1. To build rapport with a client.
2. To make the client comfortable so that he/she develops the willingness to share and accepts the worker with trust.
3. To help clients to gain insight and develop an action plan for change.

Communication has two types of content: One is the cognitive, that is, factual aspect and the other is the affective, that is, the emotional aspect. Both these play an important role in making the communication complete.

Exercise 6.2 Narrating an Event

Objective: To help the TSWs to be aware of the two aspects in a communication.
No. of participants: 2.
Time required: 30 minutes.
Material required: A dramatic event in a written form.
Procedure:

1. Ask one participant to read out the event in a monotonous tone.
2. Ask the second participant to read out the event with proper expressive tones.

Points for discussion:

1. Which narration was more effective?
2. Why did this happen?

Highlight: When we speak with our clients, we need to strike a balance between these two aspects. When clients communicate with us, we should also be able to identify both the cognitive and affective aspects in their communication and respond accordingly.

Communication also Involves Non-verbal Communication, Popularly Called 'Body Language':

The most vital non-verbal communication is through the eyes. Eye contact is very important. Appropriate use of eye contact has to be learnt consciously.

Exercise 6.3 Eye Contact

Objective: To help the TSWs to understand the impact of eye contact.
No. of participants: 2—one male and one female.
Time required: 20 minutes.
Procedure:

1. Ask both participants to stand facing each other (at a distance of about 2–3 feet) and stare at each other, without blinking, for 2 minutes.
2. At the end of the exercise, ask the volunteers to express their feelings through the entire process, that is, from listening to instructions to completion of 2 minutes.

Points for discussion:

1. What is the range of messages conveyed through eye contact?
2. What type of eye contact can make people uncomfortable?
3. How would we use eye contact in social work practice?

Our entire body plays an important role in our communication. Along with the words, the bodily movements are also interpreted.

Exercise 6.4 Mime a Situation

Objective: To help the TSWs understand the factors that contribute in our interpretation of body language.
No. of participants: The facilitator mimes one event and the class observes the same. The situation to be mimed is of a person bathing an elephant.
Time required: 20 minutes.
Procedure: The facilitator mimes the event slowly and elaborately while the class is asked to observe carefully.

Points for discussion:

1. What did the facilitator do?
2. Which movements were easily understood?
3. Which were difficult to understand?
4. What were the differences in understanding the mime?
5. Why were there differences in interpretation?

Highlight:

1. One has to be careful in using body movements in communication.
2. The previous experiences, culture, gender, and so on, would influence the interpretation.
3. The worker has to be fully aware of the cultural background and experiences of the client groups because these create the context for interpretation of messages.
4. We can also use body language to enhance our communication.

Exercise 6.5 Follow the Leader

Objective: To help TSWs understand that actions speak louder than words.
No. of participants: 10, one of them to be made a leader.
Time required: 30 minutes.
Procedure:

1. Ask the leader to do some actions like lifting or raising hands or rotating hands.
2. Ask the other members in the group to imitate the leader's movements.
3. After this game, ask the leader to give complicated instructions verbally for further body movements by group. For this, the leader has to use only words and no body movements.

Points for discussion:

1. What was the difference observed in both situations in the followers?
2. Which actions were easy to follow?
3. When and why did the participants get confused?

Highlight:

1. While communicating, we need to use simple language.
2. The receiver also receives messages from our body movements, which are easy to interpret.
3. We need to strike a balance between verbal and non-verbal communication.

Source: James, Bhaise, Marie, Brian of Training Animators in Conscientization and Education (1975) (TRACE Team), published by Janaseva Mandal, Nandurbar (Maharashtra).

Impact of Physical Set-up on Communication

Along with the non-verbal communication of the sender, the physical environment in which the worker conducts the interviews also conveys a message, especially the type of seating arrangement. Ask the TSWs to adopt different seating arrangements and identify which makes the receiver feel comfortable. For example, the client is made to sit on the ground and the worker sits on the chair or both of them sit on the ground and talk to each other. Ask the participants what different messages do the above convey? To summarise the basic concept of communication, role play could be used.

Objectives:

1. To understand the importance of planning for communication in social work practice.
2. To review the understanding of verbal and non-verbal aspects in communication.
3. To use two-way communication and to understand the role of sender and receiver in making the communication complete.

SITUATION 1

A social worker is planning to organise a talk on AIDS for a youth club in a slum. He is meeting the office bearers of the youth club.
No. of participants: 3—one has to be the social worker.
Time required: 20 minutes for preparation.
20 minutes for presentation.
20 minutes for discussion.
After the enactment, use the following points for discussion.

1. Do you think the worker had prepared well for this meeting? How?
2. Did he ask appropriate questions? In what ways?
3. Did he speak to the point?
4. What did the facial expression convey?
5. What was his tone? What did it indicate?
6. Did the worker listen carefully?
7. How do we identify 'careful listening'?
8. Did the worker respond appropriately? In what ways?
9. What were the limitations in this communication?

Highlight:

1. Clarity in communication is achieved only through appropriate planning.
2. Communication is not complete without the feedback.
3. Communication is effective when both talking and listening are appropriately directed and conveyed.

SITUATION 2

The social worker is talking to a 15-year-old girl who has been admitted to the observation home by the police.

No. of participants: 2.

Time required: 20 minutes for preparation.
  20 minutes for presentation.
  20 minutes for discussion.

After the enactment, the facilitator should use the following points for discussion:

1. How did the worker start the interview—was the planning reflected through his/her communication?
2, Did the worker make the client comfortable? How?
3. Identify the words and gestures which made the client comfortable/uncomfortable.
4. How were the questions structured: words, tones, expressions, gestures used?
5. Did the worker listen carefully? In what ways did the worker reflect or not reflect careful listening?
6. What were the appropriate and inappropriate responses?

Highlight:

1. The importance of good listening.
2. The importance of appropriate use of words, tones and expressions while asking questions.
3. The importance of encouraging a two-way process of communication.

For highlighting all the topics that are discussed earlier, the facilitator could prepare charts or OHP transparencies on the following components of communication:

1. Process of communication.
2. Filters in communication.
3. Principles of listening.
4. Charts on body language.
5. Importance of feedback in communication.
6. Qualities of a good communicator.

Types of Communication

The social worker has to use both formal and informal communication in social work practice. They could be either verbal or in written form.

Written communication is used extensively in the social work field. The social worker has to prepare many reports or documents. At the same time, he has to read letters, reports, documents, and so on. Therefore, both reading and writing abilities require to be developed consciously though we may not be very careful or we may read without really understanding the meaning.

Exercise 6.6 Test of Concentration

Objective: To give insight to the TSWs on their reading habits.
No. of participants: All.
Material required: Copies of the test paper (Annexure A 6.1).
Time required: 20 minutes.
Procedure:

1. Distribute the papers to all participants.
2. Ask them to work independently and complete the test within 10 minutes.
3. They should respond to each question.

After 10 minutes, discuss the following points:

1. Do we read instructions carefully?
2. Why are we in a hurry while reading?
3. What did you feel when you read the last instruction of the test?

Highlight:

1. Confusion can be created due to incomplete reading.
2. Importance of careful reading in understanding the message or doing a task.

The TSWs could also require abilities in formal writing. To develop abilities in writing, the following exercises could be conducted.

Exercise 6.7 Writing Skills

Instructions:

1. The TSWs could be divided into small groups (not more than six in each group).
2. Each group is to be given one exercise in formal written communication.

The following are some more illustrative situations.

1. Letter Writing

   Situation 1: You are working in a residential care institution. A child is brought to the institution by the police. You have to write a letter to the parents.

   Situation 2: You are working in a community centre and want to refer a case of a child to the medical social worker for concession for his/her medical expenses in the hospital.

   Situation 3: You are unable to go for fieldwork due to health problems. Write an application to your fieldwork supervisor.

2. Report of a Programme

   Situation 1: Your agency had a prize distribution programme for children, who have passed their final exams. You have to send a brief report to the agency that sponsored the programme.

   Situation 2: A self-help group meeting was conducted for finalising eligibility for loans. Write the minutes of the meeting.

   The participants could be asked to present their assignments. Based on the presentations, basic formats could be finalised on charts and displayed in the classroom.

WORKSHOP 2

Barriers in Communication

In spite of all the planning and understanding of the process of communication, there may be blocks in communication. Multiple factors affect the process of communication. This workshop has the following objectives:

1. To understand various factors, which create barriers in communication.
2. To understand the impact of barriers on communication.
3. To know how to overcome these barriers.

TYPES OF BARRIERS

The social worker needs to understand the types of barriers which are common.

SEMANTICS (SCIENCE OF MEANING)

1. When language is unfamiliar and hence concepts used in the language are not understood, for example, while leaving home, a person might say 'मी येते' (I will return or see you) in Marathi instead of 'मी जाते' (I am leaving or going).

2. The same word has different meanings when the context is changed. For example, the word 'sex' when used in identification data of a person indicates gender of the person but when used in the context of the relationship between a man and a woman it indicates the sexual act.

3. The same word has different meanings in different languages, for example, the word 'साला' in Marathi indicates an abuse and in Gujarati it indicates a relationship, that is, wife's brother.

4. Due to similarity in pronunciation, the meaning of the word may be lost. For example, once people started gathering in a hospital because they had heard that a woman had given birth to a child with three heads (implying God Dattatraya is born). The message was 'तीन पौंडाचे बाळ झाले' (the birth weight of a boy is 3 pounds) which was heard as 'तीन तोंडाचे बाळ झाले' (a boy with three heads is born), and so the confusion.

5. In written communication, if words are split at the wrong alphabets or clubbed together or if some other alphabets are used, the meaning would change, for example, 'साब आज मेर गये, साब अजमेर गये!'

6. Some proverbs or phrases if used in the wrong context create confusion. Instead of saying 'ते आज आपल्या समेला येउ शकत नाहीत', saying 'ते आज आपल्यात नाहीत' indicates he is 'no more' instead of 'not with us' today.

7. One word in a given sentence can create a different meaning of the same sentence if we change the place of the word. For example, Mischief of 'only'.

Only he said that he loved her.
He *only* said that he loved her
He said that *only* he loved her
He said that he *only* loved her
He said that he loved *only* her
He said that he loved her *only*

(adapted from *Management Thoughts*, Pramod Batra)

8. Use of bureaucratic language or jargon which the receiver finds difficult to follow can create confusion, or insistence on using the regional language when some words of another language are more commonly understood. For example, translation of designations in Marathi on boards in government offices. Instead of the world 'Engineer' using a complicated Sanskrit translation. Or, sometimes doctors, when conducting health education programme, use all the medical terminologies or terms in English. They only use vernacular language for the verbs in the sentence.

Many examples of semantics leading to obstacles could be discussed with various local examples.

PHYSICAL BARRIERS

Physical barriers are the environmental factors, which prevent, reduce or delay the transmission or receiving of a message. For example, distance between sender and receiver, disturbing noises (may be of traffic or loud speaker), uncomfortable seating arrangements, poor lighting or visual barriers also hinder the process of communication.

Exercise 6.8 Building Geometrical Designs from Match Sticks

Objectives:

1. To understand how different barriers create blocks in communication.
2. To understand different types of barriers, which affect the receiver's understanding.

No. of participants: 2.
Materials required: One screen to create a visual barrier and two match boxes, the match sticks to be distributed between the players randomly.
Time required: 40 minutes.
Procedure:

1. Both participants are made to sit opposite to each other on chairs with tables in between.
2. A screen is held between the two to create a visual barrier.
3. One participant will prepare a design with the match sticks.
4. While building he is supposed to give instructions to the other participant.
5. The other participant has to follow the instructions and make the design accordingly.
6. The follower is not allowed to ask questions, just follow instructions.
7. Instructions should not be repeated.

Points for discussion:

1. What did the person who was making the design state in his/her communication?
2. What feeling did the receiver experience while following the instructions?
3. What are the reasons for the differences in the design?

Highlight:

1. Various barriers in communication lead to distortions.
2. Communicator must start at the level of the receiver.

PERSONAL BARRIERS

Distortions in message occur due to various personal factors such as emotional state, attitudes, social values, intellectual level, lack of interest, memory, desire to pass judgement, sender's background. All these develop a problem of selective perception leading to distortion of messages. Lack of mutual trust between the sender and the receiver is also a contributing factor in creating barriers in communication.

Communication cannot be separated from one's own personality. Often, we communicate interpretation of facts more strongly than the actual facts. The facilitator could demonstrate the above through various statements that reflect personality factors and the impact this would have on the process of communication. For example, the following statement in a given situation could be discussed at length: The social worker is conducting a parent meeting in a *balwadi* which caters to children of poor landless labourers or casual workers. While emphasising the importance of nutritious food to be given in the tiffin box he/she says 'You can afford to give 1 or 2 rupees to your children for wasteful expenses. Then why can't you give good food to your children in their tiffin?'

Points for discussion—Tone, use of words, facial expressions and its adverse effects like blaming, defensive behaviour or aggressive behaviours needs to be discussed. How this affects relationship between the worker and the parents needs to be highlighted.

Note to the facilitator: Various statements could be prepared along the above-mentioned lines and presented, highlighting various negative personality factors like hostility, suspiciousness, anger, unrealistic expectations and prejudices.

Effects of Incomplete Communication

These barriers in communication develop distortions and arrest the process of complete communication. Incomplete communication creates the following:

- Distrust
- Misunderstanding
- Confusion
- Ambivalence
- Frustration
- Resistance to give feedback

The sender who does not trust or respect the receiver can create confusion in the receiver's understanding. This type of sender also does not encourage feedback or pretends to encourage feedback without really meaning it. The following exercises reflect many dynamics which create confusion, misunderstanding and dissatisfaction in the receiver.

The effects of incomplete communication could be understood by using the following exercises.

Exercise 6.9 Draw a Diagram

Objective: To demonstrate how different barriers created by the sender lead to distortions in message and the outcome.
No. of participants: All.
Material required: Paper and pencil for all participants and a copy of the figure (Figure 6.1).

Figure 6.1   Geometrical Human Figure

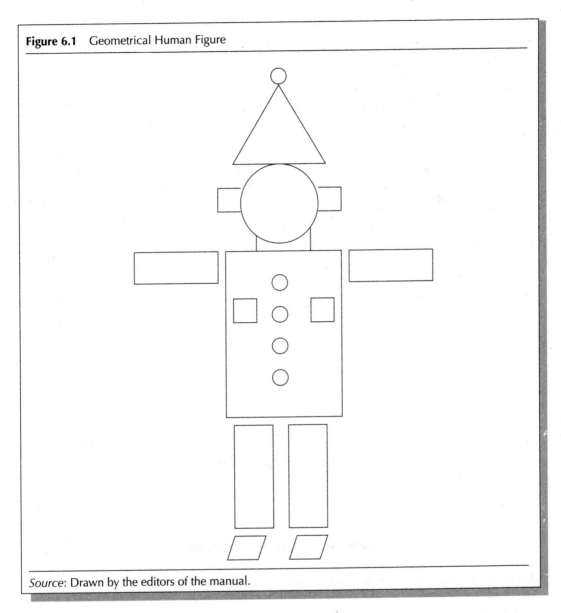

Source: Drawn by the editors of the manual.

Time required: 30 minutes.
Procedure:

1. The trainer sits with his back to the participants.
2. She/he starts drawing a diagram and simultaneously starts giving verbal instructions to the participants to draw it.

3. Instructions related to drawing the diagram are as follows:

   (a) Draw a triangle and then draw a circle
   (b) Then draw a square
   (c) Then draw two more rectangles
   (d) Then draw two more rectangles
   (e) Then draw one vertical and three horizontal lines
   (f) Draw two squares and four circles in the square

Notes to facilitator:

1. Repeat some of these instructions, without indicating that you are repeating them.
2. Give the instructions fast.
3. Do not pay any attention to the audience's questions.

Points for discussion:

1. What did the sender do?
2. What the sender did not do?
3. What did the audience feel?
4. Why were there so many differences in the diagrams drawn?

Highlight: If the communicator does not ensure that the receiver understands his expectations, there will always be a gap leading to misunderstandings and goals will not be achieved.

If the chain of communication increases, it leads to distortions in communication. Two exercises could be conducted to help the TSWs gain insight into this problem.

Exercise 6.10 Chinese Whisper

Objective: To understand how message gets distorted when the chain for message transmission is increased.
No. of participants: 10–12.
Time required: 30 minutes.
Material required: Nil.
Procedure:

1. One member prepares a sentence and whispers that sentence into the ear of the next member. This sentence should be long and complex. This chain goes on till it reaches the last member.

2. The last member has to tell the sentence aloud.
3. Go backward with each member saying about what she/he had heard.
4. Check at which points the sentence got distorted (Image 6.1).

Points for discussion:

1. Why did the message change?
2. Who felt powerful and who felt powerless?
3. Why and how did distortions occur?
4. Why was there an addition or a deletion in the sentence?

Highlight: Each person tried to add his/her own words to make the sentence meaningful. This addition led to a distortion or change in the meaning of the sentence. This is also reflected in rumours in daily life. Another exercise could be conducted to further expand this.

Source: James, Bhaise, Marie, Brian of Training Animators in Conscientization and Education (1975) (TRACE Team), published by Janaseva Mandal, Nandurbar (Maharashtra).

IMAGE 6.1   CHINESE WHISPER

Source: MUKUND D. SAWANT, PRODUCER, CENTRE FOR MEDIA AND CULTURAL STUDIES, TISS.

Exercise 6.11 Rumours

Materials required: A written paragraph with not more than 10–15 sentences.
No. of participants: 2.
Procedure:

1. Both participants go out of the class and one participant reads the paragraph to the other.
2. The second participant will narrate the paragraph to the class without referring to the written note.
3. Following this, read out the original paragraph to identify the gaps and change in narration.

Highlight: Even if there is no chain in communication, the receiver may not be able to retain everything. Hence, repetition is important or asking the receiver to ensure if he has picked up the relevant points is important. This brings out the importance of feedback for effective communication.

GUIDELINES TO IMPROVE COMMUNICATION AND MAKE IT EFFECTIVE

If one wants to be a winner in communication, some changes could be done in the following areas:

1. The physical environment.
2. Message.
3. Sender.

PHYSICAL ENVIRONMENT

1. A place which has privacy, is accessible and comfortable.
2. Time of the day to be selected—convenient to the receiver.
3. No distractions—visual or auditory.
4. Physical barriers to be minimised—distance, light, visual barrier.
5. Proper atmosphere/ethos to be created, which is supportive to the communicator/communication.

MESSAGE

1. Objectives—clear to the sender as well as to be made clear to the receiver.
2. Specific content to be selected—relevant information to be focused upon.
3. Precision is important—not too much to create confusion or boredom. Not too little to make it insignificant or vague.

4. Proper examples to be utilised to emphasise the message.
5. Avoid unnecessary repetition in messages.
6. Use of appropriate words.
7. Language should be familiar to the receiver. Do not use too much of technical language.
8. Avoid negatives, e. g. 'not allowed' instead of 'disallow'.
9. Use adequate media to strengthen the message.
10. Ensure logical sequencing of the message.
11. The message should always be clear and complete.

SENDER

1. The sender is quite crucial in the process of communication. The abilities and qualities that a sender requires to make his communication effective are sincerity, expressiveness, conviction, attentiveness, enthusiasm, patience, sensitivity, non-judgemental attitude, confidence, positive self-image, knowledge, sense of humour, warmth, interest in the subject and the receiver and openness. Continuous introspection and assessment of one's efficacy is the sender's vital responsibility. She/he must also receive feedback from the receiver without being defensive.

2. If the sender has these abilities and qualities, he/she will be able to relate well with the receiver. In establishing the relationship the following steps are essential:

   (a) Put the receiver at ease.
   (b) Empathise with the receiver.
   (c) Honour his/her feelings.
   (d) Do not discourage the receiver.
   (e) Encourage questions/opinions.
   (f) Pay attention to all and create a trusting atmosphere.
   (g) Do not impose your opinions; agree to differ with the receiver.
   (h) Listen with patience and respond to feedback.

3. Some points that need to be remembered in any communication:

   (a) You yourself are an 'audio-visual medium'.
   (b) Listen more—not only with your ears but also through your eyes, for example, when the receiver yawns, she/he tells you 'I have opened my mouth and so you shut yours'.
   (c) There is always scope for improvement. There is nothing like 'perfect communication'.

All these guidelines for improvement in communication could be demonstrated by the facilitator. Trainee social workers could be divided into small groups and asked to prepare presentation on the topics.

Note to the facilitator: Conduct the following exercise at the end of the workshop.

Exercise 6.12 Game of Boaster

Objective: To sum up all that has been discussed about communication.
No. of participants: All.
Material required: Nil.
Time required: 30 minutes.
Procedure:

1. Each person in the group goes round to the other members and tells them, in a very loud voice, his/her own virtues and qualities.
2. Within a minute they have to tell their virtues and qualities to as many members as possible.
3. The facilitator instructs the members to stop talking the moment she/he raises the arm.

Points for discussion:

1. What happened when everyone was talking simultaneously?
2. What did each one feel when no one was listening to you?
3. How did this process affect communication?
4. What did they feel about the sudden silence?

Highlight:

1. We experience frustration when people do not listen.
2. Various blocks are experienced in listening and also while communicating.
3. Importance of listening and responding in communication.

The facilitator concludes by stating: 'Now that we have understood the importance of communication in our life and as an essential component for becoming effective social workers, we the students of Master of Social Works pledge to improve our communication'. End the workshop with the pledge (Box 6.1).

Box 6.1 The Pledge

I. Statements in relation to 'Self'—The 'Sender'

1. We are responsible for our communication. Communication cannot be separated from our personality.
2. We will be careful about factors in our personality that distort communication.
3. Each one of us will understand oneself, one's own self-talk, self-image and self-concept.
4. We will improve our intrapersonal communication.
5. We will open our Jo-Hari window.

(Box 6.1 Continued)

(Box 6.1 Continued)

6. We will have attitudinal excellence.

   (a) We will be 'polite' than be proud.
   (b) We will hold our temper.
   (c) We will be task-oriented rather than self-oriented.
   (d) We will be conscious that we communicate reality as it is rather than our interpretation of the reality.
   (e) We will take a holistic view of the reality.
   (f) We will be warm hearted.
   (g) Our actions will not contradict our communication.
   (h) We will control our body movements.
   (i) Our physical appearance will be suitable to the situation.
   (j) We will look and indicate that we are interested.

II. Statements in relation to 'Others'—The 'Receiver'

1. Individuals with whom we communicate are important to us.
2. We accept the importance of trust between both of us.
3. We will be tolerant about feelings of others.
4. We will not take others for granted.
5. We will be patient and give all the time required to the receiver.
6. We will put vigour in communication by greeting people.
7. We will help the receiver to relax.
8. We will focus on the 'good' points of others rather than the negative points.
9. We will be open in our communication and help others to be open.
10. We will not interrupt the person who is responding.
11. We will empathise with the receiver.

III. Statements in relation to the 'Process'

1. We will listen more and talk less.
2. We will listen attentively.
3. We will be brief in our communication.
4. We will encode the message properly by using proper words, pictures, and so on.
5. We will choose proper 'words' and speak them in the proper 'tone'.
6. We will maintain consistency in verbal and non-verbal communication.
7. We will read carefully all written material.
8. We believe that face-to-face communication is more effective.
9. We will read and respond to body language that communicates emotions.
10. We accept the importance of touch in communication.

IV. Statements relating to 'Barriers in Communication'

1. We will reduce distractions in communication.
2. We will avoid either-or fallacies and selective observation.

(Box 6.1 Continued)

(Box 6.1 Continued)

3. We will avoid labelling.
4. We will avoid gaps in communication.
5. We will avoid incomplete communication.
6. We will avoid barriers in communication.
7. We will clarify misunderstandings promptly.
8. We will avoid being argumentative and try to be sporting losers.
9. We believe rumour is an undesirable feature of grapevine communication. We would not get affected by it.

V. Statements relating to 'Feedback'

1. We will invite feedback in communication.
2. We will take advice with thanks.
3. We will learn from constructive criticism from others.
4. If we are 'wrong', we will accept it immediately.
5. We will not steal credit due to others.

Note to the facilitator: Each sentence of the pledge could be transferred on cards, which could be distributed among trainees who take the pledge. Each participant can read aloud the sentence written on the card given to him. This pledge could be modified or only few sentences could be selected based on the facilitator's decision regarding the emphasis that is required at the end of the workshop.

WORKSHOP 3

Public Speaking

Besides one-to-one and one-to-group, social workers often have to address public meetings or large gatherings. This workshop will help the trainees to develop basic skills in public speaking.

Objectives of the Workshop:

1. To understand the importance of preparing for public speaking.
2. To get insights into specific techniques and skills to be developed for effective public speaking.

Materials required: Podium, mike (if necessary), table, chair.

Exercise 6.13 Preparing for and Making a Planned Speech

No. of participants: 3 or 4.
Time for preparing the speech: 1 week, for presentation: 5–7 minutes per trainee.
Procedure:

1. Ask the volunteer trainee to choose any one of the following topics or any other current issue for preparing a speech. This speech is to be presented in the subsequent lab session. The topics could be

    - Parental expectations from children and the resultant stress.
    - Water problem in the community.
    - Cancer awareness among middle-aged women.

2. Ask the rest of the class to note the content of the speech with reference to the chosen topic and observe the speaker.

Points for discussion:

1. Did the content of the speech reflect the topic assigned?
2. How did the speech reflect a logical flow— introduction, body, conclusion?
3. Did the speaker use appropriate verbal expressions, body language, tone and consciously check for audience involvement?
4. In what ways did the speaker reflect/not reflect preparedness, confidence and command over the situation?

Highlight: Discuss importance of Planning, Preparation and Practice for effective public speaking (three P's of public speaking).

Exercise 6.14 Equipping the Self to Make an Extempore Speech

Sometimes situations may call for making a brief speech 'on the spot'. This involves the skill to quickly prepare an outline and speak before an audience.
Examples for situations:

- Introducing the chief guest.
- Giving a vote of thanks.
- Introducing the purpose of the meeting.

Time: 10 minutes for preparation, 3–5 minutes for presentation.
Points for discussion:

1. Did the speaker begin by referring to all the members on the dais?
2. Was a reference made to the content of the previous speeches?
3. Was there clarity in the speech?

Highlight through discussion:

1. Alertness shown by the speaker to put together the content for the speech.
2. Confidence reflected.
3. Mannerism and what they convey.

Summarise the entire workshop by emphasising the different skills required for planned and extempore speech by referring to the points described in the subsection, 'Qualities essential in an effective public speaker'.

ANNEXURE A6.1 TEST OF YOUR CONCENTRATION

This is a test of your ability to concentrate. You have three minutes after the starting signal to follow the instructions as follows:

1. Read everything before doing anything.
2. Put your name in the upper right-hand corner of this paper.
3. Circle the word 'name' in sentence 2.
4. Draw five small squares in the upper left-hand corner of this paper.
5. Put an 'X' in each square.
6. Put a circle around each square.
7. Sign your name under the title of this test.
8. After the title write 'Yes, Yes, Yes'.
9. Put a circle around each word in sentence 7.
10. Put an 'X' in the lower left-hand corner of this paper
11. Put a triangle around this 'X'
12. On the reverse side of this paper multiply 73 by 9805.
13. Draw a rectangle around the word 'paper' in sentence 4.
14. Call out your first name when you reach this point in the test.
15. If you think you have followed directions up to this point, call out aloud 'I have'.
16. On the reverse side of this paper add 6950 and 9830
17. Put a circle around your answer. Put a square around the circle.
18. Count out loud in your normal speaking voice from 10 to 1
19. Now that you have finished reading carefully, do only as instructed in sentences 1 and 2.

Source: Dickson et al. 1989.

Chapter 7

USE OF AUDIO-VISUAL MEDIA

Ruma Bawikar and Nagmani Rao

Communication is facilitated and strengthened by the use of suitable audio-visual aids. Aids are facilitators of communication both for the sender and the receiver. It is said that what one thousand words cannot do, one picture can achieve. Audio-visual communication thus has a lot of potential (Figure 7.1).

Learning is facilitated if the new information makes an impact on more than one sense. There may be restrictions on the use of various aids/media, but with some imagination and effort a social worker can use a lot of media which are not always expensive. The choice of a particular method and medium will also depend upon the type and complexity of the message.

REASONS FOR USING AIDS IN COMMUNICATION

1. People get involved in the media.
2. Novelty of the media attracts people. This increases receptivity.
3. Abstract messages can be made concrete.
4. Reality can be shown.
5. Visual language holds more appeal.
6. Situations which usually cannot be seen can be shown.
7. Past events can be recreated.
8. New experiences can be given.
9. It can be interpreted through imagination.
10. It can influence the process of change.
11. It can be used again and again.

Figure 7.1 Types of Communication Channels

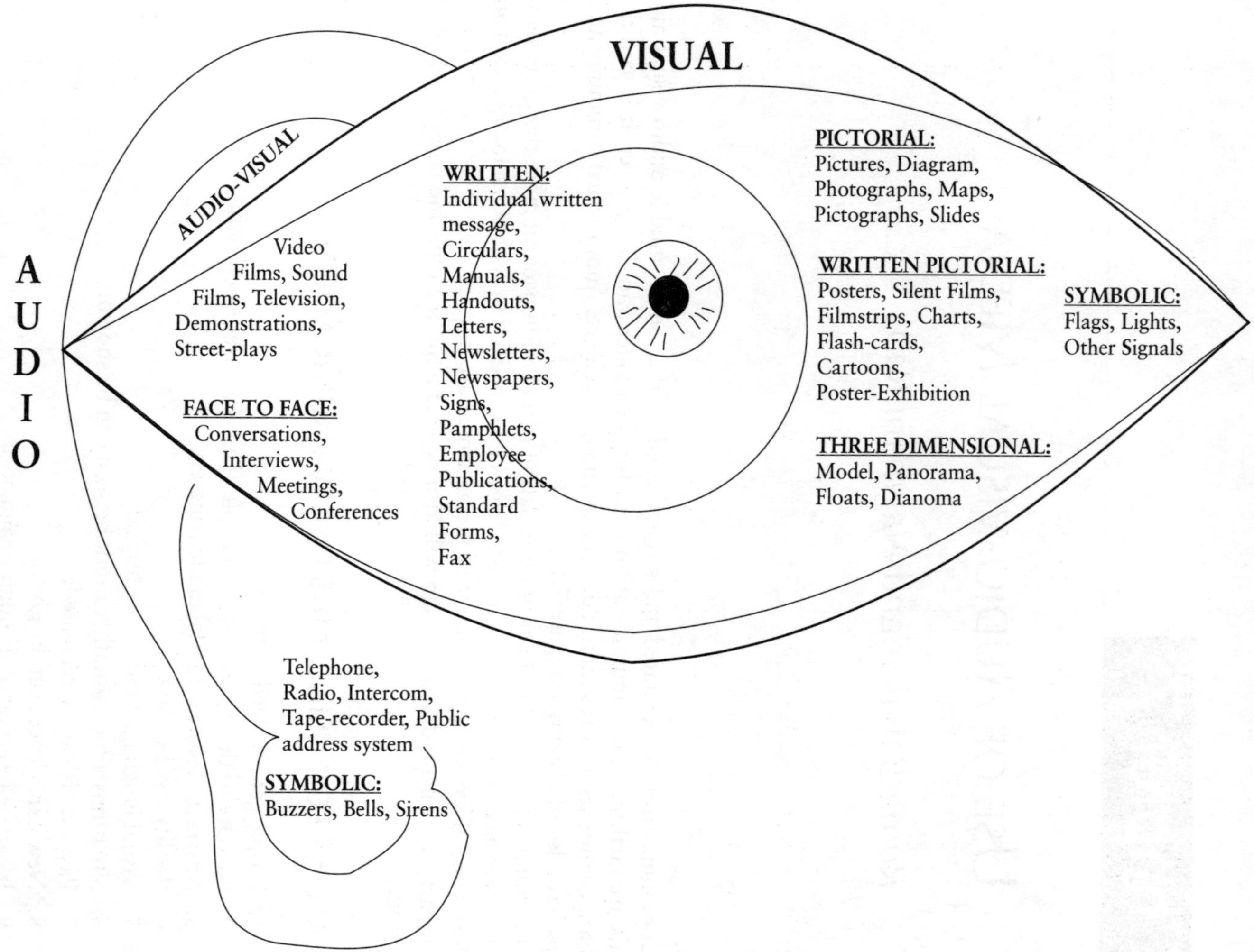

VISUAL

AUDIO-VISUAL

A
U
D
I
O

PICTORIAL:
Pictures, Diagram,
Photographs, Maps,
Pictographs, Slides

WRITTEN PICTORIAL:
Posters, Silent Films,
Filmstrips, Charts,
Flash-cards,
Cartoons,
Poster-Exhibition

SYMBOLIC:
Flags, Lights,
Other Signals

THREE DIMENSIONAL:
Model, Panorama,
Floats, Dianoma

WRITTEN:
Individual written
message,
Circulars,
Manuals,
Handouts,
Letters,
Newsletters,
Newspapers,
Signs,
Pamphlets,
Employee
Publications,
Standard
Forms,
Fax

FACE TO FACE:
Conversations,
Interviews,
Meetings,
Conferences

Video
Films, Sound
Films, Television,
Demonstrations,
Street-plays

Telephone,
Radio, Intercom,
Tape-recorder, Public
address system

SYMBOLIC:
Buzzers, Bells, Sirens

Source: Chatura Patil.

One should remember that media is not an end in itself—it is a tool for communication. Let us try to understand the strengths and limitations of media from the simple visual media to the complex technological media like the Internet.

While one uses any of the media, one is required to go by the following steps:

1. Proper preparation—planning.
2. Previewing the medium that one is going to use and pre-testing to finalise the material.
3. Practicing the use of the medium along with technical skills.
4. Presentating to the targeted audience.
5. Holding proper discussion following the presentation, highlighting the carry-home message.

Note to facilitator: Before planning the workshops, she/he should read the theoretical components of all the audio-visual media.

PART I UNDERSTANDING THE MEDIA

Visual Media

Visual media may be used along with audio tracks or it may be left to the viewer to interpret it. It is a semi-direct media, which is used to overcome the limitations of verbal communication. If one wants to prepare these visuals oneself, the first step would be to keep a scrapbook. Start collecting various pictures from advertisements, photos, captions and go on sticking them in this book. This could be the reservoir of experiences.

STEPS IN THE PREPARATION OF VISUAL MEDIA

1. Content planning—what message is to be given.
2. For whom, that is, the target group.
3. Structure the message—it should stimulate curiosity and interest

   - It must have novelty.
   - It must be effective and meaningful.
   - It must sustain attention.

4. Analyse the content: how much to be conveyed.

TYPES OF VISUAL AIDS

1. Flannel board/graph
2. Display boards
3. Flashcards

4. Posters
5. Collage
6. Charts
7. Pictures/photographs

FLANNEL BOARD/GRAPH (DEPENDENT AID)

It is prepared from a coloured *khadi* cloth or jute material, which is mounted on a wooden frame. Usually dull colours are used, so that the picture can stand out.

Preparation of cut-outs: Pictures should be properly cut into their original shape. Unwanted areas should be cut. Framing need not be done. Pictures should be big enough yet light in weight. Thin paper or card sheet can be used to prepare the cut-outs. Behind each picture, a small piece of sandpaper should be stuck. If sandpaper is not available, cotton wool and woollen thread could be stuck, fine sand or rangoli could be stuck with the help of gum. These pictures can then be stuck on a flannel board while talking to the group.

A small folder containing a 16" × 24" flannel board can be prepared, which is handy to use and can be carried easily. Within it one can prepare a small pocket to keep visuals. Visuals should be coloured. A story or logical message should be linked with the set of pictures.

Things to remember while using the flannel board:

1. The board should be kept slanting.
2. The board should not be overcrowded with pictures. One picture is displayed at a time or as the theme goes ahead pictures could be added on the flannel board.
3. It should not be used in a place where there is too much breeze.
4. Proper verbal commentary needs to be prepared.
5. Pre-planning is a must.
6. It cannot be used for a large audience.

Advantages of using a flannel board:

1. One or more pictures can be shown at a time.
2. Picture placement can be changed.
3. One can dramatise situations.
4. It attracts attention and stimulates curiosity. Appeals to all age groups.
5. It is entertaining.
6. It is cheap to prepare.
7. Easy to carry.
8. Easy to use.
9. It is dynamic. Same set could be used to convey different messages.
10. Many sets of visuals could be used on the same flannel board.
11. It increases participation.

DISPLAY BOARD/BULLETIN BOARD (INDEPENDENT AID)

These are simple hard boards or cork boards, which are hung on the wall. Sometimes things cannot be taught but are to be caught. These boards are contact points in communication.

Advantages:

1. These are simple and display one idea, hence there is no confusion in interpreting the message.
2. They are attractive —hence they catch attention quickly.
3. With a few words the message can be given.
4. These display boards create an environment to initiate communication.
5. Information is given directly.
6. Messages or information can be changed from time to time.
7. They can cater to a heterogeneous group.
8. Timely display of relevant material can help update information, such as during festivals or other public events.
9. The material displayed on the display board also conveys the commitment of the communicator to the issue.
10. There is freedom given to the receiver to view and read.

How to prepare display material:

1. Select one suitable topic.
2. Then select minimum and effective words for the message.
3. Before finalising try out various combinations then select the most appropriate placement.
4. The size of pictures and lettering should be properly matched.
5. The display board should be hung on a well-lit wall, little above the eye level.
6. It should be colourful, attractive and aesthetically prepared.
7. Visuals can be combined with textual information but the focus should be on pictures so that it carries the message to literate as well as illiterate audiences.

Things to remember:

1. Boards should be neat.
2. Proper clues should be used; familiar symbols should be utilised for the message to reach adequately.
3. Never crowd the display board, with visuals or messages.
4. Design the layout appropriately for the message.
5. When the display material is prepared, prepare it in such a way that it could be utilised on a flannel board or as flash cards also. This multiple use proves to be economical.

FLASH CARDS

It is a set of pictures with suitable captions or write-up prepared on any given theme (Image 7.1). These cards are quite small, not more than 15″ × 20″. Each card contains just one picture. Each card represents an idea and these cards are arranged in a sequence. The first card introduces the subject in bold lettering followed by others, which keep adding to information. This information has less text on it. There is continuity in the message. There should not be more than 15–20 cards in a set. Each card is shown to the audience along with the necessary verbal explanation. Bold lettering and illustrations can be used. Points to be highlighted are written on the reverse side of the card. Each card requires to be numbered.

Image 7.1   Using Flash Cards

Source: Mukund D. Sawant, Producer, Centre for Media and Cultural Studies, TISS.

The advantages of flash cards are as follows:

1. Relatively cheap.
2. Easy to make.
3. Easy to carry.
4. Flexible in utility.
5. A wide range of topics can be depicted.
6. Appealing to the audience.
7. Dynamic nature.
8. Can be reused.
9. Display time is flexible.
10. Can be discussed at the pace of the audience.
11. Dramatisation is possible.

Things to remember:

1. The series should have a title card.
2. One should not peep into the picture while talking.
3. The message has to be emphasised verbally.
4. Use only on a small audience.
5. Semicircle sitting arrangement is advisable.
6. Everyone should be able to see the picture.

POSTERS

It is one of the most creative media as one can convey messages directly or indirectly, using words and visuals. A poster contains one message or theme. Posters are self-explanatory.

The guidelines for preparing posters are as follows:

1. Design the layout appropriate to the message.
2. There should be a background and foreground for the poster.
3. Vacant space should be utilised meaningfully.
4. Alignment of material should be in relation to the dominant object—hierarchy should be maintained.
5. Common man's language can be used—rhyming captions can be used but in a smaller section of the paper.
6. The poster may be completely pictorial.

Things to remember in preparing the poster:

1. One can exaggerate the message but cannot elaborate it.
2. It should be colourful—but too many colours divert attention.
3. Blank space is important in posters. Borders should be avoided.
4. Straight lettering is better than artistic lettering. The size of the lettering should correspond with the size of the poster.

Placement and size of posters are important so that they are easily noticed.

There are two types of posters:

1. Contemporary—used for a specific purpose at a specific time.
2. Evergreen—used anytime. This poster has a universal message and appeal. For example, child labour can be a contemporary subject. While posters prepared on effects of smoking can be a message which will appeal to anyone at any time.

POSTER EXHIBITION

Here a series of posters are prepared for giving a specific elaborate message. There is a continuity of theme. The message is dramatised. These posters should not be stylised. Clear, simple images should be used. Social organisations can use them to draw public attention to current social issues.

The steps in using a poster exhibition:

1. This exhibition is displayed on streets or in public places or it could be used where large numbers of people gather.
2. Usually the members of the organisation stand nearby to answer the questions of the passers by or the group.

Note to the facilitator: A demonstration of a poster exhibition by some social organisation should be given to the trainee social workers (TSWs), followed by discussion and sharing of experiences by the members of that organisation. Discussion should be on following points:

- Why did they prepare this exhibition?
- How did they go about preparing it?
- What were their experiences with the audience?

COLLAGE

This aid is utilised to convey a broad message. It consists of pasting different pictures or cuttings of varied colours and sizes and arranging these proportionately to convey the message. Coloured pieces and black/white pieces could be properly matched for effect. Simple match sticks could be combined with pictures or words. Bordering or framing of the picture should be done with proper thought. Pasting should be done in such a way that it should convey a unified message.

CHARTS

In this aid, the interaction with the audience may be minimum. Charts are structured messages. They are not flexible. They are static but loaded with information. Hence, they have to be factually accurate and acknowledge the source of information.

Types of charts: Tabular, flow, organisational, comparative, tree, simple, and so on. A simple chart could be for giving information about disease or population profile. The information is presented in brief but proper division of the paper is a must. A comparative chart is also like a simple chart. The paper could be divided into two halves. With the help of subtitles, comparison between two comparable concepts is presented. For example, if one wants to compare two water supply schemes in a village, it could be depicted on comparative charts. Ability to present the information in precise words is very important. A tabular chart contains columns. Flow chart has picture schedule. Organisational chart shows relationship between various components—blocks and arrows are used to indicate relationships. Tree chart is used to show development of an institution, over a period of time.

The steps in preparing charts:

1. Collect all the basic information that one wants to give.
2. Classify the information.
3. Match content and format properly.
4. To make charts more effective, pictures and figures could be used for indicating comparison or difference.
5. The techniques of visual prompting can be used in the chart. Use cross, tick marks, colour prompting to emphasise differences. A change in lettering style can emphasise the different aspects. These can make the differences vivid.

PICTURE TALK

Photographs, cut-outs, stylised pictures could be utilised for this. These are based on projective techniques. One picture is shown to the group and certain questions are asked related to that picture. Based on the answers received, the worker highlights the message.

PAMPHLETS

These are used when the target is an educated population. They are prepared with more written information and comparatively less illustrations. The verbal presentation should be brief, precise and crisp. It may be used for emotional appeal. The message remains with the receiver even when the worker withdraws. It helps the receiver to learn at his own pace and time. The receiver can refer to it whenever he wants even after some time has lapsed.

LIMITATIONS OF THE VISUAL MEDIA

1. Misinterpretations are possible due to the differences in culture, experiences or exposure of the viewer.
2. Distortion in depiction is possible due to limitations of the communicator.
3. It could evoke different emotions in different individuals depending upon their age, sex and background.
4. Artists are required to prepare visuals.

A word of caution for preparation of any visual media:

1. Message must be brief.
2. Only essential words should be used.
3. Restrain is important—one should know where to stop, without sacrificing the content.
4. No visual message is complete without adequate feedback.

Audio Media

There are various forms of audio media but radio and tape recorders are commonly used aids to enhance messages.

TAPE RECORDER

This could be used to tape a conversation or a group discussion and played back to the group for highlighting certain aspects. Pre-recorded tapes of songs, stories or lectures could be used for giving information or providing entertainment.
    Advantages:

1. It is easy to carry and operate.
2. It can be used again and again.
3. It is economical.
4. Tape can be used for re-recording.
5. Immediate feedback is possible.
6. Can be used to improve one's own skills in communication in different situations.

RADIO

This medium can also be used in the social work field. After making the audience listen to special programmes, the worker can have a guided discussion. It is a familiar medium hence can be used without much technological know how. It may not require electricity. There are various programmes catering to various age groups/target groups. The communicator does not have any control over the media. He/she has to use whatever is presented by the broadcasting station.

    If the technical media are not available, the worker can use specially composed songs, which give a definite message. Such songs have to be in simple language and sung in easy rhythms. The worker has to sing the first line and the group members sing after the worker. The worker can compose new messages by using the popular film song tunes. This can help in creating an atmosphere. Along with the tune the message is remembered.

Audio-visual Media

Visual media used in isolation has its limitations because it is static. One cannot ensure holding of audience's attention over a prolonged period. This especially becomes relevant when a social worker is working in a community. For propaganda, or for organising and mobilising people, the worker may have to use other aids to make his/her communication more effective. The most effective media in today's technological world are audio-visual media. One should remember that audio-visual media are not ends in themselves. They are means for better communication.

Advantages of using audio-visual media:

1. The extent of involvement increases due to its dynamism.
2. It is closer to reality and hence identification is possible.
3. Visual language is more appealing.
4. Experiences can be given without threat or danger to the receiver.

FILMS

Projected audio-visual aids include slides, film strips and films, television and video films. Films are very useful in industrial and technical training for showing processes and events. They can also increase sensitivity to the reality and can help to develop analytical skills. They introduce new ideas.

Films should be able to stimulate creative mental activity. A film if properly used will affect habits, skills, behaviour, interests and attitudes.

The three guiding principles of film selection are as follows:

1. The use of a film should have a positive effect on the learner and it should contribute to authentic information.
2. The learner should be able to identify the film with a real need and it should also contain something which the learner does not know already.
3. It should help the audience in developing their plan of action.

For a proper selection of a film you need to know:

1. Sources from where you can borrow films and the procedure for borrowing.
2. The aims and objectives for use of a film as instructional material should be clear.
3. The details of the film in terms of the following:
   (a) Its subject matter and approach to the subject.
   (b) Its presentation.
   (c) Length and language.

The following are the special techniques used in films to emphasise certain aspects and create an impact: stills, fast motion, slow motion, infrared photography, time laps photography (plant growing), wide angle lens, microscopic lens, animation films, and so on.

The different types of films:

1. Documentary—It is a creative documentation of the reality or real incidents presented in a cinematically interesting way.
2. Narrative film—It is a film that narrates a fictional story.
3. Educational film—It is prepared for a specific target audience on a specific topic or subject and for educational purposes.

For a film to be suitable in a village or slum, it should have the following characteristics:

1. It should have a local setting.
2. It should present a single new idea or a few closely related ideas.
3. It should contain minimum abstraction and symbolism.
4. It should have a realistic approach.
5. The presentation should be simple, dramatic and not too lengthy.

Frequently, we see people using films as part of a discussion session in civic groups and social work organisations. The following steps need to be taken before using a film as a discussion topic:

1. Decide on the purpose and plan of the meeting.
2. Find out the background and interest of the participants to guide the selection of the film.
3. Preview the film to assess its content and technical soundness.
4. Analyse it—Is the purpose effectively carried out? Are the ideas interestingly presented? Is it suitable for the intended audience?
5. Plan your discussion outline. Note the basic issues, key words, highlights and significant incidences.
6. Steps in screening a film.

   (a) Introduce the film.
   (b) Screen the film.
   (c) Start discussion on the main ideas in the film.
   (d) Make transition to the agenda of the meeting consciously.
   (e) A discussion of the subject should be followed by a summary.

CD/video films can be used more conveniently, because comparatively the required equipment is easily available. An LCD projector and screen may become necessary if the audience is large.

The worker should remember that there are two goals that can be achieved through films:

1. Information: Films give detailed information and facts, hence the message may be received adequately.
2. Motivation: Films also motivate audiences. They can create a desire to find out more about the phenomenon. They inspire people to take up responsibility. Films can be very useful when shown to audiences who are in similar life situations.

SLIDES WITH AUDIO TAPE

Slides could be used as visual material with a commentary from the social worker or one can prepare slides along with synchronised audio tapes. Slides could be coloured or black and white or colour toned.

How to use slides:

1. Slides should not be shown in a hurry.
2. Once the slide is projected, use a pointer to direct the audience to the slide.
3. Adequate information has to be supplied along with each slide.
4. The room needs to be dark.
5. Project the slide on a light coloured wall, white bedsheet or screen for a clear picture projection.

Advantages:

1. Slides can be repeated, if necessary.
2. Concepts, statistical information, internal parts of body/machines can be made more clear with slides.
3. Messages can be made easier to understand.
4. Enough flexibility about number of slides, combination of slides, time for each slide and discussion along with each slide is possible.
5. The same slides can be adapted for different themes with different audiences.

Preparation of slides:

1. Theme has to be decided.
2. Theme has to be divided into definite sequential situations—preparing this description is called script writing.
3. After the script, the number of frames needs to be decided for each sub-theme.
4. These pictures could be of either real situations or graphs and charts. Laser prints or typewritten material require to be prepared and then copied with the help of a camera.
5. Slides are prepared using 35-mm black and white or colour transparency film.

Preparation of slides is a skilled job. Hence, it is advisable to prepare the slides with the help of a professional photographer or with available ready-made slides one can prepare a commentary to suit one's own message.

Limitations in using slides:

1. Electricity is essential.
2. Darkening the room affects the human touch in communication.
3. The audience is outside the media and hence sometimes the purpose of involvement or participation is defeated.
4. Social workers sometimes are not adequately trained in using this medium as a tool. It then becomes an end in itself.

With the development of computer technology, today PCs or laptops are considered more convenient than slide projectors. Now one can prepare Power Point presentations if a computer and CD projector are available. Acquiring technical skills is important to use if used efficiently and effectively.

PART II WORKSHOPS ON AUDIO-VISUAL MEDIA

Training in use of visual media and audio-visual media is not complete without actual practice. The workshop method will be very effective in helping the TSWs prepare material. Ready-made material can be made available to the TSWs and in the workshop they can be helped to learn how to use the material in a dynamic way.

Steps in Conducting Workshops in Preparing Visual Material for Communication

Input session: The facilitator should give the basic principles and steps in preparing different visual material. During this input session, the facilitator should also highlight the strengths and limitations of each type. Experts could also be invited for this workshop.

WORKSHOP 1: PREPARING VISUAL MESSAGES

Steps in preparing visuals:

1. Divide the class into small groups.
2. Give them one theme, for example, environment protection education for school children.
3. Ask each group to prepare any one visual on the selected theme. For example, one group prepares collage, another group prepares posters and charts and another group prepares flash cards.

Once these visuals are prepared, the facilitator could invite an expert to give feedback on each visual in relation to the communicability of the message.

WORKSHOP 2: USE OF AUDIO-VISUAL AIDS IN COMMUNICATION

SESSION A: USING FILMS TO STIMULATE DISCUSSION LEADING TO ACTION

The facilitator could show the TSWs a documentary film or a short film with a social message (for example, adoption, gender discrimination, problems of the aged, displacement).
Participants: All

Procedure:

1. Briefly introduce the film.
2. Screen the film.
3. Raise questions for discussion in terms of

   (a) messages conveyed
   (b) reflection on the message indicating opinions, values, facts, and so on.

Highlight: How films can be used to stimulate interest for starting a project, initiating a campaign for change, and so on.

When social workers use this medium, they can use various skills related to the selection of appropriate films/clippings, observing audience reactions during the screening, facilitating discussions and concluding the session by stimulating the development of action plans for a follow-up.

Note to the facilitator:

The discussions following a screening may be conducted by breaking the larger group into small groups. This could be followed by presentation based on guidelines given for group discussion.

SESSION B: USE OF FLASH CARDS AS AN INTERACTIVE TECHNIQUE

A set of flash cards could be given and one small group could be asked to do a role play (for example, health education of mothers/adolescent girls).

After the role play, discussion could be conducted on the following points

- How did the TSW use the flash card?
- Did these supplement his/her message?
- The style of holding the cards, speed, duration and the technique of reading.
- Did he/she ask questions that stimulated discussion and reflection?
- How interactive was the process?

SESSION C: USE OF SLIDES WITH AN AUDIO CASSETTE

Ready-made sets are available of slides along with audio commentary or the trainees could just use slides and do presentation through oral commentary.

At the end of these workshops, trainees could list out the skills required for preparing and using visual/audio-visual media.

Chapter 8

USE OF INNOVATIVE MEDIA IN COMMUNICATION

Ruma Bawikar, Anand Pawar, Manjusha Doshi, Vidya Ghugari, Anjali Maydeo, Ujwala Masdekar and Sameer Datye

MEANING AND SCOPE OF INNOVATIVE MEDIA

Communication in social work becomes complex since one has to equip oneself for various settings the worker alone cannot take the responsibility for communication. One-to-one communication relies more on oral communication. But the worker works with groups and in the field of communication organisation, he may have to use different strategies of communication. We are referring to these as innovative media because the worker needs to use novel ways of communication, either by developing new techniques or by modifying the existing media for communication.

In this chapter we have included a few innovative media of communication. These are also very commonly used media in the field of social work. These media may be used by other fields also, especially human resource development or management. But as social workers we use these media with a different perspective which aims to stimulate change. Hence one needs training in planning and implementing these strategies to facilitate the desired change.

The media presented in this chapter are from non-technical interpersonal media to highly technical Internet media.

Note to the Facilitator

Each medium is presented in a different style. The basic presentation starts with theoretical understanding of that specific medium. This is to be followed by specific workshops to strengthen trainees' abilities for using the media effectively and achieve the planned goals. Hence each workshop should be divided into two parts. Part 1—basic understanding of the medium which will include characteristics, strengths and weaknesses and guidelines for using it. Part 2—trainees to be given specific situations to develop the different media or to use the available material in specific situations.

After the actual participation, the facilitator can then discuss:

1. Steps in preparation.
2. Do's and don'ts while using the media.
3. Skills required to use the specific media to achieve objective.

TRADITIONAL MEDIA

While working with communities, the worker requires to be dynamic. She/he has to be constantly on the lookout to understand which approach will appeal to people. Especially in the rural area, the worker cannot rely on high technology media, due to various constraints like lack of resources such as space, electricity, technical assistance.

If the change process aims at not only behavioural but attitudinal change as well, then the message given should stimulate introspection or reflective thinking in the minds of the viewers.

The traditional media of *kirtan, tamasha, powada,* folk theatre could be used with newer perspectives if the worker looks at these innovatively (Annexure A8.1). One such experiment of using *bhajan kirtan* in the 'Arogya Dindi' (health procession) organised by a social organisation working in rural areas is discussed here. The main focus of their work was 'rural community health'.

Process: All the *bhajan mandalis* (groups) of the village were called for a meeting. They were asked to collect various *abhangas* (devotional songs written by great saints in Maharashtra), which convey messages on health, child care, nutrition, and so on. Some *abhangas* were prepared on relevant topics, making use of local talents. Posters were prepared on relevant topics using traditional imagery.

The route of the *dindi*[1] was planned. Each and every village on the route got involved in welcoming the *dindi*, arranging for food and accommodation, which is the tradition in Maharashtra.

---

[1] 'Dindi' is a procession of devotees, who gather from many villages and walk for days to reach Phandarpur (town in Maharashtra) which is famous for the temple of Vithoba (Vishnu).

At every stop, the *dindi* would perform a *kirtan*, arrange a poster exhibition and a film show at night. The next day *shramadan*,[2] tree plantation, gobar gas plant orientation training would follow.

The religious and emotional appeal of '*varkari*'[3] and '*dindi*' was utilised to increase participation and receptivity of the people to the new messages.

This type of awareness campaign requires lot of thinking and organisational skills. It also involves expenses. Hence the worker needs to be resourceful in involving the local leaders in these programmes.

Importance of Traditional Media

1. The popular forms of entertainment have their attraction which enhances participation of people.
2. The language, concept and methods are familiar to people—so expectations of change do not become threatening.
3. These media have been used as a channel for building social awareness over generations.
4. These media have religious, emotional implications, so they appeal to common people.

People who are experts in the use of traditional media usually belong to the masses. They can be motivated to deliver the new messages through the traditional approach for better acceptance. Many NGOs or people's organisations use this form for mobilisation and generating awareness in masses through the use of *kalapathak* or *kalajatra*.[4]

Trainee social workers (TSWs) could be given the task of preparing one campaign. The themes could be

- Cleanliness drive.
- Safe drinking water.

One group could be given the task of collecting existing *bhajan*s, *abhang*s or the folk songs which could be used for giving message (Annexure A8.2). Another group could be given the task of preparing songs, *abhang*s, by using the form but substitute with new lyrics. This would tap the talents.

---

[2] *Shramadan* is a Gandhian concept. People build public buildings or clean public places by participating voluntarily. It's like donating one's labour for public cause.
[3] *Varkari* is a religious sect established by famous saints of Maharashtra. The members of these sects are called *varkari*.
[4] *Kalapathak* or *kalajatra* is a group of artists who travel from one village to another and perform devotional songs or mythological stories. Its aim is to educate people through entertainment.

STREET THEATRE

Theatre has been an important form of communication in all cultures. It has a long history in all countries. There have been many experiments with the form and presentation of theatre.

India has a rich heritage of theatre culture. All states also have their own unique form of folk theatre. It has been a live medium, which was the main source of entertainment. But theatre also has a history as an important source of social education and conscientisation.

All over the world the socially committed theatre practitioners have questioned the purpose of theatre, which is controlled by commercial interests. They have felt that conventional theatres have ceased to provide an authentic exploratory space. On the other hand, people's theatre is for the people and by the people. It is an accessible dramatic form designed for the masses, a medium defined and controlled by the people for expressing their ideas and concerns. Street theatre is essentially a people's theatre born out of the social and political movements for change.

In this form of theatre the people's own ideas and visions find expression. It is based truly on democratic processes wherein people themselves decide the themes and how they are to be presented. The ultimate goal of this theatre is not aesthetic expression or artistic performance but to activate the people (Annexure A8.3).

The aims of street theatre is to

1. Build people's capacity to analyse the current social situation.
2. Identify and analyse ways and means of countering their basic problems.
3. Provoke reactions and actions from people.

The characteristics of street theatre:

1. Collective ownership: The group which is included in presentation works together. The theme is decided by the group. All ideas are expressed and the story line is developed by the group members. The message conveyed through this medium is the means of resisting the existing oppressive structures or situations. Hence collective commitment is the unique feature of this medium.
2. Minimum stage: Use of existing open space by breaking the artificial boundaries of stage and audience, hence there are bare minimum props. There is no glitter or glamour. There are no curtains. Everything happens before the audience, even the change of scenes, props and costumes. Open space has to be utilised.
3. Flexibility: Although the script may be prepared on the theme, it is not in the printed form. Since it addresses the current issues and actions, the actors may add their own dialogue based on the changing situation, local situation or reactions of the audience. This form is closer to the folk media, hence it uses the presentation style of folk theatre.

4. Audience participation: The medium acts as an analytical tool for testing the limits and possibilities for action. It also aims at questioning the contradictions and structures of existing society. The audience is made to reflect critically on issues of their concern in the hope that they become aware of the intricate nature of their situation. Hence the audience is encouraged to participate in the process of presentation by addressing the questions to them, by encouraging them to give reasons or solutions available. The actors have a dialogue with the audience. The audience has the freedom to leave at any time and start viewing at any point of the presentation.

5. Script form is eclectic: Use of popular tunes, songs, folk music is part of the ethos of the script. Language should be simple, colloquial and easy to understand. It should not be too long; the message must be given directly through three to four scenes. Humour is an essential component. Audiences should laugh and also start thinking critically. Slogans also can be a very important part of the script. They can be used to reinforce the message and keep the audience focused.

6. Presentation: Since the performance is in the open space, there could be many distractions like noise and passersby. Musical instruments are used to attract the audience. A chorus is used frequently in presenting important themes. Many things are presented symbolically. Actors may become objects. Rhythmic movements and dance forms are very effective in presentation.

The guidelines for presentation:

1. All actors may wear similar types of clothes, for example, kurta pyjama, kurta jeans or *dupatta*s of similar colour. This helps in establishing group identity.

2. There should be a *sutradhar* (narrator/speaker) who establishes the dialogue with the audience and gives the introduction to a new scene or he may conclude the scene. This helps in linking the theme and giving it continuity.

3. The presentation should be spontaneous and enthusiastic. Actors should be able to use their voice and also be able to use their body movements without inhibition in public.

4. The actors should have independent dialogues but at the same time some of the actors should work as a group to deliver dialogue. Group singing or group dancing is important in presentation.

5. The group cohesion and synchronisation is important. This creates a good impact on the audience.

6. Before starting the performance, start with a group song or by playing a musical instrument so as to catch the attention of the passersby.

7. After the performance, discussion with the audience is a must and street play is a tool to generate communication. The audience should get a feeling of being empowered due to this experience.

The steps in developing a street play:

1. Identify issues like urgent needs, generate public opinion to support a wider campaign, generate actions on issues like dowry deaths, apathy of municipal administration, and so on.
2. Understand an issue by holding a series of discussions in the group and collecting data.
3. Decide the details of each scene.
4. Finalise the message to be focused in each scene.
5. Decide about characters and script.
6. Prepare dialogues and songs.
7. Work out formation and movements.
8. Develop linkages with the next scenes using fillers like songs.
9. Plan the use of space, props and strategic staging.
10. Discuss follow-up activities and decide strategies for follow-up.

The duration of a street play should not be more than 20–30 minutes. The impacts of street plays:

1. At the level of the performers: The group could be youth from the community, volunteers, women or activist groups working on an issue. When this group is involved in the production process it helps in developing confidence, clarity and a proactive attitude in the individual. The group also benefits as a whole—group cohesion, team building and motivation to change builds up.
2. At the level of audience: The immediate effect is receiving information, starting to get interested in the issue. A later effect is that it may generate dialogue among the audience, if they belong to a geographical or functional community.
3. At the level of power groups or the establishment:

   (a) Arrests of actors or groups or threats/disruptions of performance.
   (b) Ban on the presentation.
   (c) Starting of negotiations with the establishment.

The advantages of street plays:

1. They can deal with any subject which is the concern of the masses.
2. They enrich performers.
3. They open communication, hence an opportunity for immediate feedback.
4. Audience is not at the receiving end.
5. The element of entertainment helps in making the message non-threatening.
6. They can be a tool in mobilising action.

Workshop on Street Play

One day will be required to help the TSWs understand the process. The facilitator can conduct this workshop by first demonstrating a street play performance and then following it up with an analysis of the performance, highlighting the theory of the media, or the facilitator could help the TSWs go through the steps of preparation of a street play leading to a presentation by groups of TSWs.

They need to understand this medium for two reasons:

1. To develop skills as performers.
2. To develop skills in facilitating groups to be able to perform.

Participants: All (for every exercise).

Note to the facilitator: Each of the exercises described later is to be short and in quick succession and aims to demonstrate various nuances that are part of street play performances.

The exercises for self-preparation are as follows.

Exercise 8.1 The Sender (The Performer)

Objective: To help the TSWs understand the responsibility of the sender.
Material required: Chart paper, markers.
Time required: 45 minutes.
Divide the class into groups.
Ask them to discuss the following points and present on charts:

1. Expectations of the receiver from a play.
2. Expectations of the performer from a performance.

Based on their presentations, the facilitator should emphasise the responsibility of the performer in identifying the expectations of the audience by observing the audience's non-verbal communication and their comments. This is the feedback.

How does one observe and how does one respond needs to be discussed elaborately, with examples.

The facilitator needs to conclude this exercise by highlighting the process of communication.

Exercise 8.2 Use of Voice

Objective: To help the TSW to develop the ability to use his/her voice effectively. Each of these is part of a set of exercises to demonstrate the use of voice and overcome inhibitions for performing.

1. Ask the TSWs to tell their name—first in the usual normal tone. Then two more times but at different pitches.
2. Ask the participants to move in a circle and while they are moving ask them to say one statement together first in a whisper and go on increasing the pitch till they are screaming, for example, 'India is my country and all Indians are my brothers and sisters'.
3. Ask the participants to express one sentence with different emotions.
4. Each participant should represent one emotion through body language. Another participant should read that emotion and express the same by articulating a sentence.

The exercise concludes by highlighting voice modulation and expression in performance.

Exercise 8.3 Reducing Body Inhibition

1. Ask one participant to laugh and then start a chain of laughter.
2. Ask participants to touch each other on different body parts—nose, cheek, shoulder, back, hand and feet—within a specific time.
3. Ask participants to lie down on the ground. Each participant has to rest his head on the stomach of another participant.

This exercise helps to shed cultural inhibition related to spontaneous expression, physical touch and proximity.

Exercise 8.4 Identifying with Characters

1. Ask the participants to walk or do some body movements as per the role.
   For example, walk like a king, walk like a soldier, walk like a person who has just ridden a bicycle uphill.
2. Give *dupattas* to all the boys. Ask them to drape themselves as girls do. And then ask them to start doing some tasks like sweeping the room and picking up a bucket.
3. Ask each participant to act out the following actions by imagining that he

   (a) picks up a small stone and throws it as far as possible,
   (b) picks up a large stone and throws it as far as possible and
   (c) goes on increasing the size and weight of the stone and pretends to throw it as far as possible.

This exercise would help the participants to understand the difference in movements and gestures as per the requirement of the role.

Exercise 8.5 Use of Body and Facial Expressions

1. Show different body postures of being tired, sleepy, reacting to a good scent or a stinking smell, perspiring due to heat, and so on.
2. Prepare a mask of newspaper, with only two holes for the eyes. Hold the mask over the face ask participants to express specific expressions through the eyes (Image 8.1).

Image 8.1   Use of Facial Expressions in Street Theatre

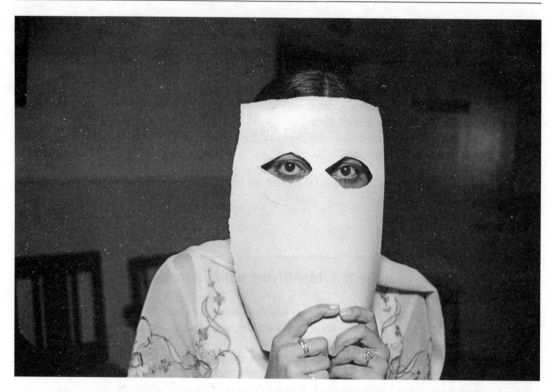

Source: Mukund D. Sawant, Producer, Centre for Media and Cultural Studies, TISS.

3. Give one pillow to the participants and ask them to show some use of it. While doing this, ask them to stand in a circle. Once all the participants have completed this task, ask each participant to repeat the action that the person next to him/her had performed earlier.
4. Give air-filled balloons to each participant. They have to keep the balloon floating in the air by blowing without touching the balloon.

The above set of exercises help TSWs understand the intricacies of using body posture, eyes and breathing to convey emotions and also understand that actions have to be logically sequenced in response to ones from other performers.

Script Writing

After these exercises, ask the participants to make a list of themes for a street play. Ask them to select one theme and prepare the objectives—What are the key take-home messages? What are the expected changes in thinking and action?

Once this is decided, divide the class into groups and ask them to prepare a storyline, characters, scenes. Ask each group to do a presentation (Annexure A8.3: example of a street play).

After the presentation, each group should select one scene and write down the dialogue with body movements, song if required and the type of music used. Ask each group to make a presentation.

Performance

To help the TSWs to be aware of the use of space available during the performance, the following exercise could be given.

Exercise 8.6 Use of Space

Situation: In a small furnished room, two people are trying to catch a hen and once caught, keep it under a cane basket.

Ask two volunteers to enact the situation without any verbal dialogue. This exercise would help the participants to be aware of the use of space, coordination, and so on.

At the end of the workshop, ask each group to perform one scene from their group presentation. The facilitator should give feedback on the following points:

1. Was the message clear?
2. Was the number of characters adequate?
3. How was the space used?
4. How was the dialogue?

Alternatively at the end of the workshop a good street play could be demonstrated.

PUPPETRY

Introduction

Puppetry like other forms of performing arts is widely accepted in life. Like theatre, puppetry presents live characters on the stage and, through the disappearance of the 'fourth wall', brings them into flesh-and-blood contact with the audience. Puppetry calls for a willing suspension of disbelief through symbolic representation of real characters through puppets. The audience is persuaded to accept the icons as representation of reality and, through this representation, gets involved with the characters and their situations.

History

According to historians, puppets are as old as civilisation. We see their references in the history of Harappa and Mohenjodaro civilisation. Mahabharata and Ramayan also have a mention of puppetry. Puppetry in India is deeply rooted in its religious ethos. Puppet shows are part of religious fairs and festivals, narrating stories of the gods and goddesses. Puppetry has been used to spread religion. It served as an integral popular medium which appealed to the masses. The traditional puppeteers were mostly nomadic artists.

The puppets have a variety and a great range of movement. Hence they attract audience of all age and types. The charm of this medium is of turning an inanimate object like doll into an animated character. Every type of puppet has a set of special movements. Some movements and gestures of puppets not only convey special articulation but also show intense emotions like agony and frustration. This is achieved through peculiar jerks of head and hands of the puppet.

Some traditional puppet theatre has a narrative text which is read or sung. The narrator or singer is not visible to the audience. The actors give each puppet a peculiar voice and give a unique identity to each puppet. Every puppet has its own style of language dialogue delivery, tempo and mannerism. Very often the puppeteer delivers all the dialogues by changing his/her voice.

The traditional puppeteers generally use stories from epics and Puranas. There is no written script and very rarely new scripts or stories are written. The scripts are usually memorised. Sometimes they use popular Hindi film songs. Comic characters are present in all the traditional puppet shows. Many traditional troupes presently perform plays on social problems like sanitation, health care, girl child and environment. The tradition of puppetry is passed from generation to generation without formal training. They learn through participation in performances from an early age.

Puppet stage is divided into two parts—first where puppets act and second where the manipulators stand. Traditional stage is simple and easy to dismantle. It is usually made of indigenous material. Traditional puppet groups use thick cloth preferably black as a back drop. Traditional glove puppeteers perform in the open and do not need any stage. Some types of puppeteers use props and painted curtains. Not much lighting arrangement is required. Many traditional puppeteers use oil lamps for the unique effect of light and shade in the performance. Music is very important in traditional puppet shows. Either one person sings songs or there is a chorus. Music is based on folk tunes and popular film songs. Use of musical instruments is also common for creating an effect, for example a war scene or a fight.

Kinds of Puppet

1. Glove/hand puppet.
2. Stick puppet.
3. Finger puppet.
4. Shadow puppet.
5. String puppet/marionette.

Roles of Puppets

1. Entertainment—puppetry for the masses.
2. Education.
3. Self-expression.
4. Social action—social role of puppetry.

Use of Puppets in Social Work

Puppets can be used for any type of group like literates, neo-literates and illiterate, young and old, and rural and urban.

Subjects like superstitions and beliefs, various social problems, alcoholism and drug addiction, health issues, environmental issues, propaganda of various developmental schemes, introducing technology and science can be communicated through puppetry.

It can also be used in therapy programmes especially for children, stimulating the group to think creatively motivating them for a particular subject, suggesting behaviour changes, and so on.

Criticism is easier to accept through puppets. Normally people do not take it personally. This helps for learning in a healthy way.

This dynamic medium could be used for giving information, education, entertainment, generating awareness and problem resolution leading to change.

Tips for Writing Scripts for Puppet Shows

The puppet play is a drama. Therefore one should conform to the rules for writing a drama. The play must be full of action. Interest should be aroused at the beginning of the play and must be held throughout. One scene follows another in sequence so that the audience follows every detail clearly.

Suspense in the story helps to arouse emotions and make the audience more attentive. Early in the play dramatic questions can be introduced. These can be subtle but the audience must be aware of it and kept in suspense until the climax.

Laughter, songs and dancing add lightness to the story. Fantasy helps but the play should be relevant to the day-to-day experiences of the audience. Otherwise they will fail to associate with it.

When teaching a lesson through a play, teach only one thing.

The characters in the play must be distinctive. They should introduce themselves or be introduced by the other characters as they make their appearance in the play. In a story, only one puppet is to be used for one character.

Speeches should be short. Quick dialogue and short speeches are easy to present as the puppets have limitations in facial expression and gestures. Avoid long pauses. The play should not be more than 20 minutes. The average attention span of the target group is to be considered. The language should be simple and colloquial with short sentences.

Each puppeteer can work with two hand puppets at a time. The size and the space of the stage are to be considered as they may create limitations for the puppeteers. It is important to consider the puppeteer's skill in using many puppets as he may have to change the puppets very fast without a pause. Changing the characters can take place between scenes or during the music. The writer must arrange for this when writing the play.

Only one puppet should show movements at a time. Use voice modulation for each character, as this would reduce the confusion amongst the audience.

Repetition emphasises a point and helps the listener to remember the main idea. As you write your play keep an eye on 'production'. Ask yourself questions as you review your play. Each word should serve a purpose in the play. Every word, gesture and action in the play must contribute something to the whole production.

Study the audience. Note its reaction. Make changes in the play, if needed.

Puppet performance could be a very effective activity while working with children. The social worker can help the group members to go through the process of selection of theme, script writing, preparation of puppets and presentation. This will stimulate creativity in children and also help them to express their feelings.

Workshop on Puppetry

Objectives:

1. To introduce the puppet as a medium of communication in social work practice.
2. To develop the skill of puppetry.

The workshop can be divided into two units:

UNIT I INTRODUCTION TO PUPPETRY

1. Input session on history, types and utility of puppets.
2. Demonstration on puppet show by the puppeteer.
   Time: 2 hours.

UNIT II COULD BE DIVIDED INTO THREE SESSIONS

SESSION I: SCRIPT WRITING

Time: 2 hours.
Participants: All.
Procedure:
Input session: Guidelines for preparing scripts and the actual performance.
Procedure:

1. Divide the class into groups of 6–7 students.
2. Ask each group to select one theme.
3. Each group should identify the main message to be conveyed.
4. Following this they should list out the characters and build the story in dialogue form, thus preparing the script. The dialogue should be prose and songs. The script should be prepared for a performance of 10–12 minutes.

Note to the facilitator: Display the chart on 'Do's and Don'ts' in script writing while the groups work on the script based on 'tips for writing scripts for puppet shows' given earlier.

SESSION II: PUPPET MAKING

Time: 3 hours.
Participants: All.
Before the groups prepare their own puppets, the facilitator could give them some ready-made puppets (hand glove puppet, stick puppet, and so on) just to handle or to get the feel of it. Then ask the groups to prepare their own puppets according to the characters planned. They should also be encouraged to prepare props.
Materials required: Cloth, needle, thread, scissors, fevicol, pencil, chart papers, coloured paper balls, empty tins/talcum powder boxes, wool, old socks, bamboo sticks, crayons and markers.

Procedure:

1. Each group should prepare puppets based on characters in their script.
2. Ask group members to cut out figures of characters on chart paper and paint them.
3. Stick these figures on the bamboo sticks.
4. Also prepare pros to depict the scene in their script, for example, trees, houses, buildings.

SESSION III: PERFORMANCE

Time: 2 hours.
Participants: All in their respective groups.
Materials required: Puppets, props made by them, a bed sheet for a screen.
Procedure:

1. Ask participant groups to practice their performance (15–20 minutes) and then each group performs in front of rest of the class. Each performance should not exceed 10–12 minutes.
2. The facilitator should give feedback on each performance along the following lines:
   - Puppet handling movements.
   - Use of voice modulation.
   - Script—language and sentence construction.
   - Use of props, songs and other material.
   - Drama in the story and its impact.
   - Techniques to make session interactive.
   - Was the desired message conveyed?

The puppets prepared by the TSWs should be used in their field placement.

THEATRE GAMES OR EXERCISES

Drama and the theatre need performers who can act at different places on different themes. These performances need skills, as the person has to adapt to the situation and perform accordingly. The theatre and drama have contributed a lot in this matter to help individuals overcome their inhibitions and fears and to contribute their best to the theatre. The theatre exercises help individuals who have constraints due to rigid social norms, values, rules as well as their own fears and frustrations.

Individuals become more open and imaginative through these experiences. It helps set free natural creativity, overcome fear/inhibitions and develop social skills and teamwork. The exercises can be used for self-development.

These exercises promote the following:

1. Emotional release through self-expression.
2. Constructive use of emotions.
3. Channelising of thinking processes.
4. Enhancing leadership qualities.
5. Respecting opinions of other persons.
6. Learning to be cooperative and social.
7. Reducing inhibitions and shyness.
8. Ability to divulge the inner personality.
9. Building of self-confidence.
10. Increasing attention span.
11. Developing cognitive skills.
12. Developing communication skills.

Use of Theatre Games in Social Work Practice

In social work practice, a social worker can use the techniques that can be used to help other individuals overcome limitations as well as for self-development. These exercises are used as ice-breakers when the group is meeting for the first time. These could be introduced in training programmes when trainees show fatigue or disinterest. Group activities lead to interaction, which is important for any development programme. While working in interdisciplinary teams or any other work teams, to break the monotony of work, to enable people to relax and to be more comfortable with each other also, these exercises could be used.

The following are a few examples of these exercises and the way they could be conducted. It is important to know that the following exercises are modified theatrical exercises. The duration for each activity is not specific as the participants may take time to open up and express themselves. It is necessary to give a chance to each participant and adequate time. The facilitator will have to be sensitive towards participants' expressions and feelings. For each exercise there is no need for any discussion as a rule, but if the facilitator thinks it is necessary to clarify certain doubts then participatory discussions can be held. Otherwise, largely, these exercises are used for experiencing from within.

Box 8.1   Modified Theatrical Exercises

Exercise No.	Exercise Title	Description
8.7	Reaching Out Group size: 20	**Objectives:** 1. To create a comfortable environment. 2. To feel comfortable with each other. **Procedure:** 1. The facilitator asks the participants to form two circles: one inner and the other outer. 2. When the music is played, one circle moves in a clockwise direction and the other in an anticlockwise direction touching each other's hands. 3. When the music stops, the facilitator asks the participants how many hands they could touch. The action can be repeated if the response is less. **Points for discussion:** 1. What feeling/thoughts came to their mind after the facilitator's instructions? 2. Differences experienced while relating to a stranger and a friend/acquaintance.
8.8	Miming Group size: 20 to form pairs	**Objectives:** 1. To overcome inhibitions. 2. To know the importance of body language in communication. **Procedure:** 1. Divide participants into pairs with different mother tongues to form subgroups, for example, one with Marathi and the other with Tamil. 2. Ask these persons to communicate by miming. **Points for discussion:** The concepts/ideas we express are thought in our own language and yet the other person understands them. It helps in breaking barriers of language.
8.9	Nonsense Talk Group size: 20	**Objective:** Understanding the importance of dialogue. **Procedure:** 1. Divide the groups into pairs. 2. In a pair one person initiates a conversation and the other person responds to him out of context. 3. Throughout the dialogue they must speak vaguely and should not answer any specific question. The response has to be irrelevant and illogical. **Point for discussion:** How do we feel when the other person does not respond appropriately/does not understand us?

(Box 8.1 Continued)

(Box 8.1 Continued)

Exercise No.	Exercise Title	Description
8.10	Passing the Action/ Voice Group size: 20	**Objectives:** 1. To enhance observation skills. 2. To overcome inhibitions. **Procedure:** 1. All the participants form a circle. 2. One person does some specific action. 3. The next person repeats the same action. 4. This is followed up to the last person. 5. Instead of actions voice can also be used. **Points for discussion:** While imitating, we change the original action. Persons are in a hurry to imitate. This game can help apathetic groups to become active.
8.11	Mouth–action Coordination Group size: 20	**Objective:** Understanding how to deliver the message in action. **Procedure:** 1. Divide the group into subgroups of three. 2. One person sits on a chair with his back to the audience. He/she speaks without any body movements. 3. Two persons perform the actions in front of the audience. **Points for discussion:** It is very difficult to predict what the other person is going to say. Unless and until one understands the matter one cannot put the message into action. Two persons perform differently although they receive the same message.
8.12	Hand–mouth Action in Pairs Group size: 20	**Objective:** Importance of understanding and coordination. **Procedure:** One person speaks and the other person acts out the statements. **Points for discussion:** 1. Importance of coordination, understanding each other. 2. How unpredictable is the other person's thought.
8.13	Orchestra Group size: 20	**Objective:** Team building. **Procedure:** 1. Form subgroups of five each. 2. Each group produces/creates a tune/rhythm. 3. This tune/rhythm is said in a continuous fashion with different volumes/tones. The beauty of these tunes is that they should synchronise with each other. **Points for discussion:** Being synchronised helps to work comfortably with each other. This helps build team work.

(Box 8.1 Continued)

(Box 8.1 Continued)

Exercise No.	Exercise Title	Description
8.14	Developing a Story Group size: 20–25	**Objective:** Team building and stimulating imagination. **Procedure:** Members are asked to select one situation/thing. All the members together prepare a story related to the selected thing/situation. **Points for discussion:** 1. Stimulating self by working in a group. 2. Usefulness of collective thinking.
8.15	Dramatisation Group size: 20	**Objective:** Building cooperation. **Procedure:** 1. Participants stand in the form of a circle. 2. One member narrates an incident and acts accordingly. 3. The next member does the supportive action to the earlier. This goes on till each gets the chance to act. 4. Normally a story/theme is built through this action. **Points for discussion:** Importance of cooperation, coordination and group efforts to achieve goals.
8.16	Quarrelling in Pairs Group size: 20	**Objective:** To ventilate pent-up feelings. **Procedure:** 1. Divide the group into pairs. 2. Two persons start a quarrel. Initially at a slow pace then faster and gradually at higher pitch. **Points for discussion:** How one feels while quarrelling and the after effects of it.

The facilitator can explain as to when these techniques could be used. The therapeutic value of this medium needs to be highlighted. For example, recovered mentally ill patients could benefit from this technique.

PHOTO LANGUAGE

Photo language is a very strong visual medium, which was introduced in the mid-1980s as part of development communication strategy.

As the name suggests, photos are used for expressing feelings and thoughts. A photographer uses photos to convey his/her own feelings, thoughts and perceptions or he/she wants the viewers to perceive the reality in a particular way. A photo directly communicates with the viewer, but simultaneously it also evokes reactions in the viewers. The viewer has the freedom to interpret the photo based on the emotions or thoughts triggered through this visual stimulus.

Photo language uses photos as a tool to stimulate the people. The viewer has the freedom to select any photo or photos and then express his feelings or thoughts with the help of the photograph. One photograph may evoke different reactions in the same person, depending upon his frame of reference. The same photograph may evoke different reactions in different individuals. It is a process of identifying with the photo and then using the photo to support our communication. Hence one can say it works as a projective technique, that is, the view gives subjective meaning to an objective reality.

In social work, photo language is not used the way photos are used in psychological tests, that is, as a projective technique (Thematic Apperception Tests). It is used more as a tool to help people verbalise their thoughts and feelings and to stimulate discussion in a supportive environment.

For photo language, the worker requires a large set of photographs (at least 60–70) of good quality—clear and sharp. As far as possible, black and white photographs should be used. These are much more powerful. These photos should depict a variety of human life situations, people involved in a variety of activities, different age groups, portraits of people, animals, naturescapes, and so on. Some photographs could be abstract in nature. Sets of such photographs are available with media agencies. Each set includes a 'user's guide' explaining the steps for using it and how to use the set with a variety of objectives. (One such agency is Low Cost Media Service, Notre Dame Communication Centre, Pattiputra P.O. Patna, Bihar, India 600013.)

Objectives for Using Photo Language

These will depend upon the needs of the clients and the broad goal of that social work activity.

1. For self-introduction or as an ice-breaker in a training situation or in a workshop.
2. To help clients express feelings about themselves and their perceptions about the self.
3. To help clients express their feelings or thoughts about their own social situation and their relationships.
4. To help clients express their views on life.
5. To help clients express their concerns about the self and others.
6. To stimulate group sharing.

If one is using photo language while training professionals, then the objectives could be:

1. To facilitate the expression of their perceptions regarding different professional roles.
2. To identify their perceptions about reality and the client systems.

Strength of This Medium

1. Photos help as support to overcome fear of expression of one's own opinions or feelings.
2. Photos also help in putting one's thoughts into words due to the visual impact.
3. Photos help in triggering recall of many other similar experiences.
4. The visual images help a person to use it as a symbol of his/her feelings or thoughts.
5. Photos touch your heart, as if the images are communicating only with that viewer. Hence the person opens up without becoming conscious.

Procedure

1. The worker should have a specific objective for using this medium with any specific group.
2. Spread the photographs in such a way that all the participants are able to see all the pictures.
3. Ask the participants to move around slowly and view each photograph carefully.
4. Give specific time for viewing.
5. Usually, members are asked to select one photo (sometimes it could be two) on the basis of instructions given by the facilitator for that specific exercise. For example, if the exercise is for understanding member perception of the self, then the instruction will be 'select one photograph which you think depicts your characteristics or yourself'.
6. Then ask each participant to talk about the photo in the context of the instruction.
7. Do not force participants to talk, keep it voluntary.
8. Highlight the points that emerged and link them to the objectives of that particular session.
9. Sometimes more than one participant may choose the same photo. Ask them to express their reasons one by one.

The facilitator may also choose a photo and express his/her opinions/feelings. This works as a demonstration.

The facilitator should never interpret the photograph for others or allow others to interpret on behalf of that specific member.

Discussion should lead to increased confidence, insight or help in building group cohesion and trust.

The same photo language set can be used with most of the population groups except for children below six years. It can be used dynamically to achieve a variety of objectives.

Photo language cannot be used with people who are visually impaired or children below six years since it heavily relies on visual images and perceptions.

Exercise 8.17 Photo Language Workshop

Objectives:

1. To orient TSWs to this medium.
2. To help them understand the procedure in using the set of photos.
3. To help them to identify the strengths and scope of this medium.
4. To equip them to use this medium as a facilitation technique.

Time required: 2 hours.
Materials required: Three sets of photo language.
Procedure:

1. Divide the class into three groups of not more than 20 in each group.
2. Each group should have one facilitator.
3. Each group should be given a specific instruction for selecting the photograph.
4. Spread the photographs, so that all can view those comfortably.

Each group should be given one theme from the following:

1. Select one photograph, which helps you in recalling one happy event in your life.
2. Select one photograph, which represents you.
3. Select any one photograph, which represents your role as a social worker.

After the selection of photographs, ask each TSW to express his/her thoughts and feelings.

Points for discussion:

1. What defines selection of photographs?
2. How do photographs help us to express ourselves?

Raise a few questions to facilitate expression if required and then summarise the discussion highlighting the gains from that exercise.

After this, assemble the groups together and discuss the concept of photo language, procedure, and do's and don'ts involved in conducting the sessions. End the session by summarising the preparation required for conducting session and various situations in which this medium could be utilised to achieve a set of objectives.

SIMULATION GAMES

Simulation games are another medium, which can be effectively used while working with groups.

Simulation means to pretend to be, pretend to have or feel, to imitate, to resemble closely, conditions of a situation. This is the dictionary meaning of the word to simulate. Culturally, games are thought of as a pastime and so simulation games can become a means to view real-life situations in the safer context of a game.

Experiences are simulated for training in various fields especially in the air force or in crisis management training, fire brigade, and so on. Learning to cope with various challenging situations or crisis situations through real-life experiences could be expensive or mortifying in view of the mistakes made.

The simulation game is a means for creating a facsimile (exact copy) of a situation indicating social processes in real life under relatively controlled conditions, which are reproducible. In social work training, we may not be able to replicate in an identical way real-life situations. However one can, through simulation games, reflect as near a situation as the TSW is likely to face in the field.

These games thus provide an opportunity to learn about oneself or about others with less harmful effects.

Why do we use simulation games in social work?

1. To increase self-awareness.
2. To develop insights into interpersonal relationships.
3. To develop skills in conflict resolution.
4. To develop awareness of one's own roles.
5. To stimulate participation and discussion.
6. To develop sensitivity.
7. To develop analytical understanding of social situations.
8. To stimulate thinking on change.

Simulation games therefore can be used in relation to practice situations such as group work sessions, therapy sessions and in different types of training.

Steps in Using Simulation Games

PRE-SIMULATION PREPARATION

1. Identify the aspect/problem or situation in which the worker wants the group members to develop skills/insights.
2. Match the game that could be utilised to fulfil the particular need—known games could be used or modified or new games could be used for this purpose.
3. Prepare clear written instructions on conducting the game.
4. Note down points that you would like to highlight after the experience and record them.
5. All the material required for the game should be prepared in advance.
6. Proper preparation of place is essential.

DURING SIMULATION

1. Clear instructions should be given and the sequence of activity needs to be explained.
2. Specific time should be given to play the game.
3. The facilitator should observe the process and take notes, if necessary.
4. In some games all the members might get an opportunity to participate. For some games, one might require few members. This could be on a voluntary basis or if the

simulation so requires the facilitator may purposefully select some members. Others could be observers.

5. When the activity is completed, clearly announce the closure.
6. You may give a break of a few minutes before you start the discussion.

AFTER SIMULATION

1. Ask questions to the participants about their feelings during the activity.
2. The facilitator should accept the feelings expressed by the participants. Caution should be exercised that participants do not feel that they are being judged as this would be very threatening.
3. Analysis should be related to key issues. Behaviour can be discussed. Individuals should not be discussed.
4. During analysis opinions may become polarised and also conflict with each other. In such a situation, maintaining a calm atmosphere that creates spaces for expressing disagreement should be ensured.
5. The post-simulation discussion should ultimately help participants reflect on their feelings when the activity was in progress and also link these to real-life parallel situations.
6. Analysis should be made in a calm environment and in supportive conditions.
7. While summing up, learning should be highlighted. Intellectualising the experience will help in reducing threat.

Advantages

If skilfully used, simulation games:

1. Create learning process which operates at both individual and group levels.
2. Increase participation and involvement.
3. Help initiate discussions that give immediate insight about behaviour and attitudes. This leads to increased sensitivity towards self and others.
4. Lead to transfer of insights by the participants to their own life situations.

Limitations

1. Games could be taken too lightly by participants, preventing their serious involvement in the activity. They may be taken as entertainment. As a result, the activity may be remembered but the key issues may be forgotten.
2. If selection of the game is not proper, then it could create adverse effects instead of giving the correct message.
3. Simulation games can be conducted only with participants who have a certain level of understanding and maturity. Therefore they cannot be conducted with young children.
4. They can stimulate hostility and resentment leading to defensive behaviours.

Simulation games require planning on the following lines:

1. Objectives.
2. Number of players.
3. Materials required.
4. Spatial arrangement (preparing the place).
5. Instructions (procedure or steps).
6. Actual process (game).
7. Points to be highlighted or questions to be raised.
8. Conclusions to be drawn.

Notes to the Facilitator

1. Games should not be used too often in the same group.
2. Appropriate selection of games is important.
3. One game can be used only once in one group.

The first part of the workshop involves conducting stimulation exercises with the TSWs to demonstrate their use. In the second part, they should develop stimulation games reflecting different situations.

Part I: Demonstration of Games

Exercise 8.18 *Eki ka Beki* (Odd or Even)

This game has two types of objectives.
The first type is from the facilitator's point of view:

1. To demonstrate the TSWs the use of simulation games for creating situations to reflect reality through *(i)* structuring the game, *(ii)* giving necessary instructions and *(iii)* facilitating the process.
2. To understand how to conduct the discussion by highlighting the significant observations of the process.

The objectives of the second type are those relating to the following:

1. To develop understanding among the TSWs about how 'unequal distribution' emerges in society.
2. To develop understanding of the emerging classes in society and their operation.

Materials required: Half-kilogram of *chana* (Bengal gram) or small beads or *chinchoke* (tamarind seeds).

Procedure:

1. Everyone has to play the game and try to collect the maximum number of *chana*s.
2. Only two participants can carry out the exchange of *chana*s at a time.
3. The one who wants to initiate should extend his/her hand to the other. If the other accepts to play, he/she will shake the hand.
4. The initiator holds out the extended fist in which a few *chana*s are held and his/her partner has to guess if an odd or an even number of *chana*s are enclosed.
5. When the fist is opened, if the guess is found correct, the initiator will give all the *chana*s held in the fist to her/his partner. But if the guess is wrong, the initiator will get the same number of *chana*s (as had been held in the closed fist) from the partner.
6. Allow the play to continue for 10–15 minutes to give everybody an opportunity to collect more *chana*s.
7. Find out the number of *chana*s collected by each person.
8. Make the groups of TSWs according to each one's collection of *chana*s as follows:

    (a) Members with more than 20 *chana*s
    (b) Members with 20–10 *chana*s
    (c) Members having less than 10 *chana*s

9. Announce that

    (a) Those who have more than 20 *chana*s will be beneficiaries of a government scheme for successful entrepreneurs by getting 10 more *chana*s for their stock.
    (b) The facilitator will collect 2 *chana*s from all the members as tax collected on behalf of the government.
    (c) Members who are interested in putting their resources for a joint venture may join together and pool their resources.

10. Once again allow them to play the game in the same way for 5–10 minutes.
11. Finally, separate the members and form three new groups as follows:

    (a) Members with more than 40 *chana*s
    (b) Members with 15–40 *chana*s
    (c) Members having less than 15 *chana*s

Points for discussion: Make them sit in the finally formed groups as above and start a discussion on the following points:

1. What was the distribution of *chana*s at the beginning?
2. By the end of the game who had nothing or reduced stock, who had collected more and increased their stock?
3. What are the feelings and experiences of members who have lost or reduced their stock of *chana*s?
4. How did the members manage to collect more *chana*s?
5. What are the reactions of members who have nothing or reduced number of *chana*s towards those who have maximum *chana*s in their stock?

6. What was the basis of forming the joint venture; who have benefited from it?
7. Who are the beneficiaries of government schemes?
8. How is this unequal distribution of resources reflected in society and what are the reasons for this?
9. What can we do to change the situation?

Instructions to the facilitator: From the earlier discussion the following points need to emerge:

1. How inequality exists in the society and the privileged tend to come together to enhance their resources through exploitation.
2. Despite being socially sensitive, the TSWs show similar tendencies as they are part of the exploitative society and influenced by this. So they have to be more conscious about their behaviour, thinking and practices in order to avoid resorting to exploitative behaviour.

Exercise 8.19 Broken Squares

Objectives:

1. To experience the intricacies of cooperation.
2. To understand how cooperation or non-cooperation affects team building or community living.

No. of participants: Teams of five members with one observer. The number of teams will depend upon the number of group members (Image 8.2).
Time required: 45 minutes.
Material required: Sets of 'broken squares' (15 pieces) as shown in Figure 8.1 for each team of five players (6″ × 6″ per square).
Procedure:

1. Cut the squares as shown in the figure. You should erase the alphabets written on the pieces after you mix the pieces and divide into groups of three piece as indicated in sequence 'AEG, BFK, CFO, HJN, ILM'. Prepare one envelope for each member which would contain three pieces from different squares.
2. Divide class into groups of six members.
3. Distribute five envelopes—giving one to each member (the sixth person will be the observer).
4. The team has to prepare five perfect squares of equal size, one square in front of each member of the team.
5. No member is supposed to speak.
6. No member can ask or signal another member to give him a piece of broken square.
7. Members, however, may give pieces of broken squares to other players in their own team on their own.

Image 8.2 Broken Squares

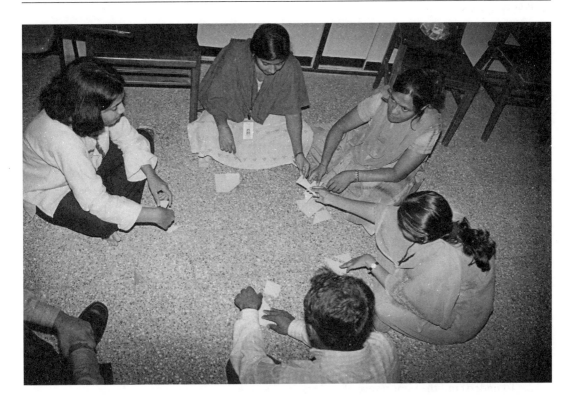

Source: Mukund D. Sawant, Producer, Centre for Media and Cultural Studies, TISS.

Figure 8.1 Sample of Pieces of Square

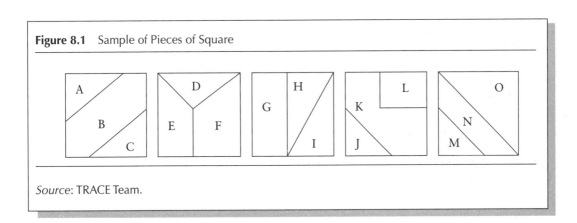

Source: TRACE Team.

Time required: 20 minutes for actually playing the game.
Points for discussion:

1. Who was willing to give away the pieces?
2. When one member finished his/her square how did he/she behave with others?
3. Who was unwilling to give away their pieces to others?
4. What were the feelings of those who were not getting the square pieces they needed?
5. Did anyone break the rules? What did this indicate?
6. At what point did the group begin to cooperate? Why some members did not cooperate?

Highlight:

1. How cooperation helps in problem solving.
2. People need to share whatever they have and also understand the unspoken needs.
3. Importance of looking at all aspects before making a final decision.

Ask the TSWs to list out situations where this game could be used in the field.

Exercise 8.20 Goal Setting

Objective:

1. To understand holistic considerations for goal setting.
2. To understand the importance of realistic goal setting.

No. of participants: 6/8 volunteers and the rest of the participants as observers.
Time required: 45 minutes
Materials required: 15–20 stones of different sizes and shapes, cloth to blindfold participants.
Procedure:

1. Instruct the volunteers to form pairs. Tell the participants that they have to build a tower from the stones with one participant blindfolded and his partner as his helper. The partner will give verbal instructions only.
2. Ask each pair how big a tower they can build.
3. Ask each pair to build the tower (Image 8.3).

Points for discussion:

1. How much did each pair succeed in building the tower?
2. Was it as per their plan?
3. What were the difficulties in performance to reach their planned goal?

Highlight: While setting goal, one must take into account the entire reality.

Image 8.3   Goal Setting

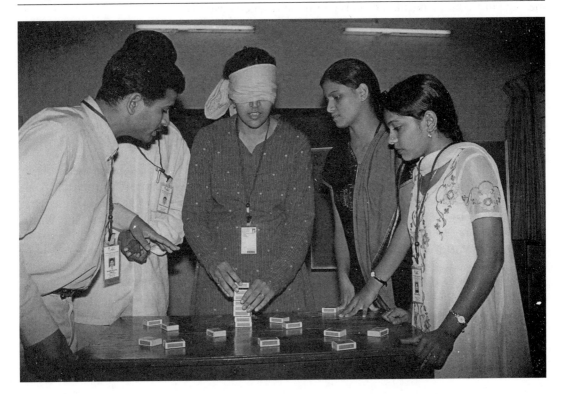

Source: Mukund D. Sawant, Producer, Centre for Media and Cultural Studies, TISS.

Part II: Developing Stimulation Exercise

Participants: All.

Process:

The class should be divided into small groups of 6–7. Each group should be given one situation and should be asked to prepare a game. Each group presents the game with proper instructions and points for discussion.

The facilitator could conclude by highlighting the skills required in using stimulation games in social work practice:

1. Skills in appropriate selection/adaptation.
2. Skills in planning games.
3. Skills in preparing instructions.
4. Skills in observation.
5. Skills in stimulating discussion and drawing out the member's feelings and thoughts.
6. Skills in summarising ideas/messages through the exercise.

Games cannot be an end in themselves. They are supportive techniques for making the message more meaningful. The carry-home message is usually:

- insight into one's won on attitudes/values,
- understanding social situations (analysis) and
- possible solutions to change the situation (action).

USE OF INTERNET (WEB) IN SOCIAL WORK PRACTICE

What is the Internet or Web?

The Internet and the World Wide Web (www) are terms that to most people mean about the same thing. While they are related, their definitions are different. The Internet is an electronic communications network and the World Wide Web is part of the Internet that allows people to use ready-made and easy-to-use tools to go about their tasks. The World Wide Web was created in 1992 by Tim Berners-Lee and continues to change and expand rapidly. The World Wide Web is known by many names like www, the Net and the Web. In our module, we will refer to it as the Web.

The Internet, which is what the Web is laid down upon, started in the 1950s as an experiment by the US Department of Defense. They wanted to come up with something that would enable secure communications among various military units. However, once this technology was out, there was no stopping it. Universities such as Harvard and Berkeley caught wind of this revolutionary technology and made important modifications to it, such as addressing the individual computers from which communications originated.

Connecting to the Web

WHAT DO WE NEED TO WORK WITH THE WEB?

OWN INFRASTRUCTURE

Computer: We need a basic computer with a browser installed. For example, Internet Explorer/Netscape/Firefox or others.
Connection: We need to make sure that we have subscribed to an Internet Service Provider (ISP) service. For example, VSNL, Reliance, Airtel, BSNL or others.
Modem: We need to make sure that we have a functional modem (any speed) installed in the computer or as an external implement.

EXTERNAL INFRASTRUCTURE

Net Café's: In many cities, we have net café's on every street. This is ready-to-use infrastructure available to us at nominal cost. Such cafés provide the complete facility on an hourly basis. They also have the facility to guide new users.
Libraries: College libraries, private libraries as well as public libraries may also have facilities for students.

Own networking: This is probably the easiest option available. Just ask your friends, family, colleagues, co-workers and teachers if they know of any place where such a facility is available for students. You will be surprised to find out that somebody will always know!

How do People Connect to the Web?

The Web is literally a global Web of computers connected to each other. Individual computers connect to the Internet through ISPs such as VSNL, Airtel and Reliance. These connections are possible using the medium of telephone lines, dedicated data lines, cable networks (like the TV cable we get in our homes) and even wireless like the mobile phones. Our computers connect with the telephone lines via an instrument called the modem. The speed of our connection to the net depends on many things like the speed at which the modem can communicate data, the capacity (bandwidth) of the medium (telephone lines) and the size of the files (actual data) that is being communicated.

On your computer, dial into your ISP from your computer.

How are Websites Found on the Web?

To put it simply, working on the Web is as simple as making a telephone call. When we are making a telephone call, we use the phone, dial a number and if the receiver picks up the phone, we start communicating. To find a website on the Web we need to do the following.

Open a computer programme that will allow you to navigate on the Web like Internet Explorer, Firefox and Netscape. These are free programmes. The following example is of the Internet Explorer icon (Image 8.4) that needs to be double clicked to start the Internet Explorer Programme.

When the programme opens, type the address you want to go to in the address box (Image 8.5). Press the 'Go' button to go to the address (Image 8.5)

Image 8.4   Internet Explorer Icon

Image 8.5

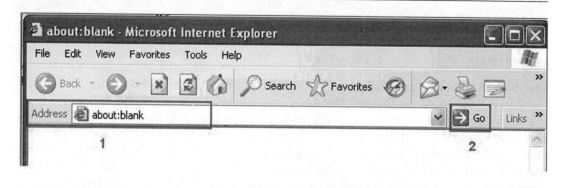

In this case, I have decided to go to www.google.com (Image 8.6). This is a free tool that allows me to search for information on the Web. You can type whatever subject you want

Image 8.6

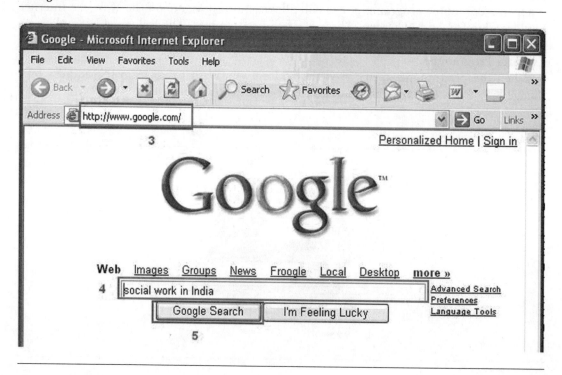

the information on in the box provided (Image 8.6) and press the 'Google Search' button (Image 8.6) to search for results.

The results are populated in the window now and you can start browsing and clicking on the links provided (Image 8.7) by the result. Normally, underlined sentences and words are links that take you further into the said subject (Image 8.7).

Image 8.7

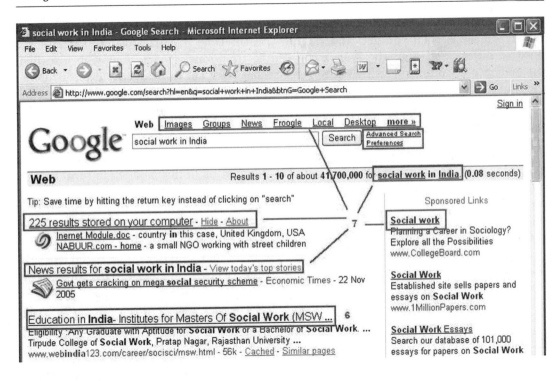

What are Domains?

A domain is a specific virtual area within the Internet. There are many different types of domains, including:

- **.com**: commercial domains, now the largest presence on the Web.
- **.org**: organisation, can be any type of organisation.

- **.gov**: government agency, usually federal, but can be state.
- **.edu**: educational institution.
- **.uk, .us, .in**: sites, organisations, networks residing or associated in a specific country (in this case, the UK, the US and India).

Why is Web Used?

The initial applications of the Web were communication, knowledge sharing and networking. Soon it evolved into a platform for many other activities like commerce, government services, information services, library services, even online matrimonial services!

Speed, interactivity, flexibility, ease of use, simplicity, self-service, openness, WYSIWYG (what you see is what you get) and JITInfo (Just-In-Time Information) are some of the positive differentiators of the Web compared to traditional media. The Web also puts the audience in command and we can choose what we want to read, see and hear unlike the traditional media.

SOCIAL WORK AND THE INTERNET

The Web has become a regular phenomenon in our lives. People living in urban areas are becoming more and more dependent on it. The penetration of this medium in rural India is a little slow till date. But it is growing at a phenomenal speed. It is up to us as community workers to make sure this phenomenon reaches our villages. By far this is the greatest global equaliser that man has ever created. With the world becoming a knowledge society, the Web becomes an indispensable tool.

Let us look at how the Web can complement us in our day-to-day work as social workers. We will also do a few simple exercises that will allow us to get the basic 'hang' of working on the Web.

The five areas where the Web can be most effective for a social worker are as follows.

COMMUNICATION

Speedy communication as we have seen earlier is the primary advantage of the Web. To optimise this strength, we need to be able to use the Web. Email allows us to stay in touch with our colleagues anywhere and instantly. The time gap required for communication with normal post does not exist. Even if we are working in a remote corner of the country, we can communicate with experts, peers, teachers, and so on instantly. Messages can be relayed quickly during good as well as bad times. The other form of Web-based communication could be 'chat'. Virtual chat rooms are available on the above-mentioned sites. If your colleague or friend is on the site at the same time you are there too (even if you are geographically in separate locations), you can start chatting. Earlier chat rooms only allowed participants to type and communicate. Nowadays you also have voice and video communication.

Research (General and Formal)

The Web offers the possibility of conducting both general as well as formal research. General research could be as simple as information you need to collect for your college project. Formal research could mean collection of validated (or to be validated) data that can be presented in a structured format. Search engines like Google.com, MSN.com, Rediff.com and Indiatimes.com are a good place to start research. They will normally lead you to the data/information that you are looking for or tell you about tools that can be used on the Web for your particular research.

Networking

Networking is really a communication possibility where many people can communicate. Often the network revolves around common needs, wants, ideas, passions, areas of work or research, issues, and so on. With the huge number of people across the world accessing the Web at any given moment of time, it is not difficult to imagine that some people out there may be interested in the same things that you are interested in. To gather a group of people like these in a group can be termed as networking. This allows people from different backgrounds, geographical locations, professions, with different passions and motivations to come together and exchange ideas, contacts, tools, experiences, knowledge and other resources. Online groups, forums, threads, and so on are examples of such virtual networking.

Advocacy

Taking the networking idea further, advocacy becomes the next obvious step. Once you have gathered enough like-minded people or people dedicated to a particular cause, they can virtually come together and try and achieve a common objective. A nice case of virtual advocacy in recent times has been the virtual advocacy carried out by people to wake up the Pune Municipal Corporation about the sad condition of roads. The Web allows us the possibility to target, recruit and engage support. It allows us the facility to inspire grassroots action. It helps give voice to a campaign and reach a broad audience. And finally, it also promotes bottom-up organising.

Fund-raising

For fund-raising, we need to have a reason why we are asking for funds and some donor out there who is willing to donate funds for our cause. With easy communication, it is natural for both the funding organisation and the fundraiser to use the Web for communication with each other and mapping the need to the resource. On the other hand, it is possible to have information on fund-raising ideas that people have used successfully elsewhere to see if you could use similar ideas with your projects.

The facilitator can conduct following exercises if computers and Internet are available.

Exercises for Social Workers in Web Communication

Exercise 8.21: Opening an email account.
Exercise 8.22: Participating in a chat session.

Expected Outcome

We would be able to send an email related to our work and carry out e-conference sessions in our group. At the end of the exercise, the TSWs would be able to share the following:

1. Artefact 1: Copy of an email exchanged.
2. Artefact 2: Copy of the transcript of a chat session.

Research

Exercise 8.23: Finding information on social work organisations in your city/village.
Exercise 8.24: Finding statistics on the population in your city/village.

Expected Outcome

We would be able to compile a list of social work organisations working in our city/village and compile a list of basic (demographic) statistics of our city/village.

1. Artefact 1: Compiled, classified list of NGOs (social work organisations in our city/village).
2. Artefact 2: Compiled demographics of the population in our city/village.

Networking

Exercise 8.25: Finding an online group which discusses World Trade Organization (WTO) policies and participating in the discussion.

Expected Outcome

We would find people willing to discuss WTO policies and participate in a dialogue.

1. Artefact 1: List of people in your network.
2. Artefact 2: Transcript of the latest communication (emails, chats, discussion board, and so on).

Advocacy

Exercise 8.26: Finding five online tools that can be useful for advocacy.

Exercise 8.27: Participating in an online advocacy campaign.

Expected Outcome

We would find advocacy tools on the Web. We participated in an online advocacy campaign.

Artefact 1: List of five online tools that social workers can use for advocacy on the Web.

Artefact 2: Details of the advocacy campaign participated in.

Fund-raising

Exercise 8.28: Finding funding agencies that entertain online applications for funding for a social cause of your choice.

Expected Outcome

We would be able to find funding agencies that were allowing online proposal submission and online processing and also make a list of fund-raising ideas that can be implemented on the Web as well as in real time.

Artefact 1: List of 10 funding agencies that accept online proposals and also process them.

Artefact 2: List of five fund-raising ideas that can be implemented on the Web and five ideas that can be implemented in real time.

Note to the facilitator: The situations above can be modified according to the kinds of task that trainees would get exposure to in the local context. It is also not essential that each and every one of the above exercises be carried out. The idea is that TSWs get familiarised and become comfortable about the use of computers and recognise its value in social work practice.

ANNEXURE A8.1 TRADITIONAL MEDIA: *KIRTAN*

A *kirtan* is a form of worship and social education rolled in one. It is a kind of sermon, but with a story and singing, aimed at proving the narrator's point and making the educational part interesting. The audience can join in the refrain at intervals.

A *kirtan*, a traditional method starts with a simple, religious story and interprets it to give a spiritual or educational message to the listeners. It usually takes place as a part of religious celebrations and can be used as an information, education, communication (IEC) measure in an IEC campaign related to social/health/sanitation/literacy and other issues.

A *kirtan* is made up of two parts, usually, the story and its interpretation. All of it is in a semi-prose form, that is, a few sentences followed by verses in traditional forms like abhanga, owi or shloka; again followed by explanation. The narrator is dressed in a traditional costume of white *dhoti kurta*, or *pagri* with a folded stole-like cloth with a border draped over his neck and shoulders. He has a pair of castanets in his hands which he plays in accompaniment to his singing. He speaks in a sing-song and not in a straight prose style.

The narrator's costume and paraphernalia are important for the *kirtan* form to be convincing because of its association with religious teachings. It is an easily accepted way of teaching moral values as well as practical wisdom to people who are largely illiterate or semi-literate. Even for the educated common people it is acceptable because of the deep-rooted faith in religious teachings.

This form can be used effectively by one with the gift of the gab. One has to improvise and a quick wit is necessary. Dramatic talent is more useful than scholarship or possessing a lot of information, for making an impact.

The example of the *kirtan* given here is written by a local person, in a simple style that is easy to understand. It gives a message about new issues like health/family planning, and so on, in a traditional manner. It is new wine in an old bottle. It goes thus: Introduction of the topic: the issue, here is family welfare and MCH (maternal and child health).

The narrator sings some verses by Saint Ramadasa about the consequences of having too many children: as more and more children are born, the family's resources get depleted and all starve. There are verses by Bahinabai depicting the drudgery of everyday life and by Saint Tukdojimaharaj, giving a message of small family norm. It ends with urging the audience to family planning operations.

Someone raises the question of having all daughters and wanting a son. The narrator answers that a girl can spread the good name of the family (in fact, of two families) just as a boy would. People are convinced and agree to the operation.

Next point: child care, health and immunisation. The narrator gives information about the immunisation schedule for a small child and the MCH programme. The programme ends with an exhortation of people to immunise their children and have a small family.

ANNEXURE A8.2 FOLK SONGS: *OWI*

Owi was a specialised verse format used by Maharashtrian women from all walks of life. (Saint Dnyaneshwar was considered a master of this form.) In the olden days women used to grind grain on a stone grinder called 'jate' for daily use, every morning. They used to make up *owis* and recite them as they went along. Like in case of all household/agricultural tasks involving drudgery, some kind of singing accompanied the performance of these tasks.

Owis mainly depict the lives of women at different ages, from early childhood onwards. *Owis* are born as the spontaneous expression of a woman's feelings, about her life, her home, her situation, her children.

Owis, because of their simple construction and gentle rhythm are easy to remember. Most of the *owis* came down from generation to generation.

These traditional forms are well accepted in the regional culture. The new message included in the familiar form makes it easy for the worker to reach out people. The tunes are common, hence the message is remembered and retained.

ANNEXURE A8.3 STREET PLAY: CHILDREN OF THE STATION

The following street play was presented by an NGO that worked for street children at the Pune station. Rather than the children being represented by the NGO staff, the children themselves were asked to express their feelings through a play because as a marginalised group, it was only right that they state their problems. The original presentation is in Marathi. This is a translation but not a word-to-word one. We have taken the liberty to loosely translate it.

The verses and dialogues given are to be loosely followed. There is a lot of room for improvisation.

Song by the street children: (The play opens with this song sung in a chorus).

Refrain: East or west/India is the best

(This refrain will be sung after each stanza.)

There is no roof over my head/I have no home
I make this platform mine/Though I am not welcome
The land is beautiful/everything is plentiful
But for me, not even a mouthful/and there is no school
India had a glorious past/It moves through the present fast
But for me there is no present nor past/and a future with darkness overcast

Scene 1a

A bustling morning at a station in a big metro.

Sanjay introduces some children: Ramu who sweeps the aisles and around the benches on the platform, Madan who polishes shoes, Salim who washes cars, Rani who is Ramu's sister and a few others.
Ramu is sweeping an aisle with his shirt. Someone nudges him with his toe.
Someone: Hey, move! Move! Dirty fellow!
Another passenger on a birth: Hey! They are my slippers. Clean them too. Bring them up here.
Another: Sweep under this bench. There's so much garbage.
People throw coins of 50 p/Re 1, and so on, at him.

Scene 1b

A few boys are polishing shoes.

Madan: Saab, it's done.
Customer: Ok. Here's two rupees.
Madan: Saab, only two rupees? The shoes are shining so–
Customer: Don't argue. For such little work—
Other boys also get paid very little. They come and talk together. One argues with a customer. A policeman is watching.
Police: Hey! What are you crowding the way for? Break up-break up. Don't hassle the passengers-get lost!

CHORUS

Is this the value of our work?/we work as hard as others
But there is no one to look/after our interests

SCENE 2

People are eating on the platform. Ramu is sweeping around a bench and Rani is cowering near it. A family of father, mother and two children is sitting on the bench.

Child 1: Mamma, I don't want this wadapav. I want Cadbury.
Child 2: I want ice-cream—(They clamour).
Mother: Ok, Ok! (To father) Please get a Cadbury for Munnu and ice-cream for both—
(Father goes to get the things.)
Mother: Beta, eat up that wadapav—there's a good boy—(Child refuse). Ok! Throw it away! Wait (notices Rani) wait—Give it to that beggar (Throws it at Rani. It falls at her feet. She picks it up and starts eating). (Father comes back with ice-cream cones. Gives them to the children.)
Father: Here, eat these fast. They will melt. (Notices Ramu and Rani eying the ice-cream.) Hey, what are you staring at?–Get lost—shoo-shoo—Dirty brats—
Mother: Casting a bad eye on my baby's food—

CHORUS

Ice cream for them/they are their children
Leftovers for us/we are nobody's children

SCENE 3

There is a television on, on the platform. M TV is playing some wild song. Some children start dancing and shouting. A policeman walks up.

Police: Hey! What's the racket? Shut up, all of you. Don't disturb people. Come—come—get lost. Otherwise, I will throw you all out.
Children grumble but quieten down.
Sanjay: See? Those children over there—in that society—they play and shout in the lane. No one says anything. But we are not allowed to express our joy—

CHORUS

Drudgery—drudgery all day/misery, pain and hunger
When we want to feel care free and gay/we arouse everyone's anger
Other children make mischief/but they say, they are innocent
We want a little relief/but they say, we are truant

SCENE 4

A few people come running and shouting, 'Thief! Thief!'–Sanjay is running ahead of them—frantic. A policeman comes along and grabs him.

Sanjay: leave me. I did not do anything. I was just passing by.

Man pursuing; Liar, you snatched that lady's purse—

Sanjay: No, no. I didn't. I don't know anything.

Man: Don't know? You must have thrown it in the gutter. Vagabond! (Slaps him. Sanjay cries)

Police: Don't argue with the gentleman—I know all about you street boys—thieves-all of you (others make agreeable noises). (The policeman beats Sanjay). Get out of here. I will break your leg if I see you again—

CHORUS

We are thieves!/We are thieves!
Although we did not steal anything
We are rogues!/we are scoundrels
Although we work for our meagre bread
No one cares/they only label us
Fie on the country/that rejects us

SCENE 5

Salim is washing a car. The owner comes. Gives him a rupee.

Salim: Saab, Saab, give me some work—anything. I am hungry!

Owner: (Starts lecturing) What can you do? Are you trained? What can you do? Why don't you go to school? You should be in school—tell your father—he does not say anything? If you don't go to school, you will become a vagabond—make something of your life—

CHORUS

We have no one/we need to earn
No school for us/no one to teach us
Father? School? Training/No training, no work
The future is without hope/totally bleak

SCENE 6

A voice from the audience: 'If life it is so bad on the streets why did you run away from home?'

CHORUS

Accused of stealing/beaten by 'bewda' (alcoholic) father
Thrown out by stepmother/Raped by uncle
No parents, no one to care/no school, our life is bare
It's no surprise/we landed here!

SCENE 7

A voice from the audience: 'Ok, Ok! Why don't you do something to improve your life?'

Sanjay: Is the onus on us? What should we do? Forgo even the simple pleasures that make life bearable? Then what is left for us?

SCENE 8

Charter of demands: (All declare) Every child wants opportunity. To grow/develop/have shelter/education/health services/nourishment/protection/livelihood

CHORUS

This is just talk/causes us anguish
Forever in want/we will languish
No, no, it must change/no more exploitation
We demand it to change/make for a better situation
We strive just to be alive/is that so strange?
We make the effort/but the world should, too, change

Source: The original Marathi version of this street play is available with the Karve Institute of Social Service (KINSS), Pune.

Section 3

METHOD TRAINING

INTRODUCTION

Once the trainee social workers have gained basic insights into understanding self and sensitivity in using communication for establishing meaningful relationship, training methods becomes easier.

Each practice method has its unique features, hence there are specific specialised skills required for each method. These will be highlighted in the following chapters. Along with the method skill training, all the previous learning should get reinforced. Hence, it would be the responsibility of the facilitator to link the skills gained from previous workshops in the method training workshops.

The figure emphasises the prerequisite steps involved in the development of appropriate skills for intervention, using any of the methods of social work in practice. All the steps are interlinked and interdependent.

Figure S3.1   Integrated Model for Professional Development

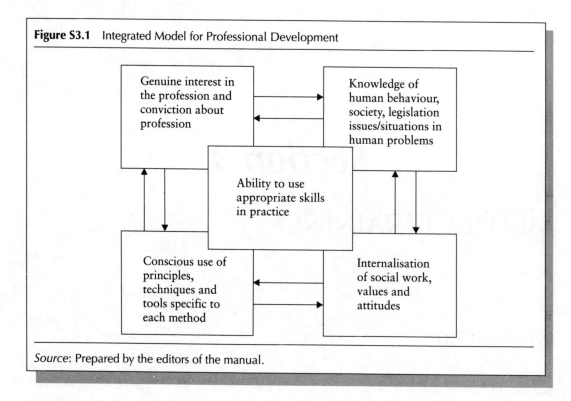

Source: Prepared by the editors of the manual.

Chapter 9

WORKING WITH INDIVIDUALS AND FAMILIES (SOCIAL CASEWORK)*

Sudha Datar and Geeta Rao

As the name suggests social casework is a method of social work practice used when working with individuals and their families. It was the first method of professional social work practice that emerged and its emergence can be traced to the concept of scientific charity that evolved through the efforts of the family visitors in the US in the later half of the 19th century.

Social casework is defined as 'A process used by certain welfare agencies to help individuals to cope more effectively with their problems in social functioning' (Perlman, 1964).

The definition clearly signifies that the method is used when remedial interventions are required while working with individual clients and their families and others who form part of the target system. The word process clarifies that it is not a one-time activity but involves a number of problem-solving operations. Process also means there is a beginning and an end, there is a movement in the positive direction, there is a change indicated. The change may be in the client or in the situation in which he/she is or both.

The problems of social functioning refer to the absence of

1. satisfactory role performance;
2. healthy interpersonal relationships and
3. positive self-image so that the individual is not at peace with himself.

---

* The name in brackets indicate the conventional name for the method, which is contemporarily called as per the main title.

The process, which is a progressive transaction, is a planned intervention done using the theory of casework and knowledge of human behaviour and social environment. For a skilful planned intervention, it is therefore necessary to internalise the values of social work on which are based the seven guiding principles of social casework and to consciously use the techniques and tools, which have evolved out of scientific practice (Annexure A9.1 of principles, tools and techniques of casework). The mainspring of the transaction is the professional, meaningful relationship between the worker and the client.

Success of an intervention also depends upon systematic and skilful application of the process. The planned process of casework involves the following phases (also see Figure 9.1).

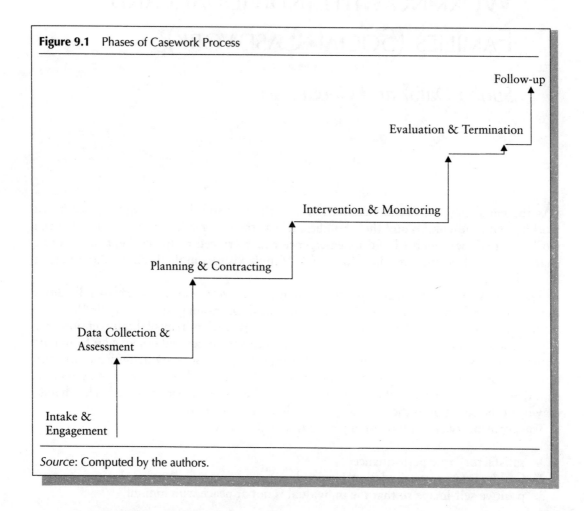

Figure 9.1   Phases of Casework Process

Source: Computed by the authors.

1. Intake and Engagement, which involves:

    (a) Establishing rapport and beginning of a relationship.
    (b) Defining the clients' concern or problem identification.

(c) Determining eligibility of service.
(d) Assessing problem-solving efforts of the client.
(e) Assessing client's motivation in seeking help.
(f) Determining urgency/emergency.

2. Data Collection (gathering facts) and Assessment, which involves

   (a) gathering information/facts which throw more light on the client and his situation so as to 'study' the problem/situation;
   (b) arriving at a tentative diagnosis, that is, what is the problem and what has caused it and
   (c) deciding what needs to be done, what can be changed and how can this be done.

3. Planning and Contracting, which means

   (a) involving the client in the problem-solving process;
   (b) collaborating in formulating objectives and setting goals and
   (c) planning tasks and understanding limits and the approximate time frame for task completion.

4. Intervention and Monitoring, which refers to

   (a) carrying out the plans leading to achievement of tasks, reduction of problem/ better coping;
   (b) monitoring the progress and
   (c) revising plans if there is stagnation or if the movement is not in the positive direction.

5. Evaluation and Termination, which indicates

   (a) evaluation of the progress achieved, assessing what brought about the progress and what led to stabilisation of gains and
   (b) both the worker and the client feel that the professional relationship can come to an end since the client has reached/attained self-reliance.

6. Follow-up, which means

   (a) continued support;
   (b) ensuring stabilisation of gains/changes that occurred due to intervention and
   (c) ensuring that the client functioning remains problem free.

As indicated in Figure 9.1, the movement is towards the client becoming self-reliant due to the skilful intervention by the worker.

These phases of the process are also termed as study, assessment, intervention, termination and follow-up. Although the phases and the tasks involved in each phase are indicated separately, they are not watertight compartments. There is a to and fro movement. For example during the study phase, the worker may ask questions tactfully, which enables the client to talk about his problem, which results in unburdening. This has an intervention (therapeutic) value/element. Similarly, as the client opens up more and more, the worker studies and reassesses the situation. It also needs to be emphasised that the principles of social casework should be necessarily used in practice and are in use simultaneously and absence of any one principle means absence of a helping relationship.

Corresponding to the tasks indicated in the process, the most essential skills required for working with individuals can be listed as follows:

1. Observation
2. Listening
3. Attending
4. Reaching out
5. Responding appropriately
6. Exploration
7. Questioning tactfully
8. Motivating
9. Assessment
10. Diagnosis
11. Evaluation
12. History taking
13. Interviewing
14. Intervention
15. Maintaining objectivity
16. Use of resources
17. Utilisation of agency
18. Communication (verbal and non-verbal)
19. Interpretation
20. Termination
21. Recording

Based on the above-mentioned framework of process and skills that are unique to working with the individual, workshops should be organised.

The complete unit of casework could be divided into five to six lab sessions for a better understanding.

Since skill training in casework method would extensively rely upon the participatory training technique of role play, the facilitator needs to discuss the use of this technique in the introduction of casework workshops.

Explain the technique of 'Role Play' and its potential in skill training for working with individuals by giving the following basic information:

1. It is a simulated situation and hence non-threatening.
2. Trainees can afford to make mistakes while playing the role of the case worker because of the simulated situation and can learn from their own mistakes. This will minimise mistakes while actually working with clients.
3. Since the focus is on the trainee social worker (TSW), discussions can focus on the theory and its application.

4. Role play gives an opportunity to prepare the TSWs to face similar situations in their fieldwork confidently and thus reduce their anxiety.
5. Trainees can learn the importance of preparing for and planning an interview.
6. Role plays also provide exposure to trainees whereby they learn to face situations which may not always be predicted, thus emphasising how spontaneity and alertness can be developed with conscious use of casework principles and techniques.
7. Trainee social workers can also learn to empathise when they enact the role of the client and develop the ability to enter into the emotional experiences of the client.
8. Lastly, emphasise that the strength of role play lies in understanding the application of casework principles, skilful use of techniques, proper choice of tools and development of skills while using the tools.

Explaining the use of role play in skill development in detail is important because in a casework lab only two trainees are involved in the role play. Out of which one has to play the role of caseworker. This situation can be anxiety producing and trainees may hesitate to volunteer. The above explanation helps in dealing with this anxiety.

Some of the casework practice situations that can be depicted through role plays are given as follows. Facilitators could select examples from their field situations.

- The first contact with the client and the intake interview.
- Home visit (Image 9.1).
- Visit to a place of work/school, and so on.
- Conducting a joint interview.
- Handling a crisis situation.
- Professional sharing.

Materials required: Copies of Annexures A 9.2–A 9.9 as many as the total number of trainees.

SESSION I: FIRST CONTACT/INTAKE INTERVIEW

Time required: 2 hours
Objectives:

1. Learning to interview.
2. Understanding the importance of the intake interview.
3. Understanding the significance of initial contact for establishing rapport and building a professional relationship.
4. Understanding the importance of creating an appropriate climate to facilitate the process of helping.

Process:

1. Read out the following role play situation:

Box 9.1   Role Play Situation

Nikhil is a 7.5-year-old boy studying in std II in an English-medium school. He has been admitted to this school in the month of June. He is showing some difficulty in adjusting, for example, not attentive in class, distracting other children and disobeying the teacher. The class teacher has written a note in his calendar three or four times asking his mother to come and see her since it is now October and Nikhil is not showing any signs of adjusting to the new school environment. In spite of being a bright boy his performance in the terminal exam has been poor.

His mother is an anxious person and is agitated and worried as to why such a letter has come from school.

It is in this state of mind that she reports to the school to see the social worker. It is the first contact between the social worker and Nikhil's mother.

2. Ask any two trainees to volunteer to perform the roles of a social worker and client's mother.
3. Ask the rest of the trainees in the class to observe and note the following when the role play is enacted:

    (a) Information gathered (verbal).
    (b) Non-verbal communication of both the client and the worker, that is, facial expressions, body posture, eye contact, stance, tone, language used.
    (c) Beginning, progress and conclusion of the interview.
    (d) Focus of the interview, that is, factual information gathering or problem centred.
    (e) Efforts at establishing rapport and whether the interview culminated in establishing worker–client relationship.
    (f) Changes in the client's stance by the end of the interview.

4. After the enactment of the role play initiate discussion along the following lines:

    (a) How did the social worker greet the client and begin the interview?
    (b) What was the focus?
    (c) How was the verbal and non-verbal communication on the part of the worker?
    (d) How did the worker display attentive and careful listening?
    (e) How was she/he responding?
    (f) What were the essential facts gathered?
    (g) Was the client given an opportunity to ventilate? How was this done?
    (h) Were the client's emotions acknowledged by appropriate response?
    (i) Did the anxiety of the client go down? How did worker contribute to this?
    (j) Did the interview end on a positive note indicating further line of action? What was this?
    (k) What were the principles and techniques used and how?

5. Highlight the importance of the following aspects of interviewing skills:

    (a) Listening and observation.
    (b) Responding appropriately.
    (c) Appropriate punctuation.

(d) Asking tactful but leading questions.

(e) Explaining purpose.

(f) Clarifying.

(g) Building and maintaining a relationship.

(h) Gathering significant information using the intake pro forma.

(i) Beginning from where the client is and going at the pace of the client.

(j) Summarising.

(k) Stating future plans.

(l) Ending on a positive note.

6. After discussion, ask two other trainees to volunteer and enact the role play again incorporating the suggestions for improvement.

7. Finally, the facilitator should play the role of a social worker and demonstrate the use of theory in practice, if required.

SESSION II: MEETING SIGNIFICANT OTHERS FOR DATA GATHERING AND RELATIONSHIP BUILDING

Time required: 2 hours

Objectives:

1. Learning to use a home visit as a tool of casework.

2. Use of relationship for understanding family dynamics, family environment and their effects on the client.

3. Gathering more information from significant others for arriving at a diagnosis.

Process:

1. Ask five trainees to volunteer to perform the roles of the social worker, Nikhil's mother, father, grandmother and teacher.

2. Ask them to enact the following three role play situations consecutively.

3. Discuss each role play along following lines:

(a) How did the caseworker enter the home and introduce herself to the grandmother?

(b) Was the caseworker able to win the confidence of the grandmother? If yes, how and if not, why?

(c) How was the communication among the family members?

(d) Describe the personalities of the significant others and the relationship between them as observed through the role plays?

(e) How was the worker responding to their interactions?

(f) To what extent were the objectives of the home visit achieved?

(g) How were these achieved? If not, why?

(h) List out the details about Nikhil and his situation that emerge from all the three role plays.

(i) How was the information sought from the teacher?

Box 9.2   Three Role Play Situations

(a)

The social worker is visiting Nikhil's family on prior appointment ensuring that the grandmother is at home and Nikhil's father would also be returning from work so that the social worker can meet him.

The interaction between Nikhil's mother and grandmother should depict the dominating nature of the grandmother and the submissive role taken by the mother. The grandmother's stance should also show her confidence in looking after Nikhil's educational and emotional needs. The father should be depicted as a passive participant in family matters. The social worker observes and tries to build a relationship with the grandmother and the father.

(b)

Nikhil's parents are meeting the social worker in her office on a scheduled appointment. The worker has called the parents to the school to ensure that they can talk freely. This is on the basis of her observations during a home visit that Nikhil's father is confused and does not know what his role is in helping Nikhil. He is also unable to become a buffer between his mother and his wife and stop them from making Nikhil a bone of contention between them.

The social worker's efforts are to give clarity of roles to the father and involve him in Nikhil's socialisation. Also there is an attempt to understand the relationship between the parents to make an assessment of the psychological environment at Nikhil's home. She explores whether it is conducive for his healthy development.

(c)

The social worker meets the class teacher to get more information about Nikhil and also shares her observations and plans only to the extent required, not sharing anything and everything with her, thus maintaining confidentiality.

  (j) What information was shared?
  (k) Was any effort made to involve teacher's cooperation in the process of helping Nikhil?

Note to the facilitator: Ask the trainees to note down data gathered during the above-mentioned discussion.

SESSION III: FILLING THE INTAKE PRO FORMA

Time required: 2 hours.
Objective: To help TSWs to develop skills in filling the intake sheet.
Process:

1. Distribute the case history of Nikhil (Annexure A9.2) and the Intake ProForma (Annexure A9.3).
2. Ask trainees to divide themselves into four groups.

Image 9.1   Home Visit Role Play

Source: Mukund D. Sawant, Producer, Centre for Media and Cultural Studies, TISS.

3. Ask all four groups to do the following tasks:

   (a) Fill in the intake sheet individually up to the identification data, that is, up to family constellation. The family constellation may also be shown by drawing the family tree diagram on the blackboard (Annexure A9.4).

   (b) Based on the four role plays (including the one on intake interview conducted in the previous session) and the case history, each group should be asked to compile relevant information about the client, the significant others, the family relationships, personality characteristics of each, and so on using the items on the intake sheet.

4. Ask each group to present the compiled information.

Recording Psycho-social History

Time required: 2 hours.
Objectives:

1. Learning to organise information.
2. Identifying gaps in information for further exploration if required.
3. Recording the psycho-social history using appropriate professional language.
4. Understanding the influence of socio-cultural factors in problem creation/resolution.

Process:

1. The facilitator should draw the family tree diagram on a blackboard showing all three generations of the family (Annexure A9.4).
2. Also write significant information about each family member on the diagram with the help of active contribution from trainees (refer notes of Session II).
3. Ask all four groups to present first the personality characteristics of the client and the significant others and compile the list on the blackboard (Annexure A9.5).
4. After the basic understanding of importance of collecting factual information and assessing the personality of each one in the family, the next task for the groups would be to analyse role performance of each adult in Nikhil's family and the interpersonal relationships among the family members.

Note to the facilitator: Give the following guidelines for the two tasks to be undertaken:

1. Analysis of role performance:
   (a) Are the roles of each family member structured? Yes/No.
   (b) Are they rigid? Yes/No.
   (c) Are the role expectations realistic/unrealistic?
   (d) Do the individuals accept the roles in which they find themselves? Yes/No.
   (e) Are the roles and responsibilities suitable for the individuals' stage of life? Yes/No.
   (f) Are the adults role models for socialisation of a growing child? Yes/No.
   (g) What are the mechanisms used by each family member while performing their roles (family dynamics), for example, pressure, keeping oneself out of the situation and blaming others.
   (h) Outline the correct roles for each family member.

2. Analysis of interpersonal and family relationships
   Plot the relationship of each member with every other member along the following continuum:
   (a) Dependency_____independence
   (b) Detached_____close attachment

    (c) Disturbed_____smooth
    (d) Dominant_____submissive
    (e) Indifferent_____involved
    (f) Hate, dislike_____love, affection
    (g) Hostility_____empathy
    (h) Suspicious_____trusting
    (i) Superficial_____authentic
    (j) Impersonal_____involved
    (k) Irresponsible_____responsible
    (l) Non-cooperation_____cooperation
    (m) Conflict_____harmony
    (n) Competition_____mutual help

3. Ask each group rapporteur to present their work and the facilitator should present compiled and finalised assessment on the blackboard.
4. Ask the trainees to fill in the intake sheets up to psycho-social history, based on the tasks done.

SESSION IV: FORMULATION OF SOCIAL DIAGNOSIS

Time required: 2 hours
Objectives:

1. Developing the ability to state the problem clearly and also identify associated problems if any.
2. Learning to identify the causes of the problem and their effects on the client and significant others.
3. Learning to prepare a diagnostic statement on the basis of history gathered.
4. Developing the ability to formulate treatment goals and plans.

Process:

1. Instruct the four groups to

    (a) analyse the effects of the family circumstances and family dynamics on Nikhil, his mother, father and grandmother.
    (b) identify the positive aspects in the family, for example, economic condition, educational status of adults, their love for Nikhil, satisfaction of basic needs and emotional needs of Nikhil.
    (c) identify what changes are to be brought about and in whom (client and target system).

    (d) formulate short- and long-term intervention goals.
    (e) convert the goals into short- and long-term plans.

2. On the basis of the presentations by the group rapporteurs compile the following on the black board:

    (a) Effects on each family member (Annexure A 9.6).
    (b) What/who needs to change (treatment goals) (Annexure A 9.7)?
    (c) How do we go about doing it (treatment plans) (Annexure A 9.8)?

3. Ask the trainees to formulate a diagnostic statement based upon the compiled information (Annexure A9.9).
4. Ask the trainees to formulate the treatment goals and plans clearly defining how interventions will be done, stating priorities.
5. Ask the trainees to fill up the intake sheets up to treatment plans.
6. Distribute handouts of annexures A9.7 and A9.8 among students so that they can com-pare and develop the skill of formulating diagnostic statements.

SESSION V: UNDERSTANDING INTERVENTION

Time required: 2 hours

Once the treatment plan is prepared, a separate workshop needs to be organised for various techniques to be used in modification of behaviour or for capacity building of the client and/or the significant others.

A series of role plays should be enacted to depict how the treatment plans are carried out, such as the following:

1. Independent interview with the mother for reducing her anxiety.
2. Independent interview with the father for making him understand his role as a father.
3. Independent interview with the grandmother to get an insight about Nikhil's father emotional needs.
4. Combined interview with both parents to appreciate them for taking interest in Nikhil.
5. Discussion/interaction with the class teacher about Nikhil's progress.
6. Gradually introducing termination by suggesting that the mother could meet the social worker once in 6 months when she comes for parent–teacher meetings, and so on.

Two or three situations could be selected and the trainees could be asked to enact role plays.

The trainees could be asked to take help from the note on treatment goals (Annexure A 9.7)
    After these role plays, discussions should highlight the following points:

1. Was the worker focused in the interview?
2. How were the options discussed?
3. How was the insight given?
4. How did the worker help the client/or the significant other to talk appropriate decisions or to change behaviours?
5. How was the caseworker–client relationship used to bring about the change?

To conclude the lab on working with individuals a final lab session may be taken as follows:
    The facilitator could prepare scripts for different types of interviews with the client and target systems to demonstrate the specific impact due to use of skills and techniques and also how the values get reflected in our communication with the client. Following is an example of the first contact with a client depicted in two ways.
    Ask two trainees to enact each of the following dialogues (Box 9.3). After each enactment, the facilitator should do the analysis as indicated in the column on the right of the box (the tone, the expressions and the choice of words by the worker):

Box 9.3 Illustration of Analysis based on Trainee Social Workers' Role Play

Interview and communication (tools) are in use	Social Worker	*Oh! Nikhil's mother is it? Glad you have come at last! Please be seated. I was wondering whether you will come.*	Non-acceptance and judgemental attitude. Lack of trust and faith in client. Hurting to the dignity and self-respect of the client.
	Nikhil's Mother	*Why did you think so?*	
	Social Worker:	*Because, you have not come when the teacher has sent you notes two or three times in Nikhil's calendar.*	Use of language and tone suggest judgemental attitude.
	Nikhil's Mother:	*Is it so? I never realised since Nikhil's grandmother sees to all matters concerning school.*	Client has become defensive.
	Social Worker:	*You people never realise how a child feels humiliated when he is repeatedly asked by the teacher why your mother is not coming to see me!*	The use of the term 'you people' indicates categorisation of client into 'irresponsible parents'. No attempt at individualisation.

Enact the same situation using the following script.

Box 9.4   Demonstration and Analysis by Facilitator

Interview and communication (tools) are in use / Use of Relationship Tool	**Social Worker:** *Mrs. Mohite? Do come in, I was expecting you. I am_____ the social worker who wrote to you.*	Addressing by name indicates individualisation (principle).
	Nikhil's Mother *May I know why I have been called? I have been extremely worried since I received the letter.*	
	Social Worker: *Won't you sit down? Let me clarify as to why I sent you the letter. It is a policy of the school to meet the parents of the new entrants to the school and generally the mother first.*	Warmth and concern communicated. Reaching out (technique and skill). Self-respect and dignity of client maintained (value). Purpose explained (clarification technique). Helping client to relax.
	Nikhil's Mother *There is nothing to worry about Nikhil then?*	
	Social Worker: *You are visibly upset on receiving my letter; no doubt I have called you to know more about Nikhil and his interests but let me assure you that there is no need to be alarmed. Nikhil is a very bright child, is he your only son? Who all are in the family? Where do you live? Are you working? Where is his father working?*	Responding appropriately to the feelings of the client (skill and technique). Giving realistic assurance (technique). Tactful questioning (skill and technique) Steering the interview towards gathering relevant factual data and not referring to the problem directly in the first meeting (use of intake interview—tool and skill).
	Glad to know that his granny was a teacher and takes a lot of interest in Nikhil's studies but that is probably the reason why the class teacher's notes have gone unnoticed by you. Never mind, now that you have come we can discuss his progress. Which school did he go to till Std I? Was it also an English-medium school? Does he talk about the school, his teachers, friends at home?	Accredition (technique). Acceptance and non-judgemental attitude. (principles). Along with acceptance, expectations also conveyed subtly.
	Will it be alright if I come to your house so that I can meet his grandmother and explain the school's functioning to her? Maybe I will also meet his father. Which day and time would suit you and them? Thank you once again for coming and as decided I will see you on __ at your place	Future plans introduced. Permission for home visit sought, objectives made clear (use of home visit as a tool with its ethical guidelines). Accrediting (technique) Summarising (technique)

Note: Client's dialogues/responses have not been highlighted. Focus is on social worker's dialogues. This will enable trainees to identify and differentiate among skills, techniques, principles and values in casework practice.

Box 9.5   Interview with Grandmother

Interview focusing on intervention	Social Worker:	*Namaste, I was so glad when you accepted my invitation to see our school especially because you have been a teacher yourself and we can benefit from your experience.*	An attempt at strengthening the relationship.
	Grandmother:	*It is nice of you to say so but I agreed to come because of my concern for Nikhil.*	
	Social Worker:	*Nikhil is definitely settling down and shares a lot of things with me and his class teacher about you taking his studies and the outings he has with his parents on weekends. I think he is feeling more secure now that his father is spending a lot of time with him.*	Using relationship for giving insight to grandmother; subtly indicating the importance of parents spending quality time with Nikhil for his emotional needs.
	Grandmother:	*I think it may be that he has started liking the school also.*	
	Social Worker:	*Yes, certainly, he has made many friends but he looks forward to the weekend outings also, I am sure you are also able to relax and have some time to yourself when they are away.*	Pointing out needs of the grandmother to her in order to give insight about parental role once again.
	Grandmother:	*Yes, yes, I am now able to invite some of my friends at home or even go out with them.*	
	Social Worker:	*I am happy things are working out well for all of you. Finally, it is Nikhil's adjustment which is important to all of us. Come, I will take you around the school.*	Focusing on the main purpose or goal of the intervention namely, well being of the client.

After the discussion the facilitator should highlight the following points:

1. Importance of internalising values of social work.
2. Conscious use of theory of casework.
3. Application of principles, techniques, tools and skills are comprehensively applied.
4. A thoughtfully planned and carried out process using theory of casework comprehensively facilitates the helping process.

FOLLOWING ARE THE GUIDELINES FOR FACILITATORS FOR CONDUCTING THE WORKSHOPS

1. Skill laboratory sessions for working with individuals and families should begin only when the theory of casework has to some extent been covered in the class.
2. Items on the intake sheet and what goes into each item should be explained to the trainees in advance as part of the theory class.
3. The facilitator should familiarise himself/herself with the case history and role play situations in advance.
4. Role play sessions should provide graded exposure, that is, from simple situations to more complex ones.
5. The lab sessions may be taken in part, for example, the session on intake interview may follow immediately after the theory of intake is covered in class. However, to understand and conceptualise the process of casework, continuous lab sessions on once a week basis should be scheduled to cover all the phases of the process.
6. The trainer may develop case studies on his/her own for the purpose of training or pick up case material from students' field work files using these by carefully concealing the identity of clients.
7. While the case given here is from a school set-up, the facilitator may draw upon cases from different types of settings like hospital, residential institution and community.
8. Students coming forward to perform role plays should be duly acknowledged for showing courage and more and more students should be encouraged to come forward.
9. While initiating discussion, always invite positive feedback first and constructive criticism later. Ensure that a healthy climate is created and maintained so that students do not feel threatened.
10. All through the lab sessions the facilitator should enact the role of a social worker and punctuate the lab with active demonstrations of how to use skills.
11. One or two lab sessions could be conducted by dividing students into groups as per their fieldwork placements and giving them the task of preparing the intake sheet for that set-up, for example, hospital social work, social worker in a community-based organisation and correctional set-up.
12. One lab session could be allotted for preparing posters on the highlights of intake interview, do's and don'ts in interviewing, and so on.

USE OF SIMULATION GAMES IN UNDERSTANDING SOME ASPECTS OF THE CASEWORK PROCESS

Following games could be used to highlight various aspects of casework process.

Exercise 9.1 of 'black spot' (also given in Chapter 1 on perception) can be used to demonstrate holistic approach in casework. This game could be used after the first intake interview role play followed by role plays on home visits, meeting the teacher, and so on.

Exercise of 'Knots' (refer to Exercise 9.1) can be used to demonstrate simple and complex problems and the need to individualise and how systematic efforts can lead to problem resolution. This game could be used after the group exercise of formulation of diagnosis for highlighting the steps in problem resolution.

Exercise of 'Tying hands with a foot ruler' (refer to Exercise 9.2) can be used to demonstrate how clients feel when in a problem situation, how closed mindedness prolongs problem and how problems can be solved by taking help. This game could be used before the session on treatment process.

Exercise 9.1 Black Spot

Objective: To help TSWs to develop an ability to look at the client in his totality.

No. of participants: All.

Materials required: A white paper with one black circle of 1″ diameter painted on it (completely black).

Time required: 30 minutes.

Procedure:

1. Show the paper to all the participants.
2. Ask them to observe whatever they see for 2 minutes.
3. Ask a few to give their reactions on what they have seen.
4. Write these reactions on a blackboard.

Points for discussion:

1. What was the instruction given by the trainer?
2. Why did most of them concentrate only on the black spot?
3. Why did other things seem to go out of focus?
4. Relating this to our client system and their environment.
5. How will this approach help in the process of diagnosis?
6. Holistic approach in casework.

Exercise 9.2 Problem-solving Process—Knots

Objectives:

1. To help the TSWs to understand that though the problem may be the same, the intensity varies in each case.

2. Depending upon the complexity of the problems, the approaches to problem solving differ and the time required will also vary from case to case.

No. of participants: All participants divided into two groups.
Materials required: Different types of threads—a few tags, a few pieces of twine and a few pieces of thin thread.
Time required: 30 minutes.
Procedure:

1. Distribute all varieties of threads to one group.
2. Ask them to tie different types of knots.
3. Give these knotted pieces of thread to another group.
4. Ask them to untie the knots within 2 minutes.

Points for discussion:

1. How did the first group tie the knots?
2. What strategies did the second group develop to untie the variety of knots?
3. When participants do understand the type of knot, they can untie it quickly (if diagnosis is accurate, problem solving becomes easier). The simpler the knot, the easier it is to untie (early identification of problem helps in problem solving); with difficult knots, many attempts and longer time is required (chronic problems, deep-rooted problems take longer to solve).

Exercise 9.3 Resource Utilisation and the Value of Cooperation—Tying Hands with a Foot Ruler

Objectives:

1. To understand the use of resources in problem resolution.
2. To gain insight into alternatives in problem solving.
3. To understand the value and utility of cooperation when people face common problems.

No. of participants: 4 or 5 pairs (8 or 10 participants).
Materials required: One dozen 12″ rulers and one dozen ribbons to tie the rulers. Dishes containing biscuits, peanuts, churmura (a type of snack). One dish of one eatable for each pair.
Procedure:

1. The rulers are tied in such a way on the elbows of each participant that their hands are prevented from bending.
2. Each pair is made to stand facing each other.
3. Between the pair a plate with the food is kept.
4. Each one is asked to eat the food and finish the plate as soon as possible.

Points for discussion:

1. What were the initial reactions of the players?
2. Did they discuss alternatives with each other?
3. Did they trust each other sufficiently?

Highlight through the discussion:

1. Reactions of the clients when they are confronted.
2. How close mindedness prolongs the problem?
3. One can overcome one's inabilities, if one is willing to share or help others or accept help from others.

ANNEXURE A9.1 CASEWORK PRINCIPLES, TECHNIQUES AND TOOLS

Principles: These are called the fundamental truths of a method. These are rules by which the conduct of the social worker may be guided.

- Individualisation
- Purposeful expression of feelings
- Controlled emotional involvement
- Acceptance
- Non-judgemental attitude
- Client self-determination
- Confidentiality

Techniques: Manner of execution or performance is called a technique.

- Acceptance of feelings
- Assurance
- Anticipatory guidance
- Accreditation
- Advocacy
- Building resources
- Constructive use of guilt feelings
- Correcting perception
- Confrontation
- Developing self-confidence
- Demonstrating warmth
- Empathy
- Education
- Encouragement
- Exploration
- Facilitating ventilation
- Guidance
- Generalisation
- Goal setting
- Humour
- Home visit
- Interpretation
- Individualisation
- Insight giving
- Judgement of situation
- Modifying environment, behaviour, attitude
- Material help
- Motivation
- Modelling
- Observation

- Partialisation
- Participation
- Persuasion
- Pooling of resources
- Putting questions tactfully
- Reassurance
- Reality orientation
- Relating to feelings
- Role playing
- Reflecting
- Stimulating
- Setting limits
- Tapping of resources
- Timely intervention
- Universalisation
- Verbalisation
- Verifying facts
- Withholding judgement
- Emotional support

Tools: These are implements for working upon something.

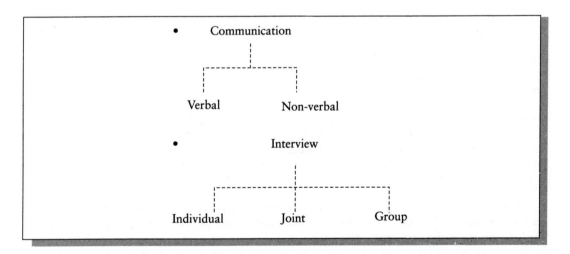

- Professional relationship or client–worker relationship
- Home visit
- Knowledge of resources
- Recording

Source: Prepared by the Editorial Team.

ANNEXURE A9.2 CASE HISTORY OF NIKHIL MOHITE

History

Nikhil Mohite is a 7.5-year-old boy studying in std II in an English medium school.

He has been referred to the counsellor in the child guidance clinic (CGC) by the class teacher.

The referred problem was stated as scholastic backwardness.

Family Background

The family belongs to the upper middle-class income group and resides in a fast-growing suburb of Pune city. The family shifted to their own flat 1 year ago.

The father is an engineer in a multinational company and the mother is a housewife. The father has had a very successful academic career and the mother too is a graduate with considerable interest in co-curricular activities. She had to give up her job after marriage.

The grandmother is a retired school teacher and has worked in schools for about 30 years.

The grandmother was widowed at an early age and was left to look after her only son after the death of her husband without any support from family members or relatives. As a result she had to undergo a lot of hardships and struggle on various fronts to educate her only son and bring him up as an achiever. She was also extremely possessive about her only son and became more so after the death of her husband.

The father had learnt to grow up as a very obedient child. In his growing up years due to the domineering nature of his mother, he used to be torn between his own thoughts and decisions and those of his mother.

His mother arranged his marriage with a girl from their native place. The marriage lasted for about a year and a half and the wife left her husband's home to go back to her parents, because she was not able to adjust to city life and could not cope with the mother-in-law's standard of perfection. There was no child from this marriage.

In due course of time the husband obtained a legal divorce and married a city girl as per his mother's suggestion.

The second wife (mother of Nikhil) came from a family with four sisters and the parents, who were traditional minded, wanted to marry off the daughters as soon as possible.

The couple gave birth to a healthy male child within a year of marriage. The delivery was normal but the mother suffered from various complications during the period of pregnancy. Though the mother was not keeping very good health she did not receive any support or help from the mother-in-law in her day-to-day household responsibilities.

Everyone was very happy at the birth of a male child and the mother felt that her difficulties had ended. During the first year of the child's life all the family members' lives revolved around this child and everyone was very protective about him. There was an obvious competition as to who was going to look after the child and gradually bickering began on this issue.

The grandmother's interference in all matters and relationships created tremendous confusion in the father's mind and he developed a tendency to escape from the situation, leaving the two women to sort out their own problems.

Nikhil was a happy child and was very curious about his environment. The grandmother decided to send him to school at an early age of 2.5 years for which the mother was not very willing. The grandmother considered herself competent to look after all the educational and developmental needs of Nikhil.

Nikhil was growing up in a confused family environment and hence found it difficult to adjust to the separation from the family. As a result, he had scholastic problems of various kinds right from the beginning of school, which never came to the attention of the teachers or his family members.

This year Nikhil had to change the school since the family shifted residence.

In Std II the class teacher noticed that Nikhil was a bright child but not very active and communicative. Due to his withdrawn personality he did not respond to the teacher's attempts at getting him involved in class activities as well as including him in the peer group.

The teacher also observed that in the absence of adults Nikhil was quite comfortable with some children.

After 6 months in school when the child did not perform well in the terminal examination the teacher called Nikhil's mother to try to find out what difficulties the child was experiencing. But there was no response from her and hence the teacher referred the matter to the school social worker.

The mother was anxious and worried about the lack of performance of Nikhil and hence reported to the social worker on receiving the letter.

Effort was made by the social worker to obtain all this information through a number of sessions with the family of the child.

Source: Prepared by the Editorial Team.

ANNEXURE A9.3 INTAKE SHEET

(Note: This intake sheet is designed for a CGC in a school. The intake sheet will change depending upon the type of agency set up, age, problem and help offered to the beneficiaries.)

Case No.:
Worker's name:
Date of initial contact:
Date of writing intake record:

I. IDENTIFICATION DATA:

Name of the client   :
Address   :
Date of birth   :
Age in years   :
Religion   :
Sex   :
Mother tongue   :
Languages known   :
Education   :
    Name of the school   :
    Standard   :
Number of members in the family   :
Type of family   :
Number of siblings   :
Ordinal position   :
Referral problem   :
Referred by   :

II. FAMILY CONSTELLATION:

No.	Name	Age	Sex	Relation with Client	Education	Income	Occupation	Remarks

III. Personality of the client   :

IV. Personality of the parents   :
    Father   :
    Mother   :

V. Description of family   :
   relationships

VI. Scholastic history   :
    Positive aspects   :
    Problematic areas   :

VII. Medical history   :
    Development history   :
    Problem   :
    Treatment   :

VIII. Psycho-social history   :

IX. Nature and/or pattern of   :
    previous contact with the agency   :

X. Diagnostic summary statement   :

XI. Treatment plan   :
    Short-term treatment goals   :
    Long-term treatment plans   :

XII. Concluding remarks   :
    Follow-up   :
    Transfer   :
    Referral   :
    Closing   :

Signature of the Worker

Source: Prepared by the Editorial Team.

ANNEXURE A9.4 FAMILY TREE

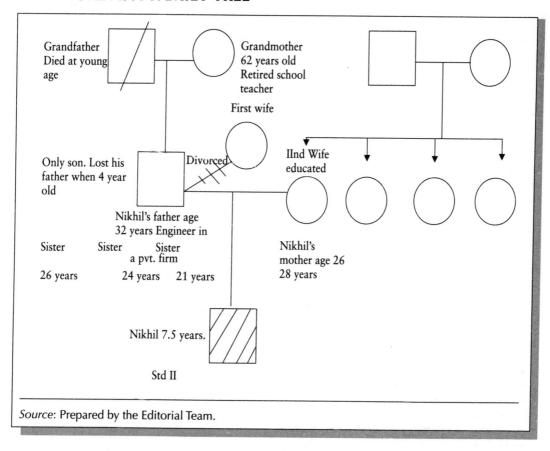

Source: Prepared by the Editorial Team.

ANNEXURE A9.5 PERSONALITY CHARACTERISTICS OF CLIENT AND OTHER SIGNIFICANT MEMBERS

Nikhil	Mother	Father	Grandmother
Intelligent	Anxious	Kind	Aggressive
Quiet	Excitable	Supportive	Harsh
Shy	Nervous	Nervous	Irritable
Disciplined	Irritable	Simple	Caring
Artistic	Critical	Affectionate	Critical
Nervous	Impatient	Vague	Boastful
Obedient	Talkative	Anxious	(Over) confident
Likable	Fussy	Disciplined	Talkative

(Continued)

(*Continued*)

Nikhil	Mother	Father	Grandmother
Confused	Obstinate	Willing	Fussy
Afraid	Vague	Weak	Obstinate
Social	Unsteady	Tolerant	Excitable
Tense	Argumentative	Shirker	Jealous
Submissive	Jealous	Irresponsible	Argumentative
Healthy	Tense	Apathetic	Ambitious
Passive	Willing		Idealistic
Curious	Suspicious		Bossy
Lacks confidence	Rude		Rude
Withdrawn	Weak		Determined
Subdued	Affectionate		Smart
Lonely			Snobbish
Detached			
Young			
Non-communicative			

Source: Prepared by the Editorial Team.

ANNEXURE A9.6 EFFECTS ON FAMILY MEMBERS

Impact on Nikhil:

- He is tense and anxious.
- His thinking skills are affected.
- Poor performance in maths.
- He does not relate with adults.
- He is not comfortable in the presence of adults.
- He is shy and reserved.
- He is lonely.
- He lacks confidence.
- Capacity to form relationships is damaged.

Impact of family circumstances
On Grandmother:

- Struggle to keep her hold (power).
- She tends to dominate, control everyone.
- She is possessive.

On Mother:

- She is suspicious.
- She also shows depression.

- Likes to seek sympathy.
- Dissatisfied with her communication with husband.
- Continuously blames the mother-in-law and has a disturbed relationship with the husband.

On Father:

- He has lost confidence and is confused.
- He is dependent on his mother.
- He is not willing to take responsibility.
- Tends to escape from the situation whenever it becomes demanding.

Need gratification of Nikhil

- All biological needs are satisfied.
- He is well looked after.
- He receives love and affection from all the three adults but expression of love is inappropriate.
- He is not properly understood by them.
- He does not get emotional security.
- He cannot mix with peers.
- He does not have freedom of expression.
- There is no communication with his father.
- There is no scope for healthy parent–child interactions/relationship.

Source: Prepared by the Editorial Team.

ANNEXURE A9.7 TREATMENT GOALS

Main Goal

Improve scholastic performance through promoting healthy interpersonal relationships in the family.
   Break-up of the main goal into subgoals for the client and target system.

Client (Nikhil)

1. Help him to relax, come out of his shell, be expressive and trust his adult environment.
2. Help him to be comfortable with his peers.
3. Help him to develop close, unique, independent relationships with adults without feeling guilty.
4. Reduce his anxiety.
5. Help him to gain confidence and become independent.

Mother

1. Reduce her anxiety.
2. Reduce use of self-defeating defence mechanisms.
3. Reduce her dissatisfaction.

4. Build up a positive attitude towards self and others.
5. Help her to be an open person.
6. Help her to gain confidence and assert herself in her roles as mother, daughter-in-law and wife.

Grandmother

1. Help her to clarify role expectations of herself and others.
2. Help her to trust other people's abilities.
3. Help her to share responsibilities with others and develop team effort.
4. Help her to be aware of her role as a head of the family and help others to grow.

Father

1. Help him to develop independent decision making capacity.
2. Help him to develop healthy relationships with his mother and wife.
3. Help him to develop healthy parenting skills so that he becomes a role model for his son.

Teacher

Help her to create a non-threatening environment in the class.

Source: Prepared by the Editorial Team.

ANNEXURE A9.8 TREATMENT PLANS

Objectives of Treatment: To develop confidence in Nikhil in order to improve patterns of relationships and performance in school.
Areas of Treatment:

1. Working with Nikhil at the CGC (main client system).
2. Working with the family:

   – mother
   – father   } (target system)
   – grandmother

3. Working with teachers in the school (target system).

Treatment Process

Nikhil will attend individual and group play therapy sessions once a week at the CGC. These sessions will be aimed at

1. Enabling Nikhil to relax.
2. Helping him develop trust in adults.

3. Providing him opportunity for self-expression without fear of criticism.
4. Enabling him to experience positive rewards.
5. Enabling him to gain confidence and independence.

Working with Nikhil will also be aimed at improving his competence in mathematics by getting the help of family members or through other resources.

Initially, Nikhil's family members will be contacted individually in order to explain gaps in ideal and actual role performances, which are contributing to Nikhil's difficulties in relationships and fulfilling expectations.

Efforts will be directed at developing awareness in family members regarding:

1. Inappropriate use of defence mechanisms having lesser coping value.
2. Importance of positive attitudes towards each other by way of positive stroking.
3. Significance of improved patterns of mutual relationships for healthy living.

Subsequently, the focus of treatment will need to shift towards strengthening the relationship between Nikhil's father and mother in the following areas:

- parenting together,
- importance of openness in communication,
- spending time together and
- respecting each other.

Simultaneously, Nikhil's grandmother will be counselled in the following areas:

- Importance of appropriate role performance.
- Lessened dominance.
- Her appropriate role in bringing up Nikhil.
- Helping her to find other avenues for ego satisfaction.

The teachers will also be encouraged to participate in the treatment of Nikhil in the following areas:

- Take her help in encouraging and appreciating Nikhil.
- Giving Nikhil positive strokes.
- Making Nikhil gradually progress in his areas of under-achievement.

Plan for Follow-up

Initial monthly follow-up will be maintained in order to ensure stability in Nikhil's relationships within the family and at school.

Six-monthly follow-up for a period of 2 years regarding his performance at school.

Termination

At the end of 2 years from the initial contact.

Source: Prepared by the Editorial Team.

ANNEXURE A9.9 DIAGNOSTIC STATEMENT

Nikhil is a scholastically backward child who has difficulties in developing meaningful relationships in his school and neighbourhood.

Nikhil is a healthy and intelligent child and is in the plastic age group. He is able to develop comfortable one-to-one relationships with peers in the absence of adults.

Nikhil is a tense, anxious, withdrawn and shy child.

Nikhil belongs to a middle-class family, which is able to gratify his physical and economic needs along with his need for love and affection.

The relationships between the adults in the family being faulty results in non-gratification of Nikhil's higher level needs for independence and a healthy parent–child relationship.

The faulty relationship between Nikhil's grandmother and mother arises due to the grandmother's dominance and inability to accept the secondary position in bringing up Nikhil. As a result Nikhil's mother has developed a strong sense of inadequacy and excessive use of defence mechanisms.

Nikhil's grandmother's excessive dominance over Nikhil's father has stunted his emotional growth and hence he is unable to perform his role as a father and as a husband.

This leaves Nikhil's mother dissatisfied in her relationship with her husband and she seeks gratification only in her relationship with Nikhil. This leads to a strong approach—approach conflict for Nikhil regarding his relationship with his mother and his grandmother.

Source: Prepared by the Editorial Team.

Chapter 10

WORKING WITH GROUPS (GROUP WORK METHOD)*

Ruma Bawikar and Ujwala Masdekar

Human growth and development is possible only through mutual dependence and meaningful interaction. Working through groups becomes an important intervention strategy in certain situations to increase the quality and relevance of help. This is due to two reasons:

1. Individuals who share common life situations get an opportunity to interact with each other in a safe environment.
2. Sharing of experiences and developing relationships with each other, in turn, help each individual to receive feedback. This feedback develops motivation for change.

Group work is based on the principle of encouraging the individual to receive help and also be able to give help to others. The following are the goals of group work applicable to any type of group:

- To socialise/re-socialise the members to acquire socially accepted norms and values.
- To develop social skills and enhance self-development.
- To educate members on various social issues.
- To develop life skills essential to perform the roles more effectively.
- To treat or modify maladaptive behaviour and areas of dysfunction in interpersonal relationships.

---

* The name in brackets indicate the conventional name for the method, which is contemporarily called as per the main title.

Group work as an intervention strategy is to be decided only after an in-depth analysis of the situation leading to a logical conclusion that group work is the best option to help the individual in particular and the group in general.

Group work is a dynamic method. At a given time the worker needs to interact with many members, and simultaneously the worker also has to focus on the individual member in the group. A group worker has to deal with the 'here & now' situation in a group for the following reasons:

1. To observe and assess:

    (a) individual behaviour;
    (b) interpersonal relationships among members and
    (c) the group process.

2. To provide insights into:

    (a) an individual member regarding his/her behaviour and his/her relationships with others and
    (b) the group regarding the group dynamics, the reasons behind the dynamics and the impact on group functioning.

3. To help members and the group

    (a) to try out new behaviours or new ways of dealing with interpersonal relationships both at cognitive and at affective levels
    (b) and to support each other in this process of change.

Group formation is the pre-planning phase, which can be called the 'Decision Making Phase'. The worker requires the following skills for assessing the needs of the prospective group members.

1. Skills in collecting relevant information of each member through individual contacts— personal interviews and/or home visits.
2. Skills in observation of the members' environment, situation and behaviour.

Information should be gathered on age-specific needs, sex-specific needs, areas of deprivation and blocks in need gratification and the impact of this on the members' present and future behaviour.

Selection of group members should be based on some or all of the following criteria: age, sex, interest, needs, problems, abilities, intellectual capacities and environmental situation. This helps in creating homogeneity of needs and interests, which is necessary for achieving group work goals.

Selection of target group should be in tune with the agency functions, goals and scope of their work. This understanding enables the worker to develop objectives, which are not only attainable but also within the framework of the agency objectives.

The skills that are expected to be developed in a trainee social worker (TSW) as a group worker are of two types—procedural skills and interaction skills.

Procedural skills mainly include the process of collecting facts, assessing the information and establishing objectives for groups. For this, the group worker requires basic skills of listening, observation, collection of information, assessment along with sensitivity, empathy and insight.

The interaction skills are as follows:

1. Accepting—individual feelings and behaviour.
2. Relating—with warmth, equality and impartiality.
3. Enabling—individual to express and accomplish.
4. Supporting—to gain confidence and decision making.
5. Guiding—for activities and group movement.
6. Alleviating—tensions, conflicts, fear and anxiety.
7. Assessing—group or individual behaviour and relationships.
8. Interpreting—roles and behaviours of individual members and group as a whole.
9. Observing and evaluating—group process.

The skill training workshops for group work which follow should be conducted after basic theory of group work method has been covered.

The objectives of these workshops are as follows:

1. To help trainees develop skills in planning.
2. To help trainees develop skills required at each stage of group development.
3. To help trainees develop skills in conducting activities.
4. To help trainees develop techniques of recording the group work process.

The workshops have the following units:

1. Group formation:

    (a) Steps in group formation
    (b) Group work plan—objectives and activities
    (c) Contracting

2. Problem solving and/or group development:

    (a) Skills in structuring appropriate activities
    (b) Skills in conducting activities
    (c) Skills in observing group dynamics
    (d) Skills in facilitation

3. Use of various activities
4. Observation and techniques of recording

UNIT ONE: GROUP FORMATION

Time required: 2 hours
Methods used: Group discussion, chart preparation, presentation and role play.

Formulation of Specific Objectives

Objectives:

1. To develop abilities in identifying needs of the target group based on the characteristics of the group.
2. To develop abilities in formulating precise, realistic and measurable objectives.

No. of participants: All
Materials required: Markers and chart paper
Time required: 1 hour
Procedure:

1. Divide the class into groups of 10.
2. Each group is given a brief description of a specific target group.
3. Ask them to list out the needs and areas of concern of the group members on the basis of the characteristics of their target group.
4. Each group will formulate objectives based on the identified needs/problems.
5. Ask the groups to present the characteristics, needs and objectives of the target group.
6. Other TSWs can give their suggestions during each presentation and the objectives for each target group could be finalised.

Some examples of the different types of target groups are given as follows: The facilitator can draw examples of target group also from the field experience of the trainees.

Set-up 1: Residential care for girls: Group of girls between the age of 13 and 16 years in an observation home. First admission, admitted by police due to parental complaints. The reason for their admission is that these girls have eloped from their homes to marry the person that they were in love with.

Set-up 2: Special school for the mentally challenged: Parents group—illiterate, age group 25–30 years. Lower socio-economic strata, having one mentally challenged child aged 8–10 years. This child has been recently admitted to a special school.

Set-up 3: Urban slum community: Married women who have been residing in the community since the last 5–10 years. Age group 25–40 years. Husbands are unskilled labourers with irregular income. All have school-going children. These women are housewives.

After each presentation the facilitator could ask the following questions:

- Were the needs identified comprehensively?
- Are the long- and short-term objectives linked logically?
- Are these objectives realistic, attainable and can these be measured in behavioural outcomes?

Process of Group Formation

Time required: 45 minutes
Method used: Brainstorming
Procedure:

1. Distribute cyclostyled copies of recording on first encounter with the women in the community (Annexure A10.1).
2. Ask the TSWs to read the recording and then raise the following questions:

   (a) How did the worker approach these women?
   (b) How did the worker use the testing out situation?
   (c) Identify the principles of social group work used by the worker (Annexure A10.2).
   (d) Identify the skills of the worker reflected in the first encounter.

CONTRACT SETTING: FIRST SESSION WITH THE GROUP

The first session with the group members is very important wherein the worker helps the group members to express their expectations and shares ideas on the extent of help the agency can offer. This helps in setting a contract, leading to mutually accepted behavioural commitments and also planning activities.
Objectives:

1. To help TSWs understand the importance of planning along with group members.
2. To help them identify the skills required for the contracting stage.
3. To help them gain insight into their own anxieties in the first session and how to deal with their anxiety.

Methods used: Role play.
Time required: 20 minutes for preparation.
                20 minutes for enactment.
                30 minutes for discussion.
No. of participants: 15.
Procedure:

1. Ask the group of volunteers to present the role play. One of them becomes the group worker.
2. The rest of the class observes the process.

The facilitator could develop two situations based on the fieldwork placements of the TSWs. For example:

1. First session with women in an urban slum community who want to start a self-help group.
2. Session with 17/18-year-old boys who are going to be released from a residential care institution in the near future.

Points for discussion:

1. How was the discussion initiated by the worker?
2. How were the members encouraged to express their expectations?
3. Was the worker able to create a supportive and comfortable environment? How?
4. How did the worker link his planning with the members' expectations?
5. What were the feelings of the worker about the expectations of the group? How did he cope with these?

In the initial session, the group worker may have to use some 'ice-breaking activity' to help members reduce their inhibitions and/or warm up to each other. These activities also help the worker to establish rapport with group members and simultaneously help them to establish rapport with each other.

USE OF ICE-BREAKING ACTIVITY

There are many ice-breaking activities, one or two of which could be conducted in the workshop. The facilitator could use any such activities. Two are given here as illustrations.

Objectives:

1. To help the TSWs understand the value of ice-breaking activities.
2. To help TSWs understand the procedure for conducting ice-breaking activities.
3. To develop skills in initiating and facilitating meaningful discussion.

Exercise 10.1 Introducing Each Other

No. of participants: All. Divide the class into pairs.
Material required: Nil.
Time required: 45 minutes to 1 hour (this will depend upon the number of participants).
Note to the facilitator: Not suitable for a very large group.
Procedure:

1. Each pair should sit together and talk to each other for 2–4 minutes.
2. The pair is expected to collect information about each other.

3. Then each pair should stand up and introduce their partners to the larger group.
4. This introduction should be based on the information received from the partner.

Points for discussion:

1. How much were the members willing to disclose about themselves to each other?
2. Did both partners listen carefully?
3. Did they introduce each other based on the information received or did they add to the information?

Note: Ice-breaking games could be used without follow-up by any discussion and the planned activity for that session could be taken immediately.

The facilitator has to help the TSWs understand that these two structures of the ice-breaking game would entirely depend upon the objectives that the worker wants to achieve.

Exercise 10.2 Animal Family

No. of participants: All.
Material required: Paper for preparing chits.
Time required: 45–60 minutes depending upon the size of the group.
Note to the facilitator: Suitable for any age group.
Procedure: For a group of about 35 participants divided into seven groups of five members each use the following procedure: Choose the names of any seven animals. Write the name of each animal on five chits and fold them.

Ask each participant to pick any one chit and find their own animal family. Once the groups are formed, ask group members to get introduced to each other and form the animal family. After 5–10 minutes, ask each group to introduce themselves to the other groups. There is no need to have any discussion after this game.

Games of introduction could be used dynamically in various situations in group work:

- If the group members are new to each other, then these games help them to get introduced and also experience a feeling of comfort.
- If the group members are familiar with each other, then the points of introduction could be linked with the objectives of the group.

For example, if the worker is using a game of introduction in a women's group who are familiar with each other and are planning to start a self-help group, the following points could be used for their introduction:

1. What are the difficulties faced by each woman in managing the household?
2. Does she save any money and how?
3. How is she going to use these savings in the future?

After the demonstration of the two games, the TSWs could be divided into small groups and given the task of preparing one game which would be used as an ice-breaker followed by its presentation.

UNIT TWO: PROBLEM SOLVING AND/OR GROUP DEVELOPMENT STAGE

Skills in Planning Appropriate Activities

Objectives:

1. To develop TSWs' abilities for appropriate selection of activities in consonance with group work goals.
2. To develop abilities in appropriate sequencing of planned activities.
3. To develop abilities to prepare a detailed process of implementation of the activities.

Material required: Chart papers or transparencies and OHP.
Time: 2 hours.
No. of participants: All.
Procedure:

1. TSWs could be divided into small groups and their previous presentations of objective formulation could be given to them.
2. Each group should be asked to prepare a detailed plan of group work. The following guidelines could be given to the groups (Figure 10.1):

   (a) Type of the group.
   (b) Objectives of the group.
   (c) Number of sessions.
   (d) Frequency of sessions.
   (e) Duration of each session and timing.
   (f) Place of the session.

Figure 10.1   Session-wise Activity Plan

No. of session	Specific	Objectives	Activity	Resources	Role of the worker

3. Each group should be asked to present their plan either by using OHP transparencies or with the help of charts (Example of plan, Annexure A10.3).

Other TSWs should be encouraged to give feedback and then plans could be finalised.
Note: Role of the worker is reflected in the plan to develop the understanding of the trainees.

Skills in Using Planned Activities

When the group is involved in an activity, the worker needs to be very alert and observant. She/he has to facilitate the process. She/he needs the following skills:

1. Skills in encouraging participation.
2. Skills in guiding interaction.
3. Ability to analyse the process.
4. Ability to be flexible.
5. Skills in summarising the process and linking it to the objectives.
6. Skills in helping members to prepare a plan of action (change in behaviour outside the group situation).

Objectives:

1. To develop skills in using activities linking it to the objectives of group work.
2. To develop skills in guiding interaction and responding to the dynamics appropriately.

Note to the facilitator: To help TSWs understand the dynamic role of the group worker, the facilitator could use the demonstration method.

Exercise 10.3 Problem Mapping Technique

Material required: Blackboard and coloured chalk.
Time required: 1 hour
Preparation time: Half an hour
No. of participants: 10–15. Rest of the class is to observe.
Procedure:

1. Ask the volunteers to identify any current academic problem that they have difficulties in coping with.

2. The facilitator can then conduct the following activity: Ask the group members to draw a tree with white chalk on the blackboard and plot the problems on the tree in the following way:

   (a) Main problems on the trunk of the tree.
   (b) Offshoots of the main problem on the branches.
   (c) Causes of the problem on the roots.

   This helps in analysing the causes and the chain of problems.

3. Then ask the members to draw a chart using three colours—problems in red, its consequences in blue and its resolution in green.

Highlight the following:

This helps the trainees to prioritise the problems and also the actions to be taken. If the members are asked to list out the actors responsible for the actions to be taken, it helps in gaining insight into the problem resolution process as a team effort.
Note: In this exercise, the facilitator should choose a problem related to the trainees' student role so that they are more spontaneous and involved in the process and also realise the benefits of an interactive reflective activity.
After the demonstration the observers could be asked to give their observations on:

- Skills demonstrated by the worker.
- Selection and structuring of the activity.
- Involvement of all and how this was facilitated.

Understanding Group Dynamics

Many group dynamics get discussed in the role plays conducted in the workshop. Hence some aspects need to be consciously emphasised.

ACCEPTANCE

Acceptance of each other by all the group members is most important in group development. There are many reasons for non-acceptance in the group. The worker has to help the members understand the importance of acceptance.

Exercise 10.4 Group Acceptance

Objective: To help the TSWs understand the blocks in the process of acceptance and its implication on individual behaviour or the productivity of the group.

Method: Simulation game.
Material required: Nil.
No. of participants: 10–15.
Time: 30 minutes.
Procedure:

1. Ask all the volunteers except one to form a circle by holding hands.
2. One volunteer will be asked to remain outside the circle.
3. This volunteer should try to break the circle and enter it.

Points for discussion:

1. Why did the group members not allow the outsider to enter the circle?
2. What were their feelings and why?
3. What were the reactions of the person who was trying to enter the group and the reasons behind the reactions?
4. What happens to the group members in the process?

   After this discussion the facilitator can ask the TSWs to list out the ways in which the worker could help members to accept each other.

TRUST

Group members need to trust each other. Only if there is trust, will members accept each other's feedback to bring about change in self. Trust helps in developing meaningful relationships.

Exercise 10.5 Game of Trust

Objectives:

1. To enable the TSWs to understand the concept of trust.
2. To help the TSWs develop capacities in building up a trusting relationship among the group members.

Method: Simulation game.
Materials required: Music cassette and tape recorder.
Time required: 40 minutes.
No. of participants: 20–22.
Procedure:

1. Ask the participants to form two circles, one inner and one outer, by holding their hands.
2. The members of the inner circle have their backs towards the outer circle.

3. The inner circle moves clockwise and the outer circle moves anti-clockwise when the music starts.
4. When the music stops the members of the inner circle leave their hands and fall backward immediately without looking behind.
5. Members of the outer circle give support to prevent the inner circle members from falling.

Points for discussion:

1. Why did the members of the inner circle hesitate?
2. How did the members of the outer circle behave?
3. What were the feelings of the members in both circles?
4. Which factors block our trust in others?

These two games will help the TSWs to understand the group dynamics. The skills that the worker needs to develop are as follows:

1. Observation of members' responses.
2. Careful listening of interactions between members.
3. Encouraging members' participation.
4. Giving feedback with sensitivity.
5. Guiding interactions subsequently.
6. Modifying behaviour tactfully.
7. Use of non-verbal communication.

Note: These games could also be used by TSWs in their group work situations to help the group members gain insight into their group dynamics.

Skills in Facilitation

GIVING FEEDBACK

The worker has to observe group dynamics to assess the group process and facilitate the interaction to achieve objectives. The worker cannot keep his assessment a secret, but has to share it with group members. This has to be at the right time.

Feedback is necessary in the group situation because the group approach believes in 'equality' of members and the concept of 'mutual aid'. Feedback could be regarding group achievement, group relationship, group dynamics or diagnosis of individual behaviour, relationship or achievement.

Giving pertinent feedback to the entire group is an important step in the group process. It is very easy to hurt the group members, so the following cautions need to be exercised while giving feedback:

1. Be sensitive to what information the group is ready to use—what will be most helpful to the group 'now'.

2. Don't 'bombard' the group with information. Too much information cannot be used. Select only two/three observations which will stimulate thinking and discussion.
3. Don't praise the group too much as learning may not take place. Mentioning accomplishments is desirable as it helps in facing the difficulties honestly.
4. Don't punish, preach or judge. The group worker cannot play the role of 'God'.
5. Discuss role behaviour rather than people's behaviour.
6. Go gently on personality clashes. It is usually better to discuss what helped and what hindered the growth of the whole group.
7. Feedback should create an enabling atmosphere and motivate the members to change.

EVALUATING INFORMATION AND DECIDING ABOUT CHANGE

The third stage of group development is based on diagnosis. It is the deliberation of what the group and its members will do to resolve the present problems and to enhance the future abilities.

Feedback from group members:

1. Members assess the observations, relate them to their experiences and test to see whether they agree with the report feedback.
2. The group examines the reasons that caused the situation to happen and ask themselves, 'Could we have recognized it earlier?'

EVALUATION

The group moves to a decision on what to do. What can be done in future in similar circumstances? What can individual members do to help themselves? What methods or procedures should be changed? What new direction can be sought? What new behaviour needs to be acquired?

This stage is the crucial one. Feedback and evaluation of group processes help the group members. Unless the members are able to gain insights into the functioning of the group and are able to find new ways of behaving, the group will not improve its functioning and will not continue in its growth and development (Annexure A10.4).

Exercise 10.6 Feedback

Objective: Help trainees understand skills in giving feedback.
Method: Role play.

Procedure:

1. Situation for role play: A group of women who are members of a self-help group and had a previous session on problems of recovery.
2. One trainee becomes the worker and other participants become group members.
3. Rest of the class observes the role play.

Role play: The worker is planning to give feedback to group members on the previous session where members had only argued and had not been very productive.
Material required: Nil.
Time required: 1 hour.
No. of participants: 10–12.
Preparation time: 20 minutes.
Role play time: 15 minutes.
Discussion: 10 minutes.
Points for discussion:

1. How did the worker start the discussion?
2. What was the reaction of members?
3. Could she/he handle the reactions?
4. Could she/he communicate the feedback constructively?

   If required another TSW could be asked to enact the role of group worker again and conduct the session in a different way based on the observations of the class. This could be followed by a discussion once again.

Termination of the Group

All groups come to an end. There are two ways in which these groups are terminated. One would be that the membership would be terminated since objectives are achieved. The second would be that the worker withdraws from the group and the group continues its association. The worker needs to prepare members well for this termination. To make this termination easy, the worker could arrange a small ceremony in the last session. If the group continues, members might give him/her a farewell.

Exercise 10.7 Skills in Termination

Objective: To help trainees understand the skills in termination of group work process.

Procedure:

Two situations could be given to the TSWs to enact the termination session.

1. In the observation home for boys, a group of 10 children were helped to settle down and follow the institute's discipline. All of them are going to be transferred to other institutes. This is the last session.
2. A group of youth has formed a youth club in the community due to the group worker's efforts. They are in the process of registration. This is the last session of the worker.

No. of participants: 12–13—one would be the group worker.
Preparation time: 20 minutes.
Presentation time: 20 minutes.
Discussion: 20 minutes.
Material required: nil.
Points for discussion:

1. How did the worker prepare for termination?
2. Was the activity appropriate for termination?
3. What else could have been planned?
4. What were the reactions of group members?
5. Could the worker handle these?
6. Did the worker help the members to conclude the learning of group experience or how did she/he summarise the group experiences?

UNIT THREE: INNOVATIVE ACTIVITIES

To stimulate group discussion or to strengthen or reinforce the content of the discussion or to attract the attention of group members or to help to release anxiety or other strong emotions, the group worker may use different techniques, tools or media. A few are discussed in the chapter on audio-visual media. The worker need not depend upon electronic or high-tech media as this means she/he has to depend upon electricity. Often the novelty of the media can have an adverse effect on the group process.

The worker can use creative literature—poems, short stories or essays—to create the necessary impact. Case studies could also be used. Common anecdotes could be distributed. With the help of these, group discussions can be conducted (refer to Annexure A10.5 for a sample case study). Mythological stories, slogans, events from history or current situations can be used for enhancing the process of learning in groups.

Newspaper clippings, editorials and letters to the editor can be used to give the group members a good glimpse into the current political and social situation.

Use of Songs

Folk media such as folk songs (Powada, Lavani), songs composed on popular film tunes can be used. Songs could be used in different ways—rhythm, dance, actions, chorus, and so on. Songs create a conducive atmosphere if used before a meeting (sample of songs, Annexure A10.6). The worker can compose songs on social issues. The worker could also help the members compose songs. This enhances participation.

Points to remember:

1. These songs have to be followed by a discussion.
2. They should be used sparingly.
3. Themes should be appealing and relevant.
4. They should be composed in simple language and tunes.
5. The trainers should be able to sing the songs without any inhibitions.
6. The members should be able to sing the songs after the trainer.
7. Also encourage members to bring/compose their own songs, where they lead the singing.
8. For achieving uninhibited participation, the focus should be on enthusiasm to sing rather than skills in tune and rhythm.

Use of Traditions, Customs

Cultural events, customs, and so on, also could be used to create insights, for example, the festival of Janmashtami in which people have to stand on each other's shoulders. The base is broad and has to reduce as one goes up. The person who is at the top has a better opportunity to get the things in the *dahihandi* (the pot holding the curd). This tradition is seen during Janmashtami. Analysis of this custom could be on the following lines:

- Indian social structure.
- Budget—national planning.
- Resource allocation.
- Exploitation, and so on.

One can make a list of various customs, traditions and use them appropriately in various group situations.

Use of Games

People of all ages like to play games. There could be outdoor and indoor games. Some games are played individually. The benefits of games could be listed as follows:

1. Help in physical development.
2. Increase interaction amongst people.
3. Help people to accept failure/success.
4. Develop teamwork in people.
5. Develop leadership in individuals.

6. Help individuals to become good followers in a team.
7. Help in learning to think beyond himself/herself.
8. Develop discipline.
9. Help in learning to give and take.
10. Develop persistence.
11. Can help in catharsis.
12. Develop decision-making abilities.
13. Learning through imitation.
14. Develop ability to persuade others.
15. Develop ability to sacrifice for others willingly.
16. Develop ability to predict/anticipate.

Games develop positive attitudes and qualities. All these qualities are important to be effective in life. While playing games, participants are supposed to take up specific roles which have assigned behavioural expectations. Due to competition or these expectations, conflicts may arise. In real-life situations also one has to perform various roles. The game situation, hence, could be a reflection of a real-life situation. The behaviour expressed through games could be 'self-revealing'.

The child expresses himself through games. For children make believe games are very important for self-expression. Children's energies are also channellised through play activities.

Points to remember:

1. One has to select games with a proper understanding of the needs and abilities of the group members.
2. Too much competition through games may disintegrate the group and the message may be lost.
3. Games should not be used as a ritual. Monotony may reduce their impact. We as social workers are not sports coaches hence developing sports skills is not the main purpose.
4. Games are an activity or a technique to increase involvement. Hence the worker should try to relate the behaviour and attitudes reflected through games to real-life situations of the members.

There could be many common games which children play or the adults have played as children. Different interpretations of these games could create a different perspective on life in the members. For example:

A simple childhood game called Queen of Sheeba or Follow the leader or in Marathi Shivaji Mhanato could be used for two purposes:

1. To help the group members relax and enjoy themselves.
2. To gain insight into power games seen in society, relating it to the patriarchal system.

There are many indoor games that could be used to enhance the group process. If the group members cannot participate actively in physical activities or if the members' intellectual abilities need to be stimulated, the worker could use puzzles, geometrical or verbal. These games are very dynamic. The worker may also use the process to give insight into the social skills required to cope with everyday challenges. Example of such game is given here.

Exercise 10.8 Nine Dots

Objective: Helping group members to develop their creative thinking in problem solving.
Materials required: Blackboard and chalk and paper and pencil for each participant.
No. of participants: 20–25 maximum.
Time required: 30 minutes.
Procedure:

1. Instruct the members to plot the nine dots as shown in Figure 10.2.
2. Ask them to join all the dots using only four straight lines without lifting the pen within 10 minutes.
3. Ask members who think they successfully completed the task to come forward and demonstrate it on the blackboard.
4. The correct way of joining dots should be demonstrated by the group worker on the blackboard.

Figure 10.2   Finding Solutions

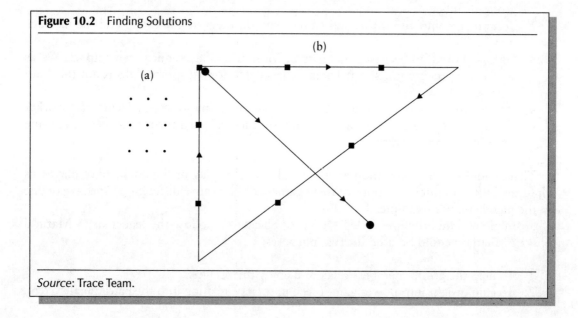

Source: Trace Team.

Points for discussion:

1. Within limited resources, how one can think of alternatives which could be very simple.
2. How is our thinking conditioned by previous experiences, preconceived notions, limitations set on us, and so on.
3. To achieve goals we may need to step out beyond established frame works.
4. Realistic planning and persistence are important for goal achievement.

Exercise 10.9 Gordian Knot

Objective: Helping group members to deal with problems using team effort.
No. of participants: 20–30.
Time required: 30 minutes.
Procedure:

1. Ask the participants to form a circle.
2. Ask each participant to link his/her hand with the alternative person in the circle.
3. After the entire group is knotted in this manner, ask the group to try to untangle the knot without unclasping their linked hands to eventually form a single circle wherein the linked partners would be standing next to each other.

Points for discussion:

1. How did members help each other while solving the common problem?
2. How did they deal with obstacles in the process of problem solving?

Highlight that when a group faces a common problem team work, cooperation and coordination are necessary for achieving desired goals.

Note to the Facilitator: One hand should be linked from the front of the person standing adjacently and the other from behind the person standing adjacently.

Role Play

It is a method whereby the members are given a real-life situation. Members are assigned different roles and are asked prepare a script. Then they are asked to enact the situation for 10–15 minutes. This enactment is followed by a group discussion.

Role playing is not a primary treatment method. It is used to enhance the treatment process. When role playing is used with a purpose to help someone with a common social problem in counselling or psychotherapy it is called psychodrama. Moreno has contributed to the application of this technique in treatment groups since 1911.

GOALS OF ROLE PLAY

1. To convey the feelings and information otherwise difficult to communicate.
2. To disclose feelings members may not have admitted to harbouring.
3. To experiment with and practice new ways of behaviour.
4. To assume and to experiment with new developmental roles.
5. To obtain feedback with reference to specific behaviours.
6. To help members see themselves as others see them.
7. To help develop expression of positive feelings towards the significant others.
8. To help members to understand the feelings and behaviour of other members in their life.

ADVANTAGES OF ROLE PLAY

1. Increases spontaneity and reduces resistance.
2. Increases participation of members who have difficulties in verbalising their problems.
3. Reduces tension and relaxes the members.
4. Stimulates involvement and identification with the group.
5. Facilitates expression of feelings and attitudes.
6. Rein projective technique, it reveals problems and motives directly.
7. Lifts the interaction from an intellectual plane to reality.
8. Preparation for, and enactment of role playing members' problems focuses on the 'here and now'.
9. Encourages each member to apply what she/he has learned.
10. Leads to empathic understanding of the significant others.
11. Helps in understanding the feelings of the other person leading to acceptance.
12. Others can give feedback which can lead to understanding of the self.
13. Gives opportunity to practice social skills.
14. One gets an opportunity to experiment with new ways of thinking and behaving in a supportive environment.

Role playing is not necessary

1. when members can discuss their problems frankly and openly;
2. can discover new and better ways of behaving and develop self-confidence and
3. have the commitment to apply what they have learnt in everyday living without further practice.

Who will be benefited?

1. One who is fumbling for words in trying to describe a problem to the persons involved.
2. A member who is trying to clarify his relationship with a significant other.

3. A member who is touched by another member's problem but is not ready to accept it as his own. This can be achieved if the member who has the problem assumes the role of the significant other with whom he is unable to relate and the non-accepting member plays the role of the other member.
4. A member who needs to develop social skills.

GUIDELINES FOR USING ROLE PLAY

The primary role player should describe the characters involved in the situation which she/he wants to depict and how she/he thinks they feel. Every member of the group should be encouraged to ask questions in order to obtain the best possible picture of the situation. Then members are encouraged to volunteer for various roles.

Members who are reluctant to take up roles could be encouraged to use puppets or dolls to speak and act for them. Members should be encouraged to feel as the character feels, express the character's feelings using their own words. While playing a scene, every actor should feel free to stop whenever he feels unable to proceed. Someone else may take up from where the other has left off.

Group worker may help in preparing the persons for their roles and in helping them put into words what they think their characters feel. She/he may clarify a situation or a relationship and help to state a feeling.

The primary role player is the director. She/he benefits from the discussion in the following ways:

1. She/he gets a chance to reveal feelings about what happened during the role play.
2. Comments upon whatever she/he discovered about the self and his/her relationship.
3. Obtains new perceptions of relationships and of his/her own functioning due to comments by others.
4. Feedback and suggestions on how she/he could try to behave helps in developing new behaviours.

Trainee social workers could be exposed to this method by actually giving them the task of helping the group members to develop a role play followed by discussion. This has to be done through role play method of training, that is, some TSWs would be group members and one of them would be the group worker.

Exercise 10.10 Use of Role Play for Various Purpose

Objective: To help trainees understand the use of role play for two different purpose.
Material: Nil.

Time: 1 hour.
No. of participants: 20.
Procedure:

Class to be divided into two groups with 10 volunteers to perform role play in each group based on the following situations:

1. Developing Social Skills: You are working with a youth club in a community. Most of the members want to take up jobs in a factory. They have to appear for an interview. As a worker you want to help them to prepare for the prospective situation. You want to use role play to develop skills in facing the interview. How would you conduct the session?
2. For Therapeutic Purpose: You are working with adolescent girls in a residential care institution. These girls are arrogant and use abusive language with the caretaker staff. As a group worker you want these girls to develop alternative communication skills with the staff. You have planned to use role play. How would you conduct this session?

Points for discussion:

1. How did the worker introduce the role play in the group?
2. How did she/he lead the discussion?
3. To what extent did this technique help the group members?

Group Discussion as a Method in Group Work

The group worker cannot rely on activities alone. Each activity has to generate discussion in the group. All members have to be encouraged to contribute in the discussion. Discussions in the group help in encouraging members' sharing and contribution to the group process. It is based on two perspectives, that is, 'interaction' and 'mutual aid'. The worker needs to emphasise the two aspects in group discussion: one, it has to be voluntary and members cannot be pressurised but must be encouraged to participate. The second aspect is 'confidentiality'. It is just not sufficient for the group worker to follow this principle alone. Each and every member needs to develop the commitment to this principle. Discussion would only be fruitful if each member is clear about the objective.

The worker needs to develop the following skills in facilitating discussion:

1. Appropriate way of responding.
2. Listening.
3. Encouraging members to talk.
4. Summarising.
5. Leading.
6. Asking appropriate questions.
7. Guiding.
8. Observation.

Exercise 10.11 Conducting Group Discussion

Objectives:

1. To help the TSWs to understand the three stages of group development—orientation, working and termination.
2. To enable TSWs to develop abilities required for conducting group discussions.

Materials required: Chart papers and markers.
No. of participants: All.
Time required: 45–50 minutes.
Procedure:

1. Divide the class into small groups of 6–7 members each.
2. Give one topic to all groups, for example, what should be the activities of the student council.
3. Each group will appoint one leader and one rapporteur.

Guidelines for the leader:

1. Introduce the topic in such a way as to provoke response from the members.
2. Introduce the topic briefly in 2/3 sentences.
3. Once the discussion starts the leader should raise some relevant issues related to the topic.
4. She/he should point out some facts or opinions by reading from a newspaper or a magazine or any relevant material.
5. Ask one or two direct questions to the members, either general or specific.
6. The leader should observe the interaction and behaviour of the group members along following lines:

    1. Who takes the lead?
    2. Did all members participate? Yes/No, Why?
    3. Atmosphere—Whether the members felt free to express themselves?
    4. How did they respond to each other?
    5. How did the discussion progress?
    6. Were there attempts to summarise or highlight?

Guidelines for members to observe in the leader:

1. How did the leader lead the group discussion?
2. How did she/he respond to a member's behaviour?
3. How did she/he play the role of the facilitator?

After the exercise on group discussion, divide the class into six groups again. These groups are given the task of chart preparation. Three groups are to prepare highlights of a good group discussion. The other three groups are to prepare highlights of a bad group discussion.

UNIT FOUR: TECHNIQUES OF RECORDING GROUP PROCESS

There are three commonly used techniques of recording the observations of member behaviour, relationships and communication pattern in the group.

Socio-gram: Who Talks to Whom?

This is a graphic method of depicting the choice relationship formed in the group, by the use of a socio-metric test. The most common questions asked are 'With whom does one prefer to sit?' or 'With whom does one prefer to relate?' This is based on a group situation in which there is freedom to choose and the selection does convey a message. The socio-gram may be used as a recording device indicating not only choice but also factors like 'Who spoke to whom? How many times?'

Moreno has developed this 'snap shot' way of recording relationships in a group. Drawing this 'Acceptance–rejection' pattern gives awareness about the group structure, that is, subgroups, leaders and isolates in the group.

This is a picture of a given phase in the group process. It depicts only specific moments in the session. This picture may change constantly. It does not give the reasons for observed phenomena. The socio-gram is an instrument for observation. This mode alone cannot be used in making decisions with regard to group intervention.

The number of lines made by the observer in Figure 10.3 indicates the number of statements made in a 10—15-minute period. The alphabets in Figure 10.3 present the names of members.

The comments made to the group as a whole are shown by arrows. Arrows at each end show that the statement made by one person was responded to by the recipient. This also helps us to identify which member made the maximum statements. The small straight lines cutting the arrow at the tail indicate the initiator in communication. The broken lines indicate the negative contributions by the members.

To draw a socio-gram the worker should first plot the seating positions of the members using their initials and then plot interactions with the help of arrows.

The socio-gram can be drawn using different coloured arrows or different types of arrows. The worker should then provide the key to interpret them.

A series of socio-grams help the group worker in diagnosis of various aspects of the members' behaviour. A socio-gram indicates the following aspects, which help the worker in his/her analysis and intervention plan for the group.

1. Seating arrangement.
2. Leadership.
3. Isolated member.
4. Initiator.
5. Hostile or aggressive member.

Figure 10.3   Socio-gram

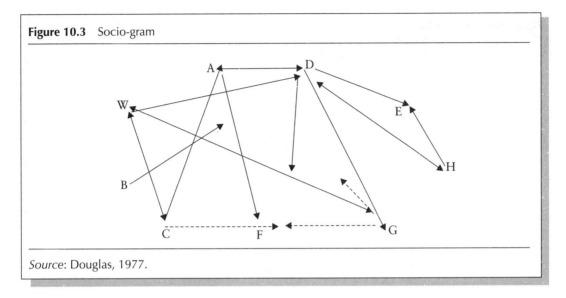

Source: Douglas, 1977.

6. Active participant.
7. Subgroups/pairs.
8. Extent of participation.
9. Nature of participation—positive/negative.

The worker must be keen and quick in observation and collecting information. She/he also requires the ability to sort out the identified behaviour and depict it with a diagram.

Wheel Chart: Contribution Rates

How much each member said during the session can be recorded by a simple 'wheel chart'.

Each member is assigned a segment of the wheel with the initials of the members written on the curve of the segment as indicated by alphabets in Figure 10.4. The worker makes a mark for each statement made by each member, regardless of its length, content or direction.

A series of such recordings would give insight into the member's rate of participation in each session. This in turn helps the group worker to facilitate better participation of members.

Figure 10.4   Wheel Chart

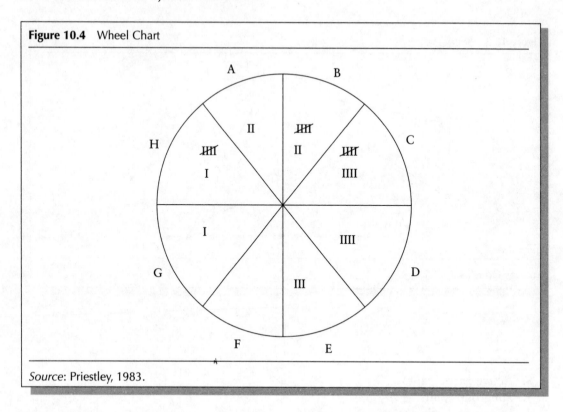

Source: Priestley, 1983.

Observation Categories Chart: Who Makes What Kind of Contribution?

Table 10.1 can be used to depict the types of contributions of members over a number of sessions. The horizontal column represents the members whose initials should be entered in each column. The vertical column gives a list of behaviour expressed by the members.

Table 10.1   Types of Contributions of Members over a Number of Sessions

Observation categories	Members									
	NM	GR	UM	RB	SS	VK	AP	AM	MT	DD
1. Encourages				√						√
2. Agrees, accepts	√					√				
3. Arbitrates					√			√	√	
4. Proposes action	√									
5. Asks suggestions				√						
6. Gives opinion										
7. Asks opinion	√		√			√		√		
8. Gives information										

(Table 10.1 Continued)

(Table 10.1 Continued)

Observation categories	NM	GR	UM	RB	SS	VK	AP	AM	MT	DD
					Members					
9. Seeks information										
10. Poses problem			√							
11. Defines position										
12. Asks position					√		√		√	
13. Routine direction	√									
14. Depreciate self										
15. Autocratic manner			√		√				√	
16. Disagrees										
17. Self-assertion			√							
18. Active aggression										
19. Passive aggression					√					

Note: Based upon observation categories discussed in R.F. Bale's book (1950) 'Interaction process analysis'.

During the session, the worker will tick mark the type of behaviour expressed by the members below his/her initials. One sheet is to be filled in for each session. Based on these observations, the worker can identify members who positively or negatively contribute to the group process and also decide the interventions required for changing behaviours of members.

Note: The list of observation categories can be changed according to the requirements and objectives of the group.

Exercise 10.12 Use of Techniques of Recording

Time: 1 hour
Method: Role Play
Material required: Nil
Participants: All
Objective: To develop the abilities of observation and the use of techniques of recording.
Procedure:

1. Class to be divided into four groups.
2. A topic for discussion to be given to each group.
3. Each group will have two observers.
4. They will record the group process for 5 minutes during the session. Socio-gram and wheel chart are to be used for recording.
5. Based on the Bale's observation categories chart (Table 10.1), one observer will fill in the chart by observing the complete group discussion session. The observer can make his/her own list of categories to be used for observation.

Group Growth Scale: A Measuring Yardstick

This is a detailed format but easy to use due to the key provided. This scale helps to plot the group growth at several stages of the group process. It also helps to identify areas in which there may be difficulties which are blocking progress (Table 10.2).

Table 10.2 Group Work Session Analysis Guidelines

1. What was the general atmosphere in the group?

Formal	———————	Informal
Competitive	———————	Cooperative
Hostile	———————	Supportive
Inhibited	———————	Permissive

   Comments

2. Quality and quantity of work accomplished.

Accomplishment	High	☐	Low	☐
Quality of production	High	☐	Low	☐
Goals	Clear	☐	Vague	☐
Methods	Clear	☐	Vague	☐
Worker Comments	Flexible	☐	Inflexible	☐

3. Leader behaviour

   Attentive to group needs   ☐

   Supported others   ☐

   Concerned only with the topic   ☐

   Dominated the group   ☐

   Took sides   ☐

   Helped group   ☐

   Worker Comment

4. Participation

Most people talked	☐	Only few talked	☐
Members involved	☐	Members apathetic	☐
Group united	☐	Group divided	☐

   Worker Comment

Source: Adopted from Douglas (1977).

Observation of Functions Performed by the Group Members during the Sessions

While observing a group, one might simply note those modes of participation (verbal and non-verbal) by the members, which help the group to complete its task successfully and/or those, which hinder the process. The worker should give particular attention to how a member functions. These functions could be classified as follows:

TASK FUNCTIONS

The task-oriented behaviour is the one which helps the members to accomplish a goal or to be productive. Some of these types of behaviours are listed below as guidelines.

1. *Initiating*—proposing tasks, goals or actions, defining group problems, suggesting a procedure.
2. *Informing*—offering facts, giving an opinion, seeking opinion or information.
3. *Clarifying*—interpreting ideas or suggestions, defining terms, clarifying issues before the group.
4. *Summarising*—pooling together related ideas, restating suggestions, offering a decision or conclusion for the group to consider.
5. *Reality testing*—making a critical analysis of an idea, testing an idea against some data, trying to see if the idea could work.

MAINTENANCE FUNCTION

The maintenance-oriented behaviour is the one which helps in building relationships in groups. A few functions of this type are listed as follows.

1. Harmonising—Attempting to reconcile disagreements, reducing tensions, getting people to explore differences.
2. Gatekeeping—Helping to keep communication channels open, facilitating the participation of others, suggesting procedures that permit sharing.
3. Encouraging—Being friendly, warm and responsive to others, indicating by facial expression or remarks the acceptance of others and their contribution.
4. Consensus testing—Asking to see if a group is nearing a decision, checking with the group to see how much agreement has been reached.
5. Compromising—Offering a compromise when involved in a conflict, admitting error, modifying opinion in the interest of group cohesion or growth, sometimes maybe at the cost of one's own position.

SELF-ORIENTED FUNCTIONS

This behaviour is shown by members who think only about themselves. Achieving their own goals is their major concern. The following are some examples of self-oriented behaviour:

1. Aggression—Deflating another's status, attacking the group or its values, joking in barbed or semi-concealed way, seeking recognition through ways not relevant to the group tasks.
2. Blocking—Disagreeing and opposing 'beyond reason'—stubbornly resisting the group on its values.
3. Dominating—Asserting authority or superiority, manipulating the group or some members, interrupting contributions of others, controlling by means of flattery or other forms of patronising behaviour.
4. Special interest solicitation—Using the group as a vehicle for extraneous interests (for example, political interests, gaining power), personal biases and stereotyping used for one's own individual needs.

Exercise 10.13 Observation of Member Behaviour in Group Work Practice

Objective: To develop the ability to identify and categorise member behaviour.
Material required: Handouts of lists of member functions for each trainee observer.
Time: 1 hour.
Procedure:

1. Eight to nine TSWs to form a group. They are given a specific task: With the resources available within the classroom they have to prepare a message: 'protect the environment from pollution'. The resources may include the members themselves.
    Following are the instructions to a participant group:

    (a) Brainstorm on how you will convey the above message.
    (b) Prepare the presentation.
    (c) You are given half an hour for planning, preparation and presentation.
    (d) The rest of the class is going to observe and judge your presentation.

2. After giving the above instructions, send the group out for a few minutes with another facilitator/faculty member with the instruction that they should not start brainstorming till they come back to the training hall.
3. While the participant group is outside give the following instructions to the rest of the class after distributing these handouts:

    (a) Refer to the sheets regarding observation of functions performed by group members.
    (b) Use these as guidelines to observe the group process as they plan, prepare and present the message.
    (c) Record the observations of member behaviours during the process.

4. After the presentation, observers are asked to present what they have recorded.

All the workshops in this chapter should enable trainees to develop skills in working with groups from identification of group to recording the group process.

ANNEXURE A10.1 VILLAGE SITUATION CASE STUDY: WORKER'S ROLE IN GROUP FORMATION

While passing by Shantibai's house, the worker was surprised to see two ladies smoking *bidi*s. The worker stopped beside them, smiled and asked whether they smoked regularly and one stated that she had begun it a long time ago. She found that it stopped pain in her stomach.

At that point, an old lady approached asking the worker her name and whether she was married. On learning that the worker was not married, she said that this seemed to be true of all girls who wanted to take up studies. Pointing to her daughter and daughter-in-law she said that they had their first babies at the age of 15 and 16, respectively. As for herself she had been married at the age of 9 and since then she had suffered very much and she hoped that in her next birth she will be able to pursue education and enjoy life. The worker immediately commented that it is still possible for them all to have a class of their own where they could get together to learn, to read and to write and also discuss topics of their common interest.

Choti, another old lady who was an onlooker, remarked 'Yes, yes, it is a good idea! Education is becoming so important who knows even God may ask us to sign before entering heaven.' All the women laughed and hearing them, a few more came forward to see what was going on.

Banubi came forward, addressed the worker and said that her daughter-in-law was seriously ill following her delivery. On hearing her, the worker asked if she could visit her a little later. Banubi appeared hesitant. The worker sensed her hesitation and inquired 'Will it be alright if I come to see your daughter-in-law?'

Banubi smiled and said, 'Oh no, the thing is nobody is supposed to visit the mother and the baby for a week after the delivery. They say "NAZAR lag jati hai". I know all this is superstition but you can come after 4/5 days.' The worker nodded and said, 'Ok, I will certainly do that'.

Then the worker again addressed the group and explained the various programmes of her agency which were meant to help women. She told them about the various groups which were functioning in other communities with the help of her agency. The women listened and then the worker said that they could meet at a time which would not interfere with their household chores.

Banubi said that it was an important point. The worker then asked if she came next week at the same time, would they meet her. They agreed and the worker promised to bring samples of what other mandals were doing, particularly crafts which were being made by women to supplement incomes.

Points for discussion:

1. How did the worker approach the women?
2. How did the worker use the 'testing out' situation?
3. Identify the principles of social work used by the worker.
4. Identify the skills of the worker.

Source: Group work record, Delhi School of Social Work.

ANNEXURE A10.2 PRINCIPLES OF GROUP WORK

1. Principles of planned group formation.
2. Principle of specific objectives.
3. Principle of purposeful worker–group member relationship.
4. Principle of guided group interaction.
5. Principle of progressive programme planning.
6. Principle of democratic group determination.
7. Principle of flexible functional group organisation.
8. Principle of continuous group evaluation.

Source: Trecker, H.B. 1970. Social Group Work Principles and Practice.
New York: New York Association Press.

ANNEXURE A10.3 GROUP WORK PLAN

Set-up: Community Centre in an Urban Slum
Basic information about the group:

Women's age group-Between 20 and 40 years

Number of members (20) –	Undergoing sewing training for 6 months.
Long-term objective –	To organise a work centre after their sewing class training is complete.
Short-term objectives –	To develop group bond amongst the women.
–	To motivate the women to start the work centre.
–	To develop the essential skills and know-how required in members to run a work centre.
Session planning –	Number of sessions—5
	Number of visits: 2
	Frequency of meeting—every day for 5 days
	Duration: 2 hours, timing: 2.00 p.m. to 4.00 p.m.

Place: Sewing class
Visit plan: One visit to the work centre run by Samajwadi, Mahila Sangathana
One visit to bank to submit the loan proposal.

(Annexure A10.3 Continued)

(Annexure A10.3 Continued)

Sr. No.	Specific Aim	Activity	Resources	Role of Worker
1.	To enable the members to understand the need and importance of additional income for the family To help the members to understand the importance of working together	Small group discussion topic: Need of finances for quality of life Small group discussion followed by presentation	Charts of family life cycle high-lighting needs of each stage Two case studies: (a) One woman working alone (b) A group of women working together	Facilitator, initiator, summariser, opinion giver, seeker Clarifier, enabler, motivator, encourager
2.	To discuss the elements required to be effective as a group–trust, cooperation, sharing	Two simulation games: trust walk and co-operation	Handkerchiefs for blindfolding, 6 rulers and 12 ribbons	Encourager, facilitator, Summariser
3.	To give specific information about working of a work centre and financial aspects for starting the centre	Lectures	Two experts: – Secretary of a work centre – Officer from bank	Liaison, networking, mediator
4.	To help the members to understand the important qualities required to compete in the market To plan the functioning of the work centre	Game: Preparing paper boats Discussion activities and responsibility planning	Old newspapers, Chart paper, sketch pens	Guide, clarifier, facilitator, encourager Organiser, expert, giving/seeking information, testing consensus
5.	To introduce all the members with the representatives of the organisation, which wants to place the order for aprons To finalise the contract and procedures of order and delivery	Discussion	Resource persons representatives	Networking, gate keeping, liasoning, encouraging, negotiating, directing, interpreting, and so on

(Annexure A10.3 Continued)

(Annexure A10.3 Continued)

Follow-up Plan

– Once a week meeting with members for the initial 3 months.
– Once a month meeting after 3 months.

Source: Prepared by the authors of this chapter.

ANNEXURE A10.4 EVALUATION FORMAT (FEEDBACK FROM GROUP MEMBERS)

Evaluation formats could be prepared by the group worker depending upon the literacy level and writing abilities of the group members.

A general format is given here:

	Name of group member
1.	What do you think the aims of this group were?
2.	How do you think these aims have been achieved?
	• Completely
	• To some extent
	• Not at all
3.	Three things you liked
4.	Three things you did not like
5.	In what way has being in the group helped you?

Source: Prepared by the authors of this chapter.

ANNEXURE A10.5 A CASE STUDY: A VILLAGE EXPERIENCE

It was a small village without any educational facilities. The local and other political leaders were indifferent to the development of the village. Some young men in the village, who were in the age group of 18–22 years and were members of a political youth group, came together and, after much thought, decided to do something about this situation. They started planning although they did not consult anyone in the village in this matter—neither the established leadership nor officials like the *sarpanch*.

This group of 6/7 youths started working with enthusiasm. They prepared plans about meeting their requirements of land for the school, building and school materials, capital to be raised, trained teachers to be hired and the like; and about how to make things available. The work started according to their plan.

The *sarpanch* of the village was a member of the political party in power in the state. He was not informed about any of this. When he came to know about it, he was very angry. His ego was hurt because he was not consulted nor even informed. Till then nothing in the village had happened without his knowledge and approval. He was stunned by this sudden emergence of this situation. When he came to know more about who had done it and how, he was greatly disturbed.

He started thinking about how to create a hindrance to the work going on, an obstruction that would totally stop the process. The boys were working hard but the work had not yet progressed much. He started and fed a rumour of money being misused and misappropriated. He caused problems with the building permit, and so on, by bringing pressure on the *gramsevak* who was earlier helpful to the youths. So far, the youths were well thought-of in the village because of their good work. But they quickly lost the good will of the villagers. In fact the villagers stopped being cooperative. The school construction stopped.

No one was ready to examine the reality of the situation. But at the same time all were aware of the need to appease the *sarpanch*.

What are the key factors in this?

What would you do to resolve this situation?

Note: These types of case studies can be prepared by the facilitator to help trainees to understand the type of material that can be used while working with groups.

ANNEXURE A10.6 ENGLISH TRANSLATION OF MARATHI SONGS WITH SOCIAL MESSAGES

1. SONG OF THE SELF-HELP GROUP

This song tells about the new concept of self-help group: The key concepts are:
The whole village should adopt the concept. The idea of circulating money among themselves should be taken to the women.
The money will grow and give strength and confidence to the group. New development will occur. The group can get rid of the moneylenders.
After awhile, when the group has money, they can think of starting an enterprise and be self-reliant.

2. SONG OF LIFE

I will clean my house and won't throw the garbage into my neighbour's yard.
I will start a small venture and take vegetables, milk, eggs to the market.
I will throw away blind faith and say no to black magic.
I will help my neighbours and when my son gets married I will demand no dowry.
I will think of my old age and save whatever I can.
I will go to evening school and learn to read and write like my children.

3. BEING TOGETHER

We are all equal/we will not fight
Everybody has the same right
We will sell our possessions/to pay off our debts
We will not drink/it will make us bankrupt
Men and women are equal/both are equally wise

Our daughters will study/we will not batter our wives
Mother-in-law, daughter-in-law/sisters-in-law as well
Fight no more/love will serve us well
My little girl I married off/came back in pain
I will educate her/her life will not be in vain
No more castes/no more discrimination
We all are children/of our one nation
The village will come together/all our troubles will fly away
Injustice-poverty-misery/will, for happiness of us all, make way

4. PRIMARY HEALTH CENTER

In a backward village/There was a hut
One evening from the hut/cries were heard
A woman was in labour/a baby was born
The midwife cut the cord/the woman had a convulsion
The woman died at once/no one knew how
What could we have done/we must know
For eighty thousand people/there is a primary health center
Convenient for all/for every one's health care
Scientifically run/free medical advice
Nurse examines every pregnant woman/doctor is nice
Women should go to the center/without anxiety or fear
When the delivery is in the center/childbirth is a happy hour

5. THE LITTLE PRINCE

Mother sings a lullaby/the little prince sleeps well
Taking good care of the baby/everything will be well
When a pregnant woman/takes care of her health
The baby is nourished well/it's good for its health
The baby is breastfed/it's a happy baby
Getting extra vitamins/it becomes chubby-chubby
The mother is alert/takes him for BCG
The baby will be/protected from TB
Give it triple vaccine/give it polio doses
They will protect it/from childhood diseases
Give it vitamin 'A'/give it nourishment
It will grow healthy/it will grow content

The original songs 1–5 are written by local people on topical subject matter in Marathi. They are easy to remember and to sing along. So, they become quickly popular and are used to initiate women's meetings, rallies and other programmes.

6. Ode to Jyotiba Phule

This is an ode to Mahatma Jyotiba Phule who started the movement of women's education in the year 1848. He lighted the lamp of learning for women who were confined to the home without education.

He rebelled in 1848. He taught his wife Savitri to read and write. The orthodox Hindus were furious and persecuted him but he started a school for girls.

The orthodox Hindus attacked him but he did not hesitate. He opened his own water reservoir for the poor backward classes. He spent his life in working for the uplift of women, dalits and the common people.

Let us get together for the emancipation of women/let us use this weapon break down the walls of tradition. This song about a social reformer Mahatma Jyotiba Phule is written by a regular poet. Such poems can be used for inspiration. Many such poems by known poets can be used in different languages.

The songs included here are of two types: one type is prepared by the common people who are involved either in implementing social programmes or the people themselves like women.

Second type is songs prepared by activists and these are sung to express the situation and try to inspire people to revolt or to unite.

Source: The original Marathi version of these songs are available with the Karve Institute of Social Service (KINSS), Pune.

Chapter 11

WORKING WITH COMMUNITIES

Nagmani Rao and Ujwala Masdekar

WHAT IS A COMMUNITY?

A geographically defined locality or a larger functional group where members are bound by common concerns, lifestyles and socio-cultural orientations, which guide or organise their lives and collective norms of functioning.

What types of communities can we work with in the context of their geographical location)?

1. Urban slums.
2. Rural communities.
3. Tribal communities.

At the first year level, the direct work area would most likely be urban slum communities although through visits and camps, there could be opportunities for some exposure to rural and tribal communities. It is important for a trainee social worker (TSW) to understand that each type of community has its characteristic features and specific needs.

Working with communities is one of the practice methods in social work. It involves a process whereby communities are organised to work towards their development. In this process of development, a professional change agent enables a community action system (comprising of individuals, groups and organisations) to engage in planned, collective action in order to deal with commonly felt problems. This process is initiated within a democratic framework, which lays emphasis on collaborative efforts, consensus building and building one's potentials and capacities through participation. Beginning with a process of relationship building, community work seeks to identify and prioritise needs, focusing on discontent and the desire for change. Community sections are encouraged and enabled to come together to seek alternatives and get mobilised for action. Through this process the community develops attitudes and practices of collaboration and solidarity.

The approach in community work ranges from a welfare approach (where 'target' populations are beneficiaries of services) to a developmental orientation (which seeks to enhance community capacities to work towards change) or social action and advocacy which is oriented towards mobilisation to bring about systemic changes, including changes in power relations. The nature and level of participation of community members vary according to the specific approach(es) adopted by an organisation. The TSW's roles would be defined within the framework of the agency's orientation with respect to community work. Apart from this, at the first year level, the TSW is given such exposure as would enable her/him to develop some basic skills and attitudes for working in communities. This is carried out through assigned tasks, which involve interaction with community members, gathering information to understand the community situation and needs and organising projects/ activities/campaigns, which draw the participation of community subsections and other relevant partners in the system.

Given the levels of practice and the multiplicity of skills required for working with communities, ideally speaking, students should be imparted with some basic skills in the first year and more advanced skill training should be given to students in community placements (in particular community development students) in the second year.

The sessions at the first year level would therefore cover the following units:

1. Entering the community: Making a positive representation of one self and the organisation; initiating community contacts and beginning a process of relationship building.
2. Understanding the community: Widening community contacts, gathering comprehensive information about the community and its problems, preparing the community profile and mapping.
3. Organising meetings with community groups: Identifying issues for bringing groups together; planning and conducting meetings that arrive at specific, goal-directed action plans.

The above units may span over four to six sessions, depending on the size of the group. Each session could last between 1.5 and 2.5 hours. The primary methods used in conducting the sessions are brainstorming (in small and the larger group), role plays, small group discussion followed by presentations and open discussions. Where time and group situation permit, feedback discussion can be followed by partial replay of simulated situations. Each session ends with concluding remarks, including some learning guidelines.

The skill lab sessions in community work try to initiate a process whereby TSWs can develop the skills and attitudes that would help TSWs develop an orientation towards community work. These are listed as follows:

SKILLS IN COMMUNITY WORK

Interactional Skills

These are used when

1. introducing oneself and seeking introductions;
2. expressing the purpose of a visit;
3. seeking information;
4. responding to reactions (both positive and hostile);
5. drawing participation/eliciting response(s);
6. motivating community members towards action for a planned activity or project and
7. developing positive image about workers and the organisation (represented), amongst community subsections.

Information Gathering and Assimilation Skills

These are used to gather pertinent information, which are useful for understanding community and planning programmes. The skills are used to:

1. Identify relevant sources of information.
2. Ask pertinent questions. Verify and confirm information by tapping different sources.
3. Record, classify and organise information into an integrated whole.
4. Utilise information to analyse community situation(s) and draw up plans for activities/programmes/campaigns within the framework of assigned tasks.

Observation Skills

These skills are important to understand both the obvious as well as the less obvious aspects of the community situation and dynamics. Keen observation helps the TSW to analyse the complex web of interactions and problems that exist in a community. This in turn helps to foresee obstacles and support in dealing with problems while working in communities. Observation therefore involves not only the use of the senses but also the development of analytical abilities 'to look below the surface' and 'read between the lines'.

Observation Skills are Drawn Upon When a TSW

1. walks around the community and assesses living patterns and conditions;
2. observes interactions between people (for example, at street corners, water taps, central meeting points—the *addas* or *kattas*);
3. observes reactions/responses to outsiders (for example, agency workers, officials, TSWs, and so on) or during conflict situations within the community and
4. visits homes in the community.

The understanding drawn from the observation also helps the TSW to develop maturity in both interaction as well as intervention as she/he develops the ability to anticipate probable reactions from different subsections to initiatives taken in the process of development.

Listening and Responding Skills

The TSW expresses these through facial expressions, body language and tone and manner of talking. They should be such as would evoke interest and enthusiasm of the community members. The development of these skills involves:

1. Alertness to a variety of communication messages—direct and subtle, simple and complex, verbal and non-verbal, and so on.
2. Showing interest in ways that stimulate response and help to draw people out to express their interests.
3. Responding to information queries, opinion seeking efforts, clarifications sought by community members, and so on.

Organising Skills

Since the purpose of community work is to stimulate people to become proactive, the worker is a key entity to bring them together for planned action. As an organiser the worker recognises the value of people's participation, creates spaces whereby community members get involved at their own pace and in accordance with their potentials. Procedures are devised that encourage and nurture participation. By drawing their involvement, the worker facilitates the development of capacities and leadership amongst the community members. Organising skills therefore enable the TSW to:

1. motivate and encourage people to come together;
2. arrive at consensus;
3. develop mutual sensitivity and remove blocks to participation;
4. provide or create access to information and exposures that would motivate joint action;
5. deal with some aspects of group dynamics;
6. facilitate planning and review by community members and
7. deal with and dissipate negative, hostile reactions.

Box 11.1 presents an illustrative overview of task areas of community work and the skills that would need to be used.

While the above-mentioned task areas appear to indicate a sequential nature, in reality they are interlinked and many of them could be performed simultaneously. Some of the skills would be used continuously while others may be specific to particular tasks.

The community worker plays a range of roles such as enabler, guide, expert, social therapist, advocate, activist, while also carrying out roles that involve fund-raising and

Box 11.1   Task Areas of Community Work and Skills Needed

Task Area	Skills
Understanding the community	Information gathering and assimilation, interactive communication, observation and responding skills
Building community relations	Communication and interaction, listening and responding skills
Community diagnosis and power structure analysis	Close, critical observation, in-depth inquiry using formal as well as informal methods of interaction, triangulation, social mapping and other participatory methods, socio-political analysis skills
Assessment and prioritisation of community problems	Conducting meetings to focus on discontent and raise issues for action, drawing participation, handling conflicts/hostilities/apathy, negotiation and arbitration skills; planning and organising skills
Preparing and implementing action plans	Skills in training for team building, budgeting, planning, resource mobilisation, use of local culture and media for awareness generation and community mobilisation, public speaking and writing skills for campaigning support, and so on.
Sustaining action for change	Skills for tapping and developing local leadership, liaison and networking, documentation and recording, making critical evaluation and review as base for future planning, drawing media and public support (addressing press conferences, preparing press releases, mass level programme/event management skills, and so on)

Source: Prepared by Nagmani Rao.

networking. However, many of these roles are carried out at a more advanced stage of training and experience and are hence more specialised in nature. The first year skill training confines itself to those aspects that are required for an essentially primary level of work, which involves developing skills for relationship building and community understanding.

One of the factors that need to be emphasised at the outset of orientation to community level work is that bringing change in the communities is often a slow process. As an outsider coming into the community, the TSW has to consciously work towards removing barriers (created by differences in ideological values, social and economic background, and so on) if she/he seeks to draw response to the efforts made.

This is imperative for gaining acceptance to work in the communities. It involves the development of attitudes that evoke respect and draw people towards oneself.

Some of the important attitudes that therefore need to be highlighted through the skill lab sessions are as follows:

1. Patience to work at the pace of the people rather than pushing or dragging them along.
2. Warmth, reflected in interaction and sharing in the lives of people and showing compassion for their situations.
3. Flexibility and openness in adapting to new situations, overcoming biases and not imposing one's own values.
4. Sensitivity, with a belief in democratic values and acceptance of differences.
5. Respect towards and faith in people's abilities and experiential knowledge. This means being able to learn from the people also.
6. Optimism reflected in persistence and sustained enthusiasm even when faced with difficulties.
7. Orientation towards people shown through non-hierarchical behaviour, simplicity of demeanour and a commitment to equality.
8. Constantly seeking new learning and sharing and spreading knowledge.

CONDUCTING THE SESSIONS

The basic orientation for working in communities can be divided into three units.

Unit One: Entering the Community

Unit One takes the TSWs through sessions(s) that help them to be comfortable while entering into an unknown community, being able to interact purposefully and projecting a positive image about one self and the organisation in the community (Image 11.1).
Methods and time required:

1. Open Discussion: 20 minutes.
2. Group Discussion: 20–30 minutes.
3. Enacting Role Play: 10–15 minutes
4. Feedback and discussion on role play and partial replay: 40 minutes

Material required: Open space to perform the role play.
No. of participants: 6–8 volunteers for each role play situation, others as observers.
Objectives:

1. To identify situations for making first contact in the community and learn techniques for locating individuals/households.
2. To understand how to begin and end a conversation.
3. To know how to respond to queries and clarify doubts/overcome suspicions.
4. To understand how to build a positive image of the self and organisation in the community.

Image 11.1   Enter the Community Role Play

Source: Mukund D. Sawant, Producer, Centre for Media and Cultural Studies, TISS.

Process:

1. Brainstorm about task situations that would involve first contact with the community. These would be based on the agency situation of TSWs.
2. Select a few situations. Possible situations that can be portrayed:

    • A number of parents have not paid the fees for the Balwadi programme. To avoid reminders they have stopped sending their children to the pre-school. The TSW is assigned the task of locating the houses in an urban slum and meeting the parents regarding this issue.
    • The agency wants to begin work in a new community. The TSW is assigned the task of meeting key persons and after self-introductions, discusses the organisation's work and intention to start working in this community. The TSW has to indicate

through the role play how key persons were identified and located and the process of conversation with them.

- In an area where the agency has been working for sometime the TSWs (group of 2–3) are sent to the community for the first time. The TSWs are instructed by their agency supervisor to walk around the community to observe living conditions, infrastructural amenities and facilities and common patterns of interaction in the community. They are to record their impressions and experiences.

3. Divide the class into role play performing and observer groups.
4. Ask each of the (role playing) groups to move out of the main hall and discuss how they want to present the situation.
5. Discuss with the observer group key aspects to be observed.

Note to the facilitator: The types of situations to be portrayed can be modified/adapted to local conditions/field placement situations. While developing the role play, instruct the performers to integrate the following situations that a trainee worker will need to handle:

1. Responding to queries.
2. Addressing curious questions regarding the purpose of a visit.
3. Explaining about the organisation that she/he is representing, and so on.
4. Responding to reactions of the parents and neighbours.

Highlight:

1. How did the TSWs approach the community members while trying to identify locations?
2. How did they introduce themselves?
3. How did they convey the purpose of their visit to the community informants and respond to their questions?
4. In what way did they provide information about the organisation?
5. How did the workers introduce the purpose of visit and how did the visit conclude? Why did it conclude in the way it did?
6. What kind of attitudes and values did the TSWs reflect through the style of talking, content and tone of conversation, facial expressions and reactions?

After discussion replay selected parts based on the above-said feedback. This would help observe if TSWs have consciously absorbed the critical feedback to make improvements. Sum up the session by:

1. Highlighting important 'Do's and Don'ts' while making the first visit (Box 11.2).

Box 11.2   First Impressions Count

Do's	*Don'ts*
1. Greet people politely ('Namaste', 'I am looking for ...') 2. Introduce self and organisation briefly, giving essential information only. 3. While moving around the community, acknowledge people with a nod, a smile, and so on. Stop to have brief conversations with them. 4. Speak in a language that people can understand. 5. Accept tea if people insist and offer on their own. But also tell them that you would be coming to the community regularly and they should not bother to give you special treatment. 6. First impressions count. It is therefore important to be sensitive to local cultural norms. Therefore, be conscious while showing reactions, ways of dressing and behaviour, and so on.	1. Don't share unnecessary information with people who are not concerned with the issue. 2. Even if you see disagreeable sights (for example, filth all around) don't show your discomfort in an obvious way. 3. Don't raise false expectations by making unrealistic commitments of what you/the organisation can do. 4. When in a group, don't behave/interact in ways that draw negative attention towards you (for example, talking and laughing loudly, teasing each other). 5. When people show indifference or negative reactions to you or about the organisation don't get agitated and don't get into arguments. 6. Don't project your values and ideology at the first instant.

2. Highlighting important details and attitudes to be developed for establishing a positive impression during first contact.

Unit Two: Understanding the Community

In this unit, a TSW develops an understanding about the relevance and content of community study, sources to be tapped and the process of drawing information and presenting the community profile (Annexures A11.1 and A11.2.

The unit is divided into three parts. Part I discusses the importance, content and sources for compiling the community profile, the second part demonstrates the process of gathering information about the community and the last part is the community mapping exercise. These may be conducted as consecutive sessions on different days or as a day-long workshop.

Methods and time required:

Part I

1. Group discussion (brainstorming) and presentation—75 minutes.
2. Finalising the outline for community profile—15 minutes.

Part II

1. Recap of previous session and instructions—20 minutes.
2. Preparation and presentation of role play—45 minutes.
3. Discussion, summing up—45 minutes.

Part III

1. Recap of previous session and instructions for community mapping—20 minutes.
2. Mapping exercise—45 minutes (restrict the area to be covered).
3. Drawing the map(s)—45 minutes.
4. Summing up—20 minutes.

Materials required: Many chart papers (at least two for each group), pencils, erasers, markers and sketch pens; community pocket for mapping; space for role play.

No. of participants: All for Parts I and III; for Part II, 7–8 role play performers and the remaining as observers.

Objectives of the unit:

1. To understand why community study is important for working in communities.
2. To draw up the list of relevant information required for understanding the community as well as list key informants for the same.
3. To get insights into the process of gathering community information and likely obstacles that one may face.
4. To obtain guidelines for assimilating the information for presentation as a community profile (Annexure A11.3).
5. To understand how to prepare and utilise a community map.

Note to the facilitator: The first and second objectives can be covered in the first session, the next two in the second session and the last objective can be covered in a separate, independent session.

Process:

Part I

1. Introduce the session outline and its three parts.
2. Break up the entire class into small groups (maximum 10 members) to discuss the following:

   (a) Why is it important to understand the community?
   (b) What do we mean by 'understanding the community'?
   (c) What is the information we need to gather?
   (d) Who/what would be the key information sources?

3. Give chart papers and markers to each group with the following instructions:

  (a) They should list the components of community profile under categorised subheads.
  (b) They should list sources for each set of information.

4. Display the charts in the training hall, discuss and fill in gaps, if any.

Note to the facilitator: At the end of the session, integrate the group discussion into a comprehensive outline and prepare a systematic, formal outline and instruction sheet for the community profile prior to the next session. Circulate this to the field supervisors for them to reinforce the learning during field work discussions.

Part II

1. Begin with a recap of the previous session and highlight that the finalised content of the community profile must be thoroughly understood before information gathering begins.

2. Discuss the process of information gathering which involves:

  (a) observation;
  (b) discussions with individuals;
  (c) small group informal discussion;
  (d) focus group discussions with specific community subsections and
  (e) looking through available secondary sources.

3. Invite volunteers for role play for community study. Facilitate role play planning that portrays a situation of information gathering from a variety of sources and the use of different methods (Annexure A 11.2).

4. Give instructions to the observers to observe:

  (a) How TSWs introduced themselves and explained the purpose of seeking information.
  (b) How questions were sequenced.
  (c) How resistance of key informants was tackled.
  (d) How data gathered was recorded.
  (e) How information was verified/cross-checked.
  (f) Images projected by TSWs during information gathering process and what kinds of impressions are made on community members, as a result.

5. Presentation of role play, followed by open discussion. Highlight through a open discussion:

  (a) Need for prior planning and preparedness of TSW for information gathering.
  (b) Identification and selection of key informants: extent to which they represent different community interests.
  (c) Type of information sought from each set of informants (asking questions relevant to informant's capacity to answer). Effective techniques to draw out key informants.

(d) Spontaneity, natural behaviour and informal techniques of information gathering.

(e) Need to be sensitive to cultural specificities, time priorities and interests of key informant(s).

(f) Barriers created to the process because of TSW's anxiety to 'collect information as a task given' rather than the conviction about establishing community contact through the process.

(g) Manner of recording—during discussion or after; if during discussion, taking prior permission from the informant to write down the information.

(h) Manner of giving opinions/reactions to questions raised by informants—whether it takes forward the process or evokes hostility leading to premature closing of discussion.

(i) Persistence shown to overcome resistance/apathy.

6. Based on the earlier discussion sum up with 'Do's and Don'ts' while seeking community information (Box 11.3).

Note to the facilitator: This is a suggestive list, which may have add-one/modifications according to local situations.

End the session by sharing 'Qualities for an Effective Community Worker' (Annexure A11.4) and ask TSWs to reflect on which are the qualities they have and which they need to develop in themselves.

Part III: Preparing a Community Map

Method: Guided discussion followed by practical exercise.
Materials required: Rough papers, pencils, chart papers, markers and sketch pens.
Participants: All.
Objectives:

1. To develop skills to draw a community map.
2. To gain an understanding about the use of maps to analyse the community situation.

Process:

1. Do a recap of the previous session and break the entire class into small groups of 5–6 TSWs.
2. Discuss with the groups:

   (a) Importance of the mapping exercise.

   - Gives the worker an idea of the approximate layout and spread of the community.
   - Helps locate infrastructure and amenities in the community.
   - The base map could be used to locate and analyse:

Box 11.3   Seeking Community Information: Guidelines

Do's

1. Be polite, pleasant in your manner while talking to people.
2. Begin conversations with an informal interaction or ice-breaking questions.
3. Be clear about explaining the purpose of seeking information and how this information will help you/the organisation to carry out work in the community.
4. If people raise doubts/suspicions clarify these honestly and sincerely.
5. Talk to people when they are available: flexibility of work time is important.
6. Be sensitive to people's time. If they are resting, busy in some other activity, getting ready to go out, and so on, show that you are willing to come back at a time more convenient to them.
7. Use words to address people that reflect respect and facilitate rapport building (for example, 'Tai'—elder sister, 'Bhau'—brother, 'Maushi/Kaki'—aunty, 'Mama/Kaka'—uncle, 'Ajji/Azoba'—grandmother/grandfather)
8. Frame questions in a simple form, using words that people can understand.
9. Use colloquial language, familiarise yourself with the local words.
10. Allow people to talk and express opinions.
11. Personal questions may be addressed to you. Answer these to the extent necessary without going into detailed information about oneself.
12. Remember to draw the lines between personal and professional relationship. This is particularly essential while interacting with the opposite sex.

Dont's

1. Don't force people to respond to you. You can be persuasive, but not insistent.
2. Particularly during the initial period of contact, don't get into arguments about sensitive/controversial issues that reflect strong ideologies. Even later, once you have been accepted, you may express your viewpoints in a non-imposing, non-judgemental way.
3. Don't frame negative questions that can put informant(s) on the defensive.
4. Don't block hostile/negative reactions to you/your organisation. Instead, probe to understand why such reactions have emerged.
5. Request people not to address you as 'sir' or 'madam' or 'saheb'. This creates unnecessary hierarchies.
6. Consciously avoid using foreign words (English, and so on) or jargon-heavy language that tend to widen distances between 'you' and 'them'.
7. Don't make the information gathering process sound like a formal interview unless you are conducting a survey.
8. Avoid standing and talking down to people. Sit with the group (for example, if people are sitting at ground level, join the circle instead of sitting on a chair).
9. Don't be so anxious to please people, that your appreciation seems artificial and hypocritical.
10. Don't try to collect all information at one shot.
11. Don't write down the information/tape record without obtaining prior permission or if informants reflect discomfort about this.

(b) Economic distinctions (class/occupational groups).

(c) Social distinctions in spatial patterns (regional/caste/religion-based segregation in housing patterns).

(d) Mapping location of organisation's beneficiary/participant groups.

(e) Mapping household locations of key persons/opinion shapers/influential leaders.

3. Ask the groups to go to different clusters.

4. Give instructions on how to carry out mapping exercise as follows:

(a) Establish directions

(b) Locate important landmarks as you walk across and through the community, covering it as comprehensively as possible as a group [transect walk technique of Participatory Rural Appraisal(PRA)].

(c) Identify central and periphery points and mark these on the map.

(d) Draw up list of symbols index (*kirana* shop (neighbourhood grocery store), *anganwadi* (a government sponsored child-care and mother-care center in India), dispensary, barber shop, community hall, toilet units, and so on).

(e) Draw up colour index for economic and social components you want to highlight through mapping.

(f) Draw a rough map.

(g) Show and discuss this with various groups with whom you have established contact (for example, *mahila mandal* members, youth group members, senior citizens from the community, agency field workers, older children).

(h) Make modifications/corrections additions as required.

(i) Finalise the maps on a larger sheet (including thematic maps) and attach this to the community profile. Note: The map need not be to scale.

5. Carry out a practical exercise of mapping. Depending on availability/access, this may be done:

(a) On the campus.

(b) By sending the TSWs to nearby, small communities where the institution has contacts.

(c) By guiding students to do it in their community agency settings and later sharing their experiences.

See Annexure A11.5 for an example of a community map prepared by a TSW. One can prepare different types of maps to get better insights to the community situation.

At the end of the exercise, ask the trainees to present their finalised maps and conduct a critical discussion on these. Take them through a small demonstrative exercise on how they can analyse the content. Caution the trainee workers that in the actual fieldwork situation mapping should never be carried out during the initial period of community contact as this can arouse fear and suspicion.

Note to the Facilitator: The mapping exercise can take a long time, sometimes taking several days. It would be effective, if during the lab session, the area for mapping is restricted to a small pocket that would take up to a maximum of 45 minutes to cover.

Unit Three: Conducting Meetings in the Community

This unit involves deciding on relevant issues for which meetings are required, planning and preparing for the meeting, inviting/gathering the participants for the same and conducting meetings to arrive at logical conclusions.

Methods: Brainstorming, role play and group discussion.

Time required:

1. Brainstorming and themes selection—15 minutes.
2. Preparation for the role play—20–30 minutes.
3. Group discussion and open sharing—45 minutes.

No. of participants: All for brainstorming and discussion, 10 for the role play and the rest as observers.

Material required: Space (preferably on an elevated area or at the centre in a circularly arranged room) and blackboard or chart paper.

Objectives:

1. To understand the relevance and purpose of conducting meetings.
2. To learn how to prepare for and organise meetings.
3. To get an understanding about the stages involved in conducting meetings that arrive at logical conclusions.
4. To enhance skills required to conduct meetings that are participatory in nature.

Process:

1. Ask the class to brainstorm (open discussion) on possible themes for conducting meetings in the community.
2. List the themes that emerge on the blackboard/chart.
3. Select any of the situations through consensus (any two could be selected).
4. Draw volunteers for the role play and facilitate preparation for role play.
5. Give guidelines for observation to the observer group.
6. After the role play break the class into groups for discussion about the role play.

Highlight through discussions:

1. Manner of inviting people for the meeting.
2. Sitting arrangements and how these facilitated/blocked participation.

3. Assessment of worker's preparation for taking the meeting through its stages:

   (a) Ice-breaking.
   (b) Introducing purpose of meeting.
   (c) Presentation for a discussion (style, tone, clarity, simplicity).
   (d) Arriving at conclusion and deciding follow-up.

4. Assessment of techniques to draw audience participation.
5. Manner of tackling disturbances and cross purpose discussions.
6. Handling dominating influences during the meeting.
7. Handling disagreements and manner of arriving at consensus.
8. Assessment of techniques used in conducting the meeting taking into consideration availability of time, resources and audience background.

Sum up the session by emphasising:

1. The importance of prior preparation and practice at public speaking.
2. Controlling hesitation, showing confidence.
3. Adapting style, techniques and language of presentation keeping in mind the audience (age, literacy, socio-cultural background, and so on).
4. Necessity that the meeting must end with some decision arrived at, through consensus, regarding follow-up action/responsibilities sharing, date, time, venue for next meeting and contact points during the interim period.

CONCLUSION

As already mentioned, community work is a highly complex area of practice requiring the development of multifarious skills. Within the short span of skill training sessions, it is difficult to capture all the complexities and also equip the trainees comprehensively and specifically as lab situations would be limited by the fact that every possible field situation cannot be predicted or replicated in a simulated environment. The challenge before the educator is therefore to keep improvising and evolving according to new experiences faced.

ANNEXURE A11.1 SOURCES OF INFORMATION FOR COMMUNITY UNDERSTANDING

- Trainee social worker's own observations.
- Agency supervisor, field workers in the agency of placement.
- Local *mandal*s (men, youth, women).
- Senior citizens.
- Opinion leaders/community influentials.
- Formal leaders.
- Ward officers/other government employees directly dealing with community problems or issues.
- School/*balwadi* teachers and *anganwadi* workers.
- Doctors running clinics/dispensaries in the community.
- Available reports/data compiled by agency or others.
- Municipal Corporation records (if accessible).

Source: Prepared by the authors of this chapter.

ANNEXURE A11.2 ROLE PLAY SITUATIONS FOR INFORMATION GATHERING FROM KEY PERSONS FOR 'UNDERSTANDING THE COMMUNITY'

1. Talk to the *balwadi/anganwadi* workers to get information about the children in the community.
2. Go to the ward office and collect official demographic data about the population, infrastructure facilities, legal position of households, survey number, and so on.
3. Meet community leaders and find out about organisations and *mandal*s working in the community, government schemes, occupational pattern, political influences, common community problems, political affiliations, their contributions.
4. Meet members of *mandal*s, workers of NGOs and other community-based organisations to find out about their work and their perceptions about community people and their problems.
5. Meet senior citizens/old time residents in the community and collect historical information about the community.

Source: Prepared by the authors of this chapter.

ANNEXURE A11.3 COMMUNITY PROFILE (GUIDELINES)

Method of collecting information, discussion with community members and leaders, observations of community situations and data from secondary sources:

1. Name of the Community
2. Geographical Location (Give following details)

    (a) Survey
    (b) Prominent landmarks near and around the community
    (c) Direction bearings (north, south, east, west)

(d) If possible, locate your community on area/city map

(e) Landmarks like temple, daily provision store

3. Origins of the community and its development

   (a) When and how established

   (b) Important stages of expansion/development

4. Type of Community (Urban/Semi-urban/rural)

5. Community Characteristics (Give Proportion/Percentage wherever possible)

   (a) Demographic: Population composition in terms of age group, gender, religion, region (or origin), caste, and so on.

   (b) Occupational patterns (Male + Female differentials), skilled, unskilled.

   (c) Literacy and educational status (Age and Gender Differentials)

   (d) Common Leisure Time Activities (Age-wise, gender-wise)

   (e) Special cultural characteristics
   (Common festivals and events in which community members participate, their cultural significance, manner of celebration, and so on.)

6. Infrastructure Status (Facilities and Amenities)
   (Describe facilities numerically in proportion to population, their quality and location—whether within the community or outside, if outside, distance from the community.)

   (a) Housing patterns, types of structures (*pucca*, semi-pucca, kutcha)

   (b) Water supply (frequency of supply, timings, include also sources, whether individual connections or public/shared facilities)

   (c) Sanitation (Toilet, drainage + garbage disposal)

   (d) Road (Nature: [*kutcha*/tarred], width: [narrow/wide])

   (e) Electric Supply (domestic, public)

   (f) Health Services (government and private, type of practitioners (BAMS, MBBS, traditional healer, nature of illness treated, and so on)

   (g) Education Services (government/private, up to which level)

   (h) Daily use consumer good services (market, provision store, ration shop, wheat grinding unit [giran] public telephone booths, and so on)—list all available services and their location

   (i) Other miscellaneous (barber, cycle repair, places of worship, and so on)

   (j) Transport and communication (public/private phones)

   (k) Recreational facilities

7. Formal and Informal Associations (*Mandal*s in the Community)
   Details such as member composition (age, occupation, socio-political leaning, and so on) their activities and how different community sections perceive them.

8. Organisations (Government and NGOs) Working in the Community

   (a) Type of organisation

   (b) Nature of organisation

   (c) Since when working in this community

   (d) Programmes and activities

   (e) Outreach (what sections of the community benefited, approximately how many benefited by these organisations).

9. Dominant Political Groups/Parties Exerting Influence on the Community
10. Profile of Community Leaders

    (a) Who they are

    (b) Their background (social, economic, political, since when residents of the community)

    (c) Whose interests do they represent?

    (d) What kind of issues/problems do they tackle in the community?

    (e) Their contributions to the community (to be cross-checked through discussions with community sections whose interests they claim to represent)

    (f) Nature of relationship with other identified community leaders—cooperative allies/indifferent/in conflict or competition.

    (g) Leader's opinion about and their relationship with the organisation where the trainee social worker is placed.

Based on the above-said information students should make an analytical assessment of the leadership structure and their potential in blocking or furthering the community development efforts of the agency.

11. Existing resources within the community (list both material and human resources from the point of view of development intervention)
12. Common problems identified for intervention (list in priority order)
13. Of above, which are the problems addressed by your organisation and which are the problems not addressed and reasons for the same.
14. Diagnostic statement about the community
   (The statement gives in brief the trainee worker's assessment about the scope of work in the community and what could be the possible strategies)

Note: While presenting community profile, specify

1. Sources of information
2. No. of days spent in collecting information
3. No. of hours required

Instruction to facilitator: The community profile is prepared over two terms. In the first term, only a general understanding is expected and the detailed profile as per above-mentioned guidelines is submitted in the second term. However, this may be modified according to local training requirements.

Source: Prepared by the authors of this chapter.

ANNEXURE A11.4 DESIRABLE QUALITIES FOR BECOMING AN EFFECTIVE WORKER IN COMMUNITIES

(Note: The list is suggestive rather than a comprehensive list and can be expanded through discussion.)

- Conscientious.
- High awareness and variety of source of information.
- Having vision, commitment and progressive attitude.
- Open, non-biased and flexible.
- Selfless.
- Non-partisan.
- Good organising ability.
- Inspiring personality.
- Optimistic and enthusiastic.
- Good stamina.
- Calm tempered.
- Confident.
- Simple in dress and manners.
- Warm, with ability to relate to all kinds of people with spontaneity.
- Belief in equality (democratic values) and non-hierarchical behaviour.
- Reliable (fulfils commitments).
- Having leadership and decision making abilities.
- Knowledge seeker and knowledge giver.
- Good speaker.
- Having firmness and courage.
- Compassionate and sensitive.
- Patient and persistent.
- Ability to communicate in a simple and direct way.

Source: Prepared by the authors of this chapter.

ANNEXURE A11.5 EXAMPLE OF A COMMUNITY MAP

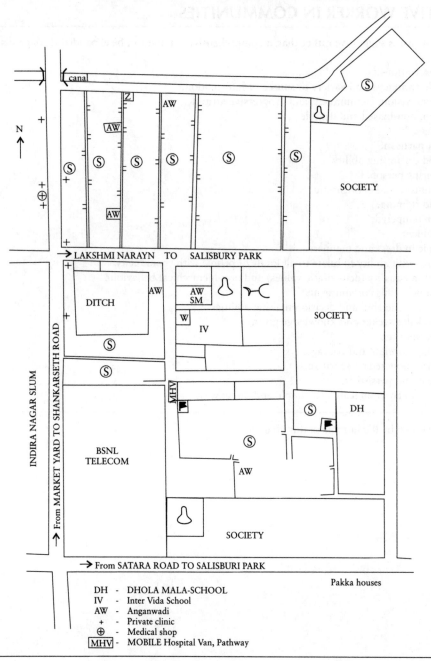

DH - DHOLA MALA-SCHOOL
IV   - Inter Vida School
AW - Anganwadi
 +   - Private clinic
⊕ - Medical shop
MHV - MOBILE Hospital Van, Pathway

(Annexure A11.5 Continued)

(Annexure A11.5 Continued)

General Map Signs

The thick cluster of houses, slum (Basti)	Ⓢ
Hindu temples	⚑
Mosque	⊤⊂
Gallis	═
Roads	─
Bridge	)(
Nagar shed office	Z
Cow shed	CS
Open cement platform	CP
Samaj mandir	SM
Toilets	⬙
Garbage bin	●
Ambedkar chowk	●

Source: Map is prepared by a student social worker as part of his fieldwork task.
Note: This map is not to scale and does not depict authentic boundaries.

GLOSSARY

Advocacy The act of directly representing or defending others; in social work, championing the rights of individuals or communities through direct intervention or through empowerment.

Affect A vital feeling, mood or emotion characterised by specific physiological (psychological) changes and states.

Agency An organisation and facility governed by a board of directors and usually staffed by human service personnel (including professional social workers, members of other professions, sub-professional specialists), clerical personnel and sometimes indigenous workers to provide a specified range of social services for members of a population group that has or is vulnerable to a specific social problem.

Assessment The process of determining the nature, cause, progression and prognosis of a problem and the personalities and situations involved therein; the social work function is acquiring an understanding of a problem, what causes it and what can be changed to minimise or resolve it.

Attention Acts or faculty of applying one's mind; notice.

Attitudes A learnt and enduring tendency to perceive or act towards persons or situations in a particular way. It is useful to see attitudes as involving three elements: (*a*) a cognitive component—beliefs and ideas; (*b*) an affective component—values and emotions; (*c*) a behavioural component—predisposition to act and actions.

Audio media A channel of communication which depends upon auditory messages alone, in the form of speech, music (vocal or instrumental), sounds, etc.

Audio-visual media	A channel of communication that uses auditory and visual images in combination to make it more dynamic and attractive to the audience.
Behaviour	Any observable action of a person or animal. It is a response of a living organism to its environment. Behaviour could be covert or implicit. Environment which is the cause of reaction is called stimulus. It could be internal or external.
Casework	The orientation, value system and type of practice used by professional social workers in which psychosocial, behavioural and systems concepts are translated into skills designed to help individuals and families solve intra-psychic, interpersonal, socioeconomic and environmental problems through direct face-to-face relationships.
Channel	The medium through which the message travels.
Client	The individual, group, family or community that seeks and is provided with professional services.
Cognition	It encompasses the processes by which knowledge of an object is attained, including perception, memory and imagination.
Communication process	The steps between a source and a receiver that result in the transfer and understanding of meaning.
Communities	A set of social relationships operating within certain boundaries, locations or territories.
Community action system	The organisation of groups to achieve change within the community.
Congruence	Suitableness of one thing to another; agreement; consistency.
Conscientisation	Learning to perceive social, political and economic contradictions—developing a critical awareness—so that individuals can take action against the oppressive elements of reality.
Decision making	The processes by which individuals or groups and organisations, decide actions or determine policies.
Dependent aid	A channel while using to enhance communication, depends upon other aids like electricity or technical support.
Empathy	The capacity of a person to put oneself in somebody else's situation and understand the feelings and emotions involved.

Feedback	It is transforming information about the results of an action to the individual who performed that action. The check on how successful we have been in transferring our messages as originally intended. It determines whether understanding has been achieved.
Group acceptance	Recognition by members of a group of each other's positive worth as a human being without necessarily condoning an individual's actions.
Group development	How the relationships in a group are changing in time and in relation to specific situations and events in the life span of a group. Generally, the well-known models of group development identify a linear arrangement of development stages, where one stage is expected to precede or follow the other stage, such as forming, storming, norming, performing and adjourning.
Group dynamics	The flow of information and exchanges of influence between members of a social collective. These exchanges can be modified by group leaders or helping professionals and used to achieve certain predetermined objectives that may benefit the members.
Group formation	Bringing together a number of people to interact with each other on a regular basis, with a common identity, a feeling of unity and shared goals and norms.
Group	A number of people who interact with each other on regular basis.
Independent aid	The channel which is complete in itself and can be used as it is by the communicator.
Inference	An act of conclusion, the act or process of deriving logical conclusions from premises known or assumed to be true, act of reasoning from factual knowledge or evidence.
Interactional skills	Interaction in a group is a natural phenomena; it begins as people come face to face in a situation, interaction skills involve listening, responding, feeling, paraphrasing, clarifying, information sharing, reflecting and referring.
Interactive techniques	The use of skills by the trainer to draw out the involvement of the participants in the training sessions. This helps trainees to express themselves and brings out their potentials.

Interpersonal relationship	Interaction/rapport between a group worker and individual members and also between members which facilitates group interaction. It is the ability to relate to and work with others in achieving specific social goals.
Meaningful relationship	Interaction/rapport established for a purpose which could be a problem resolution, minimising of the problem or enhancing coping.
Message	The actual physical product from the sender's encoding.
Networking	The social worker's therapeutic efforts to enhance and develop the social linkages that might exist between the client, such as family members, friends, neighbours and associates.
Non-judgemental	A term pertaining to a fundamental element in the social worker-client relationship, in which the worker demonstrates an attitude of tolerance and an unwillingness to censor the client for any actions. The worker does not suspend judgement but conveys to the client that the working relationship takes precedence over any possible feelings of disapproval.
Non-verbal communication	It includes body movements, intonations or emphasis we give towards facial expressions and the physical distance between the sender and receiver.
Objectivity	The ability to evaluate a situation, social phenomenon or person without prejudice or subjective distortion.
Observation	It refers to the ability of a person to understand things by using simple observation techniques, a keen observer is able to observe small and simple facts which others ignore or consider unimportant.
Participatory learning	It includes the ways in which a learner contributes in diverse ways to individual and shared learning goals. It includes the ways in which new technologies enable learners (of any age) to contribute in diverse ways to individual and shared learning goals. Through games, wikis, blogs, virtual environments, social network sites, cell phones, mobile devices and other digital platforms, learners can participate in virtual communities where they share ideas, comment upon one another's projects, and plan, design, advance, implement, or simply discuss their goals and ideas together. Participatory learners come together to aggregate their ideas and experiences in a way that makes the whole ultimately greater than the sum of the parts.

Participatory methodology	It refers to the methods used in the teaching learning process which encourage/stimulate active involvement and contribution from the learners.
Personality	An integrated dynamic organisation of the physical, mental, moral and social qualities of the individual as they manifest to other people in the give and take of social life.
Person/individual	A single human considered apart from a society or community.
Photo language	A set of black and white photographs which are consciously compiled such that the photographs 'talk' to the people there by stimulating their selection. The people then 'talk through' these photographs to express their thoughts, feelings, visions or experiences.
Planned intervention	It is the use of well thought out steps to be taken based on the diagnosis. This could be to prevent or alleviate a problem situation.
Problem	A situation, matter, or person that presents perplexity or difficulty.
Procedural skills	Knowing how-that is, skills. The correct way of doing something following a clear and systematic sequence.
Professional change agent	A social worker or other helping professional or group of helpers whose purpose is to facilitate some improvement.
Professional self	It reflects the professional personality which gives focus, content and direction to social work processes and assures accountability to society. Knowledge, attitudes values and skills are crucial for social workers and when internalised it reflects professional self.
Receiver	The object to whom the message is directed.
Response behaviour	Usually the term is used to indicate a discrete form of behaviour such as a knee jerk, salivation or pressing of a key, but the term also applies to broadly defined behaviours such as bringing home flowers for one's spouse or expressing anger to the social worker after being turned down in a request for assistance.
Role	A concept taken primarily from sociological theory. A role is the behavioral and attitudinal content of a social position.
Self-acceptance	Self-awareness presupposes self-acceptance which generates self-esteem. Knowledge of one's own strengths builds up self-esteem and self-esteem is necessary for the social worker for building up confidence and hope with regard to the tasks of helping.

Self-awareness   This involves developing awareness of one's own thoughts, feelings, attitudes, strengths, weaknesses, biases, behaviours and their effect on others.

Self-concept   It is a detailed pervasive set of ideas about the self. It develops in early childhood and persists throughout life. It is a cognitive accomplishment but has its roots in social interaction.

Self-disclosure   A revelation of personal information, values and behaviours to the clients.

Self-esteem   An individual's sense of personal worth that is derived more from inner thoughts and values than from praise and recognition from others.

Self-image   It is supported by normalising fears and reactions and validating strengths or successes.

Self-respect   It is to consider worthy of esteem; to regard with honour.

Self   A mental construction of the person, by the person, but inevitably formed from social experience. Thus the person sees himself/herself reflected by others, in their reactions, and these are interpreted through the lattice of self perception. MEAD (1934) is particularly associated with this idea of the self as being a social construction; self cannot exist without society—the self is where knowledge resides, but the knowledge is about society, which surrounds it.

Semantics   The subdivision of linguistics concerned with meaning. It attempts the systematic study of the assignment of meanings to minimal meaning-bearing elements and the combination of these in the production of more complex meaningful expression.

Sensitivity   The capacity for or an act of responding to a stimulus.

Simulation game   A technique whereby reality situations are nearly replicated such that learners can go through the experiences in a controlled and less threatening environment whereby they can become critically aware about their own thinking, behaviour, attitudes and reactions.

Skills   The familiar knowledge of any art or science, united with readiness and dexterity in execution or performance, or in the application of the art or science to practical purposes; power to discern and execute; ability to perceive and perform; expertness; aptitude; as, the skill of a mathematician, physician, surgeon, mechanic, etc.

Social action   Coordinated efforts to achieve institutional change in order to meet a need, solve a social problem, correct an injustice or enhance the quality of human life.

Social awareness	It is creating our understanding about one's own and social realities based on information, insights and knowledge.
Social change	Variations over time in a society's laws, norms, values and institutional arrangements; the difference between the current and antecedent condition of any selected aspect of social organisation or structure.
Social education	Educational philosophies and methods that use informal/non formal methods such as group discussions, educational media and laboratories as instructional techniques to educate people about social situations such that they lead to expected change in their values, attitudes and behaviour.
Social work method	It is a systematic planned mode of intervention based on knowledge and values of social work.
Source	The point at which something springs into being or from which it derives or is obtained.
Stimuli	It excites or produces a temporary increase of vital action or process, either in the whole organism/activity.
Street theatre	A form of performance which focuses on developing socio-political understanding amongst the masses. Marked by minimal props and presentation at street corners or open public spaces, it draws the audience into an interactive dialogic process.
Systematic/structural changes	A change in the social, economic and political institutions which would serve to alter power relations and structures in society.
Termination of group	To bring the intervention to a close; an assessment of an individuals' dependence on group should be done carefully.
Termination	The conclusion of the workers-client intervention process; a systematic procedure for disengaging the working relationship.
Traditional media	It refers to the folk media, indigenous media, cultural media or people's media. These are oral communication among the people used for religious and/or social awareness purpose for generations.
Trust	Confidence in the reliability of a person or a system.
Verbal communications	Communication which allows the receiver to respond rapidly to what he thinks he hears.
Visual aid	Material that depicts pictures, signs or symbols to clarify the communication and used as a supportive mechanism in training.
Visual media	Channels that use symbols, signs or pictorial depiction to convey messages for generating social awareness or to direct social behaviour.

Welfare approach   The approach towards a condition of physical, health, emotional comfort and economic security; also, the efforts of a society to help its citizens achieve that condition. The term is also used popularly as a synonym for public assistance or other programmes that provide for the economic and social service needs of the poor.

CONSOLIDATED BIBLIOGRAPHY

Alissi, A.D. 1980. *Perspectives on Social Group Work Practice: A Book of Readings*. New York: The Free Press.

American Association of Social Workers. 1931. *Social Casework: Generic & Specific*. New York: American Association of Social Works.

Balgopal, P.R. and T.V. Vassil. 1983. *Groups in Social Work—An Ecological Perspective*. New York: Macmillan Publishing Co. Inc., The Haworth Press.

Bales R.F. 1950. *Interaction Process Analysis: A Method for the Study of Small Groups*. Reading, Massachusetts: Addison–Wesley.

Batra, Pramod. 1992. *Management Thoughts—A Collection*. New Delhi: Thomson Press (India) Ltd.

Batten, T.R. 1965. *The Human Factor in Community Work*. London: Oxford University Press.

Biesteck, F.P. 1957. *The Casework Relationship*. London: Unwin University Book.

Boldock, P. 1974. *Community Work and Social Work*. London: Routledge & Kegan Paul.

Brandler, S. and C.P. Roman. 1999. *Group Work, Skills and Strategies for Effective Interventions*. New York: The Haworth Press.

Briscoe, C. and D.N. Thomson (eds). 1977. *Community Work: Learning and Supervision*. London: George Allen and Unwin Ltd.

Brisley, M.S. and V. Burton. 1934. *Social Casework*. New York: Y. W. C. A.

Brown, A. 1989. *Group Work*. England: Grower Publications.

Burnard, Philip. 1989. *Teaching Interpersonal: A Handbook of Skills: Experimental Learning for Health Professionals*. London: Chapman and Hall.

Calouste Gulbenkian Foundation. 1968. *Community Work and Social Change*. London: Longman Group Ltd.

Cannon, M.A. and P. Klein. 1933. *Social Casework*. New York: Cambridge University Press.

Claude, Shannon and Weaver Warren. 1949. *Mathematical Theory of Communication*. Urbana: University of Illinios Press.

Commonwealth Secretariat. 1998. *Handbook Working with Communities*. UK: Commonwealth Secretariat.

Commonwealth Secretariat. 1999. *Common Wealth Diploma in Youth Development Work: Tutor's Manual*. Commonwealth Youth Programme. UK: Commonwealth Secretariat.

Council on Social Work Education. 1959. *Social Casework Method in Social Work Education*, Vol. 10. New York: Council on Social Work Education.

Cournoyer, Barry. 2000. *Social Work Skills Workbook*, third edition. California: Wadsworth Publishing Company.

Darison, E.H. 1970. *Social Casework*. London: Bailliere, Jindal and Cassell.

David, W. Johnson. 1986. *Reaching Out-Interpersonal Effectiveness and Self Actualization*. New Jersey: Prentice Hall.

Dembar, William M. 1960. *Psychology of Perception*. New York: Henry Holt and Company.

Dickson, D.A., O. Hargie and N.C. Morrow. 1989. *Communication Skill Training for Health Professionals: An Instructors Handbook*. Chapman and Hall.

Doel, Mark and Steven M. Shardlow. 2005. *Modern Social Work Practice—Teaching and Learning in Practice Settings*. Aldershot, UK: Ashgate Publishing Company.

Douglas, Tom. 1977. *Group Work Practice*. UK: Tavistock Publications.

Dunham, A. 1970. *The New Community Organization*. New York: Crowell.

Elkins, Dov Peretz. 1972. *Teaching People to Love Themselves—A Leader's Handbook of Self-esteem & Affirmation Training*. New York: Growth Associates.

Ernest, Bharper and Arthur Dunham. 1966. *Community Organization Action—Basic Literature & Critical Comments*. New York: Association Press.

Ferard, M.L. and N.K. Hunnybyun. 1962. *Caseworkers Use of Relationship*. London: Tavistock Publications.

Fisher, J. 1978. *Effective Casework Practice an Electric Approach*. New York: McGraw Hill.

Flexner, A. 1975. 'Is Social Work a Profession?' Proceedings of 42nd National Conference on Charities.

Forbes-Greene, L.M. 1983. *The Encyclopaedia of Icebreakers*. USA: Jossey-Bass/Pfeiffer.

Gambrill, E. 1983. *Casework: A Competency Based Approach*. Englewood Cliffs: Prentice Hall Inc.

Gangrade, K.D. 1971. *Community Organization in India*. Bombay: Popular Prakashan.

Garland, J.A. (ed.). 1992. *Group Work Reaching Out: People, Places and Power*. New York: The Haworth Press.

Garwin, C. 1987. *Contemporary Group Work*. New York: Prentice-Hall Inc.

Goldstein, Bruce. 1999. *Sensation and Perception*. New York: Books/Cole Publishing Co.

Heun, Linda R. and Richard E. Heun. 1978. *Developing Skills for Human Interaction*, second edition. London: Charles E. Merrill Publishing Company/A. Bell and Howell Company.

Hollis, F. 1939. *Social Casework in Practice*. New York: Family Welfare Association of America.

Hollis, F. 1964. *Casework: A Psychological Therapy*. New York: Random House.

Jary, David and Julia Jary. 1991. *Collins Dictionary of Sociology*.

Johnson, David W. 1996. Reaching Out-interpersonal Effectiveness and Self Actualization 301.15 J50R Pg.22

Johnson L.C. 1995. *Social Work Practice–A General Approach* (5th edition). Newton: M.A., Allyn and Bacon.

Jones, D. and M. Mayo (eds). 1974. *Community Work*. London: Routledge and Kegan Paul.

Kadushin, Alfred. 1990. *The Social Work Interview*. New York: Columbia University Press.

Keats, Daphne. 2002. *Interviewing—A Practical Guide for Students and Professionals*. New Delhi: Viva Books Pvt Ltd.

Kemp, C.G. 1970. *Perspectives on the Group Process*. Boston: Houghton Mifflin Co.

Khera, S. 2002. *You Can Win*. India: Macmillan.

Klein, A.F. 1970. *Social Work Thought Group Process*. New York: School of Social Welfare-State University.

Konopka, G. 1970. *Social Group Work*. New Jersey: Prentice Hall Inc.

Konopka, G. 1983. *Social Group Work: A Helping Process*. Englewood Cliffs: Prentice Hall Inc.

Kurlnd, R. and R. Salmon. 1998. *Teaching a Methods Course in Social Work with Groups*. Alexandria: Council of Social Work Education.

Laxmi, K.S. (ed.). 2000. *Encyclopaedia of Guidance and Counselling*. New Delhi: Mittal Publication.

Leaper, R.A.B. 1970. *Community Work*. London: National Council of Social Service.

Lennox, Daphne. 1982. *Residential Group Therapy for Children*. London and New York: Tavistock Publications.

Mathew, Grace. 1992. *An Introduction to Social Case Work*. Bombay: Tata Institute of Social Sciences.

McCaughan, N. (ed.). 1978. *Group Works Learning and Practice*. National Institute, Social Service Lib No. 33. London: George Allen and Unwin.

Middleman, R.R. *The Non-verbal Method in Working with Groups*. New York: Associated Press.

Morgan, T., R. and A. King. 1986. *Introduction to Psychology*. New York: McGraw-Hill Book Company.

Munn, Norman L. 1969. *Introduction to Psychology*. Boston: Houghton Mifflin Co.

Murphy, C. 1954. *Community Organization Practice*. Boston: Houghton Mifflin Co.

Northen, H. 1969. *Social Work with Groups*. New York: Columbia University Press.

Nursten, Jean. 1974. *Process of Casework*. GB: Pitman Publishing.

Perlman, H.H. 1964 (1971). *Social Casework: A Problem Solving Process*. Chicago: University of Chicago Press.

Phillips, J. 2001. *Group Work in Social Care: Planning and Setting up Groups*. London and Philadelphia: Jessica Kingsley Publishers.

Pippins, J.A. 1980. *Developing Casework Skills*. California: Sage Publications.

Prasanna Counselling Centre. 2001. *A Manual on Counselling for Lay Counsellors*. Bangalore: Prasanna Counselling Centre.

Priestley, Philip and James McGuire. 1983. *Learning to Help—Basic Skills Exercises*. London and New York: Tavistock Publications.

Priestley, Philip, James McGuire, David Flegg, Valerie Hemsley and David Welham. 1978. *Social Skills and Personal Problem Solving—A Handbook of Methods*. London: Tavistock Publications.

Robinson, Reginald. 1975. *Serving the Small Community—the Story of the United Community Defense Services*. New York: Association Press.

Roland, Lwarren. 1965. *Studying Your Community*. New York: The Free Press.

Rogers, C.R. 1961. *On Becoming a Person*. Boston: Houghton Miffin.

Ross, Murray G. and B. W. Lappin. 1967. *Community Organization—Theory, Principle and Practice*. New York: Harper and Row Publication.

Sainbury, Eric. 1970. *Social Diagnosis in Case Work*. London: Routledge and Kegan Paul.

Sheafor, Bradford, Charles Horejsi and Gloria Horejsi. 1992. *Techniques and Guidelines for Social Work Practice*. London: Allyn & Bacon.

Stempler, B.L. and M. Glass. 1996. *Social Group Work Today and Tomorrow: Moving from Theory to Advanced Training & Practice*. New York: Haworth Press.

Sundel, M., P. Glasser, R. Sarri, and R. Vinter. 1985. *Individual Change through Small Groups*. New York: The Free Press.

Sussman, M.B. 1959. (ed.) *Community Structure and Analysis*. New York: Crowell.

Suttles, G.D. 1972. *The Social Construction of Communities*. Chicago: University of Chicago Press.

Taft, F. 1940. *Social Casework with Children*. Philadelphia: Pennsylvania School of Social Work.

Thompson, Neil. 2006. *People Skills*, second edition. New York: Palgrave McMillan.

Timms, N. 1964. *Social Casework: Principles and Practice*. London: Routledge and Kegan Paul.

Tata Institute of Social Sciences (TISS). 1998. *NACO—HIV/AIDS Counselling Training Manual*. Mumbai: TISS.

Toseland R.W. and R.F. Rivas. 1995. *Introduction to Group Work Practice*. Boston: Allyn and Bacon.

The Calouste Gulbenkian Foundation. 1973. *Current Issues in Community Work: A Study by the Community Work Group*. London and Boston: Routledge and Kegan Paul.

Trecker, H.B. 1950. *Social Group Work*. New York: Women's Press.

———. 1970. *Social Group Work: Principles and Practices*. New York: Association Press.

Twelvetress, A. 1982. *Community Work*. London: Macmillan.

Warren, R.L. 1995. *Studying your Community*. New York: Free Press.

Wilson, G. and G. Ryland. *Social Group Work Practice*: The Creative Use of the Social Process. Boston: Houghton Mifflin Company.

Yelaja. 1982. *Ethical Issues in Social Work*. Springfield, IL: Charles C. Thomas Publisher.

ABOUT THE EDITORS AND CONTRIBUTORS

THE EDITORS

Ruma Bawikar has been a senior faculty member at the Karve Institute of Social Service, Pune for the last 30 years. She has worked as a trainer and consultant in various consortiums in partnership with international organisations for Rural Drinking Water Schemes for the Government of Maharashtra. She has extensive experience of working with networks involved in child rights and has conducted various researches funded by the UNICEF and the Ministry of Social Justice and Empowerment, Government of Maharashtra.

Sudha Datar is retired senior faculty at the Karve Institute of Social Service. She has extensive experience as counsellor in the field of Mental Health and Community Health and has conducted many studies on 'Acceptance of Self and Others' with various target groups, especially with social work trainees. She is also consultant to the Fulfilling Peoples Aspiration India (FPAI), Pune for their extension projects.

Geeta Rao is a senior lecturer at the Karve Institute of Social Service. She has been practitioner for 14 years in the field of Medical and Psychiatric Social Work, with special focus on 'Caring of the Aged'. She is team leader and project incharge of many researches and evaluation studies in the field of health. She is an expert in skill training in counselling and her work has been with individuals and families. Also, she is member of the Visitors Committee of Regional Mental Hospital, Yerawada, Pune and visiting faculty at the Cipla Palliative Care and Training Centre, Pune.

Nagmani Rao has been working in the field of development since 21 years and has been teaching at the Karve Institute of Social Service since 1995. She has been part of the women's movement since 1978, in mobilisation, research and training. She has written extensively on issues of women and rural toilers as well as academic writing related to teaching social work students. She has been consultant with research and community development organisations and has been involved in research projects related to women, community development, functional review of government departments and Total Literacy Campaign. She has conducted training on development issues and participatory research for senior government functionaries, NGO field staff, professional students of agriculture and engineering, college teachers and development practitioners.

Ujwala Masdekar is part of the faculty at the Karve Institute of Social Service for the last 14 years. She has worked as Gender Expert and consultant on various projects funded by the International organisations for Rural Drinking Water Schemes of the Government of Maharashtra and has extensive experience of working with NGOs involved in Saving and Credit group for women. She has also conducted various research studies which are funded by the Kibi International University, Japan; Government of Maharashtra Ministry of Women and Child Development, Mahila Aarthik Vikas Mahamandal (MAVIM), UNICEF. She has written manuals for NGOs and village committees on conflict resolution, women's participation in Drinking Water and Sanitation programme. She is also a trainer on gender sensitivity and equality for different NGOs and MAVIM districts level implementers.

THE CONTRIBUTORS

Anuradha Patil is a senior lecturer at the Karve Institute of Social Service. She has been working as the master trainer for NACO counselling training and teaches values and attitudes to counsellors while dealing with HIV/AIDS patient. She also conducts communication workshop with NGOs for their staff development programmes and for new entrants to the MSW course at the institute. She is also an Ethics committee member at the National AIDS Research Institute and at the B.J. Medical College and committee member on Visitors Committee at the Regional Mental Hospital.

Anand Pawar is Executive Director, Samyak Communication and Research Centre on Gender and Masculinities. He is a visiting faculty at training institutions for professional social work and has conducted numerous trainings for the government and NGO functionaries on gender, violence and masculinities and communication. He is associated with networks like FEM (Forum for Engaging Men) and MenEngage. These networks address gender equality and gender rights through working with men.

Manjusha Doshi has a Master's degree in Social Work from Pune University and a Post Graduate degreee in Ecology and Environment. She has worked with NGO in designing and ex-ecuting programmes for community development and is an expert in conducting training and sessions on family life education, health, decentralisation, people's empowerment, soft skills. She worked as programme officer for German Technical Cooperation (GTZ), which supported basic health services of Maharashtra government. At present she is working with Child Fund India as Area Manager of Udaipur area office, Rajasthan.

Anjali Maydeo is a member of the faculty at the Karve Institute of Social Service since 1981. She has been teaching Social Policy and Community Organisation and has worked as a consultant for government and civil society organisations in the fields of water and sanitation, child rights based community development projects and capacity building of the organisations. She has contributed to the development of manuals to be used by various cadres of workers in development projects such as village committees, para-professionals and trainers in different programmes. She also has extensive experience of working with organisations involved in women's rights. She has conducted evaluation studies of NGOs or development projects of the government for the donor agencies. Her major interest areas include capacity building, participatory methodologies for assessment, planning and evaluation, human rights issues—mainly for women and Dalits.

Sameer Datye is the Pune Head of Tieto India, an IT corporate. After years of experience in the field of communication he moved to the IT sector. He is also founder trustee of the Identity Foundation, which works with street children in Pune, Maharashtra.

Vidya Ghugari is an M. Phil in Education from the University of Pune. She has been the training officer for the Centre For Learning Resources, Pune and Chaitanya Rajgurunagar, Tal Khed, District Pune and has been the programme coordinator for the Door Step School, Pune, and the CASP-PLAN Project, Pune. She has independently conducted children's camps at various slums. She has organised puppet shows and workshops on puppet making for various institutions and communities. She has also organised training programmes and workshops for grassroots level workers for Gramvardhini, Vanchit Vikas, and Senior citizens of the Khoja community.

INDEX